UNIVERSITY OF CHICAGO STUDIES IN LIBRARY SCIENCE

DETERIORATION AND PRESERVATION OF LIBRARY MATERIALS

DETERIORATION AND PRESERVATION OF LIBRARY MATERIALS

The Thirty-fourth Annual Conference of the Graduate Library School August 4–6, 1969

Edited by HOWARD W. WINGER and RICHARD DANIEL SMITH

THE UNIVERSITY OF CHICAGO PRESS
CHICAGO & LONDON

THE UNIVERSITY OF CHICAGO STUDIES IN LIBRARY SCIENCE

The papers in this volume were published originally in the
LIBRARY QUARTERLY, *January 1970*

Standard Book Number: 226-90201-3
Library of Congress Catalog Card Number: 78-115971

THE UNIVERSITY OF CHICAGO PRESS, CHICAGO AND LONDON
The University of Toronto Press, Toronto 5, Canada

Published 1970
Printed in the United States of America

TABLE OF CONTENTS

DETERIORATION AND PRESERVATION OF LIBRARY MATERIALS

INTRODUCTION

The deterioration of library materials, constant since libraries began, has accelerated to alarming proportions in 1969. Researchers have predicted that all paper-based records of this century, as well as those of earlier years, face imminent ruin. Without new and effective efforts for their preservation, most will not be usable in their present form in the next century. The danger of destruction threatens not only research library collections but also the world of knowledge and scholarship that they support. For not only paper is involved. Similar dangers of destruction confront other cellulosic products, such as film, which may substitute for paper as the material base of records. And not only research libraries are involved. The surprisingly rapid deterioration of printed materials, even those that have been produced with some eye to permanence, creates problems and expenses for other libraries as well.

Paper deterioration is not a discovery of our time, nor is an identification of its causes new. Certain trends and events, however, have converged to focus attention on it in recent years. Some are worth mentioning briefly here, although they will be elaborated in the papers that follow this introduction. The trend toward devoting a greater proportion of the social effort to research and advanced scholarship places a higher priority on the preservation of the library research collections that support them. Events particularly impressive for librarians but also acknowledged as important by others have been the dramatic demonstrations by W. J. Barrow of the unexpected speed with which library materials are deteriorating and his publicization of the major cause as excessive acidity in paper. His experiments thus offered hope and direction for solution as well as warning of danger. Finally, the Council on Library Resources has helped promote a feeling of urgency among librarians. It gave financial support to the work of Barrow and also supported the Library Technology Project of the American Library Association in studying the preservation of materials as well as other library problems.

These developments have inspired librarians to undertake programs of study, research, and action about the problems of the deterioriation and preservation of library materials. They have also helped foster a community of interest and inquiry among others involved in the production and preservation of library materials. Paper makers, publishers, printers, binders, suppliers of photographic materials, environmental scientists, conservators, and others have pursued or continued to pursue their own investigations. Study is proceeding on many fronts, and we seem near technological solutions to many of the most pressing problems of preservation.

Because of the importance of the problems and the pace of investigation and events, the faculty of the Graduate Library School of the University of Chicago chose "The Deterioration and Preservation of Library Materials" as the most timely topic for their thirty-fourth annual conference held at Chicago August 4–6, 1969. The papers that follow were first presented there. Collectively they include discussions of the scholarly needs for preservation, the physical nature of the materials to be preserved, the means and care required in manufacture and storage and handling to achieve the greatest possible permanence, the effects of different manufacturing techniques, programs for conservation and restoration, and personnel needs and requirements.

The schedule of a three-day conference precluded a comprehensive discussion of the subject. The number of speakers was limited, and the task of selecting from all those doing significant work in the preservation of library materials was not easy. Not all the materials preserved in libraries today, not to speak of some that may bulk large there in future, were discussed. But it is hoped that the wide representation here of various parties concerned with the problems of preservation may contribute to a wider communication of knowledge and cross-fertilization of ideas so important in scientific advance.

Grateful acknowledgement is made to the Joseph Fels Foundation for assistance in defraying the expense of the conference.

HOWARD W. WINGER
Conference Director

DETERIORATION OF LIBRARY COLLECTIONS TODAY

EDWIN E. WILLIAMS

In discussing the deterioration of library collections today, it would be possible to deal with the topic very briefly—not quite as briefly as with the subject of snakes in Ireland, but in a single sentence. This would read, *Everything in library collections is deteriorating today, was deteriorating yesterday, and will continue to deteriorate tomorrow although we ought to retard the process.*

Enough is known to justify this statement; it is when details are examined and countermeasures are considered that complications arise and the limitations of our knowledge become evident. It is hardly easier to generalize about the deterioration of books than about the aging of human beings. Beginning as identical twins, two copies of the same book may deteriorate at very different rates as the result of use and of storage conditions, which vary, even within the stacks of a single library, from one shelf to another. Life expectancies of different kinds of paper range from a very few years to centuries, and paper, of course, is not the only substance with which we are concerned. The conference will also deal with bindings and with photographic films; perhaps the conference program should also have provided for consideration of magnetic tapes and other things on which increasing stores of information will be recorded as the computer extends its empire. There are those who wonder why we worry about the deterioration of something as obsolete as the book.

This line of thought, however, would get us into tomorrow before we have dealt with today, much less with yesterday. It seems to me that we must begin with a glance at least toward the past; if some familiarity with history were not essential to an understanding of the present, perhaps we would be foolish to deplore or resist the deterioration of our library collections. Our problem has a long history. It occurs to me that the most serious mistake in that long history may have been made at an early date when knowledge began to be recorded on substances more pliable and more perishable than the baked clay tablet, which will not tear, will not burn, and will not turn into a pulpy mess when it is soaked in water. Have not library collections been highly perishable ever since? Have we not repeatedly sacrificed permanence for convenience and economy?

Vellum, to be sure, was more durable in many respects than papyrus, but vellum, after a few centuries, was superseded by a Chinese invention, paper. We were warned as early as the twelfth century, when the emperor of the Occident, Frederick I, Barbarossa, prohibited the use of paper in deeds and charters because he feared it was too perishable [1]. The account of "Paper Deterioration—An Old Story" by Lee E. Grove [2], which was published five years ago, begins with a fifteenth-century Benedictine abbot, Johann Tritheim, who believed that vellum would last for a millenium but had his doubts about paper.

I wish only to give a few names,

dates, and quotations in order to suggest how frequently the problem of paper deterioration has been considered during the past century and a half. In July 1823 two different British periodicals called attention to it. An item in the *Annals of Philosophy* entitled "Frauds and Imperfections in Paper-making" protested the practice of mixing sulphate of lime or gypsum with the rags and gave directions on how to detect this fraud; it also referred to "the slovenly mode in which the bleaching by means of chlorine or oxymuriatic acid is effected [3, p. 68]. In *The Gentleman's Magazine* for the same month, John Murray wrote:

> Allow me to call the attention of your readers to the present state of that wretched compound called *Paper*. Every printer will corroborate my testimony; and I am only astonished that the interesting question has been so long neglected and forgotten. It is a duty, however, of the most imperative description;—our beautiful Religion, our Literature, our Science, all are threatened.
>
> . . . I have in my possession a large copy of the Bible printed at Oxford, 1816 (never used), and issued by the British and Foreign Bible Society, *crumbling literally into dust*. I transmitted specimens of this volume to the Lord Bishop of Gloucester, and to Mr. Wilberforce. No doubt it must be difficult to legislate on such a subject, but something must be done and that early. I have watched for some years the progress of the evil, and have no hesitation in saying, that if the same ratio of progression is maintained, a century more will not witness the volumes printed within the last twenty years. *MS. Records* are in the same fatal condition. [4, pp. 21–22]

Murray concluded that "the chief causes of destruction consist in the employment of sulphate of lime, &c. in the pulp, and bleaching the rags previously, or the paper subsequently, with oxymuriatic acid gas *(chlorine)*." A footnote by the editor added: "It is notorious that the great mass of printing papers are now made of *cotton* rags; and that to produce a better colour, the pulp undergoes a chemical process, which materially injures its durability" [4, p. 21].

Leaving it to the experts to judge the validity of Murray's chemical diagnosis, I should like to observe only that his remarks have a very modern sound and that it is not encouraging to reflect that he seems to have enlisted no support, although he followed up his article with two monographic publications [5, 6, 7].

Within the literature of paper deterioration there is a whole subliterature on newspapers. Here the chronology appears to begin with Justin Winsor; at least it was reported in 1891 that "fifteen or twenty years ago" (that is, before he became the first president of the American Library Association or the librarian of Harvard College) Winsor had tried to persuade Boston newspapers to use more durable paper [8, note at end, signed "Eds. L. J."]. Long afterward, from 1910 to 1913 and again from 1918 to 1920, the ALA had a Committee on Deterioration of Newsprint Paper; there were distinguished chairmen—Frank P. Hill and Harry Miller Lydenberg—but the committee was no more successful than Winsor had been.

As we all know, the problem of newspapers has been solved, at least in one sense. The reservation is added because it could be argued that the preservation of newspapers in their original form has been abandoned as a lost cause; we rely upon microfilm to preserve the text, and a subsequent paper of this conference will inform us regarding deterioration of the film copies on which we depend.

Certainly microfilm is much more durable than newsprint; yet the history of our success in this field may not be entirely reassuring. My point is that our present solution to the newspaper problem seems to have been technically feasible long before Hill and Lydenberg tried to find a solution, and even before Winsor made the first attempt. I say this because in 1870, during the siege of Paris, microfilm had been successfully used to reproduce documents. The pigeons who flew film copies over the German lines were never entirely forgotten, and there was a European article in 1907 on "a new form of book—the microphotographic book" [9]; but it was not until the 1930s that American libraries began to use microphotography to any significant extent. If its possibilities were almost entirely overlooked for more than sixty years, one naturally wonders what possibilities we may now be neglecting.

During the sixty years that followed the publication of John Murray's book in 1829 there appears to have been relatively little interest in deterioration of paper, but the closing decade of the nineteenth century produced a number of contributions to the subject. In 1891, for example, Rossiter Johnson wrote on "Inferior Paper a Menace to the Permanency of Literature" [8], and in 1897 J. Y. W. MacAlister told the Library Association that, "as librarian of the Leeds library, I made certain simple experiments and observations which convinced me that many of the books on our shelves there, even if left untouched, would not outlast the present generation of readers" [10, p. 295]. Specifications for book papers were formulated in a report made during the following year to the Society of Arts by its Committee on the Deterioration of Paper [11]. In 1898, also, the librarian of Congress discussed the subject in his annual report, [12, pp. 45–6, 58–62], and the Italian government was petitioned by a conference of librarians to establish paper standards [13, p. 147].

The first year of our own century brought the publication (on paper that is now extremely brittle) of the *Procès-verbaux et mémoires* of the International Library Congress at Paris, including a paper by Pierre Dauze, who observed (I translate) that "Relatively recent works have completely disappeared from circulation or become more rare than incunabula. . . . Librarians, on whom rests the responsibility for leaving in perfect condition to their successors the precious stores in their care, show themselves gravely disturbed [*se montrent sérieusement inquiets*]" [14, p. 228–29]. He recommended that governments buy only books on paper meeting standards approved by official laboratories, and that good paper be required in copies supplied to libraries under the provisions of legal deposit.

In 1907 Cyril Davenport wrote that "there is no doubt that the large majority of our modern books will not be in readable condition in about a hundred years' time from the date of their publishing" [15, p. 82]. During this period the Bureau of Chemistry of the United States Department of Agriculture published results of research on the durability of paper [16], and some twenty years later, as reported in early volumes of the *Library Quarterly* [17, 18], a series of studies by the Bureau of Standards included in its findings a number of recommendations on optimum storage conditions for the preservation of records.

Our present efforts may be regarded as belonging, in the long history of deterioration and preservation, to a chapter that began about a dozen years ago. Thus far there have been two major figures in this chapter, and they are important, regardless of how their technical contributions may be appraised, because of the attention they have drawn to the problem. I refer to the Barrow Laboratory and Association of Research Libraries (ARL) committee that I serve as secretary; the two have been related, and both have been greatly indebted for assistance and counsel to Verner Clapp and the Council on Library Resources, Inc., which he served as president from 1956 to 1967.

On June 1, 1957, "the Virginia State Library, under a grant from the Council on Library Resources, Inc., and with the technical supervision of W. J. Barrow, began . . . a study of the deterioration of modern book papers" [19, p. 7]. The findings were published in a seventy-page booklet. Subsequent grants and studies produced two more booklets which, like the first, appeared as publications of the Virginia State Library [20, 21], and these have been followed by a series of W. J. Barrow Research Laboratory publications [22].

In 1959 the report of the first study gave "actual findings of the physical condition of 500 typical non-fiction books printed in the United States in the first five decades of this century [19, p. 7]. Its most striking and widely quoted conclusion was that "if material which should be preserved indefinitely is going to pieces as rapidly as these figures indicate, it seems probable that most library books printed in the first half of the 20th century will be in an unusable condition in the next century [19, p. 16].

If one recalls the closely similar statements that have been quoted from Murray (1823), MacAlister (1897), Dauze (1900), and Davenport (1908) —to say nothing of others that could have been cited—one might suppose that this would not have been regarded as news. On the other hand, it was based on a far larger sample than any of the previous statements, and this sample had been subjected to careful testing. There was also an encouraging prospect that financial assistance for further work on deterioration and preservation could be obtained from the Council on Library Resources. The result, in any case, has been a more systematic and persistent effort than had been prompted by any previous cry of alarm. This conference is both an evidence that the effort is continuing and an opportunity for review of what has been done thus far. Leaving technical questions to those who are qualified to deal with them, I propose to consider problems of organization and strategy that librarians face; hence I shall have much more to say about the ARL committee than about the Barrow Laboratory.

Interest aroused by the report of 1959 led the ARL to discuss paper deterioration at its meeting in Montreal on June 18, 1960, and it was decided at this meeting to establish a committee "to develop a national program for the preservation of research library materials with its primary concern directed toward the preservation of retrospective materials" [23, pp. 6–7]. Closely related efforts were already under way. The Subcommittee on Micropublishing Projects of the American Library Association Committee on Resources, under the chairmanship of Raynard Swank, had recently drafted a proposal for a cooperative national microfilm deposit, with objectives that included preservation, bibliographical control, and physical accessibility [24]. Wesley Simonton was at work on bibliographical control of microforms [25], and in

Washington on September 16, 1960—a week before the first meeting of the new ARL Committee—there had been a discussion of permanent/durable book paper at which Robert Kingery of the New York Public Library had presented a working paper on "The Extent of the Paper Problem in Large Research Collections and the Comparative Costs of Available Solutions [21, pp. 36–41].

These were all questions that must be considered by the ARL committee. At the outset it assumed that the solution to its problem would probably be found in microreproduction; at the first meeting it agreed "that the study should not neglect chemical treatment of books as a possible alternative to filming for preservation, though such treatment would not offer the desirable by-products of economy in space and increased accessibility of resources [26, p. 3]. It should be added that the committee has never seriously considered what might be called the "rare-book aspects" of preservation. It has assumed that it ought to deal with the great bulk of research collections, which will have to be rescued by relatively inexpensive mass-production techniques; and consequently it has not investigated conservation and restoration methods that are too costly to consider except for very valuable books, manuscripts, and bindings.

An essential first step, in the opinion of the ARL committee, was to determine the quantitative extent of the problem. Consequently its first special project, a study made for it by the Research Triangle Institute and financed by the Council on Library Resources, was a statistical sampling of the National Union Catalog. This indicated that, in 1961, the National Union Catalog listed 14,376,000 different volumes containing 2,999,998,000 pages; slightly more than 57 percent of these pages were in volumes published since 1869, and 56 percent of them were printed abroad. These figures take no account of serials. Though the findings were published over my signature [27], I have never been convinced that they make a great contribution toward solution of the problem.

The second project, at any rate, was far more significant. Late in 1962 a grant from the Council on Library Resources enabled the ARL committee to engage one of its members, Gordon Williams, director of the Center for Research Libraries, to make a comprehensive study [28].[1]

Two points regarding this study should be emphasized. First, the questions with which it dealt were discussed repeatedly and at length by the ARL committee; during many of these discussions it appeared that agreement might never be possible, but the final report won the support of all members. Second, it was unanimously adopted in principle by the Association of Research Libraries at its meeting of January 24, 1965; it stands therefore —until changes are approved—as a statement of the association's position, a plan of action that has been approved by librarians of the institutions most vitally concerned with the problem of deteriorating library materials. Hence it can be described as the most significant single document on the subject, and it seems to me that its major recommendations ought to be kept in mind as we consider the papers that are to be presented here. It is five years old, and we should try to judge how much it may have deteriorated. Are modifications indicated by what has been learned since it was prepared?

[1] This study also appears in *Library Journal* [29].

Do we need further research to test the validity of some of its recommendations?

Evidently I must attempt to summarize it, though it is not a verbose document and condensation is difficult. It begins by citing evidence of deterioration; here its source is the Barrow report of 1959, which dealt only with American publications printed between 1900 and 1939. This section might now be strengthened by reference to findings of the Barrow report of 1967, which analyzed the results of testing fifty books from each decade of the nineteenth century [30]; but this further data would not seem to call for any modification of the conclusions.

The objectives of an effective and efficient preservation program are stated as follows:

> It must preserve all books of significant value ("books" is here used in the general sense to include all forms of written records); it must preserve the maximum amount of information carried by the original books; it must provide for the longest period of preservation practicable with present technology and compatible with the other requirements; it must provide for the continuous and ready availability of the preserved materials to anyone who needs them; and it must avoid unnecessary duplication of effort and expense. [28, p. 12]

The report then deals with the question of preserving original books as opposed to photographic copies only:

> the primary importance of most books lies in their text, . . . but books can also be important in other ways. . . . There are those in which the primary interest is in some other intrinsic part of the book—the paper or binding, for example, or the decorative illustrations. . . .
>
> . . . A copy can indicate, but cannot reproduce precisely, most of those qualities that make a book significant as an artifact . . . [but] most copies, which are made primarily to reproduce the text, do not even indicate some of these characteristics. Microform copies, for example, do not usually show the binding, end papers, . . . watermarks . . . ; neither do they identify cancels or show gatherings. Characteristics such as these are sometimes of critical importance in evaluating the authenticity or priority of the text, and sometimes are important . . . for the evidence they supply about the taste and technology of the society that produced the book.
>
> . . . [Moreover] even photocopies are not infallibly accurate, . . . they can copy illegibly; . . . and operator carelessness can omit whole pages or sections. . . .
>
> . . . We must therefore conclude that in order to preserve all the information that may be significant in a book it is essential to preserve the original itself, and that even though copies of books are adequate for many uses, the availability of the original is also necessary to verify the accuracy of the copy. Further argument for preservation of the original for as long as possible is the recent evidence . . . that negative microfilm may have a shorter life expectancy than the original book. [28, pp. 12–14]

Originals cannot be preserved as long as possible, however, unless they are used as little as possible—used only when a copy will not serve the purpose. It follows, if photocopies must normally be supplied to the user, that "physical preservation of the original book is not simply a prudent alternative to the preservation of the text in microfilm, but is another operation which must be judged on its own merits" [28, p. 16]. However,

> this cost need not be purely an additional cost. . . . Many books are infrequently used and, if physically preserved, copies of them would not have to be made until someone wanted to consult the text, or until the preserved original was no longer usable, and in either case this would not be for a great many years for many books. If, however, . . . the original were not preserved, a microform copy of every deteriorating book would have to be made as soon as possible. Data is presented [in this report] . . . showing that to microfilm a book is more expensive than physically to preserve it. . . .

> Still further, the possibility of future improvements in methods of microcopying urges deferring this operation for as long as possible. [28, p. 17]

The decisive consideration clearly is economic, which means that cost estimates supporting the choice are constantly subject to change. Moreover, technological changes can alter the processes and products of filming, while specifications for optimum storage conditions may be altered from time to time as our knowledge increases.

If needless filming is to be avoided, there clearly must be a central record, if not a central collection, of master negatives. Likewise, any plan for the preservation of original books will be wasteful unless it provides for preservation of a single copy only of each ordinary book, and this obviously entails a national system supported by research libraries—the single preservation copy must be "nationalized" in some way, though this need not mean that all such copies would be physically assembled in a single national center.

Preservation of originals was a question on which opinions changed as the study proceeded, and there was another major point on which economic considerations proved to be decisive in changing the views of the ARL committee or some, at least, of its members. This was the question of selecting materials to be preserved. At the outset it had been supposed that selection would be a difficult problem; yet the report recommends simply that we preserve what has been selected and added to research libraries, since it would cost too much to review that selection—that is, it would cost more to identify volumes that could be discarded than to preserve these volumes.

To be specific, the cost estimates indicated that one would have to eliminate approximately 4 percent of books examined to justify the reappraisal project economically. Would it in fact prove impracticable to eliminate this much from our research library holdings? From the Harvard University Library, for example, this would mean weeding more than 300,000 volumes. There are certainly more than this that need not remain forever in the Harvard stacks. Yet the weeding in question here is an elimination of books from the world's collection, a decision that each book discarded is no longer to survive anywhere. Undoubtedly juries could be found who would be ready to condemn books by the millions, but books presumably should be judged by those who know them. Indeed, should not each book be judged by the scholar most likely to be interested in it, and, if he judges it to be useful—or even potentially useful—will it not have to be reprieved? Anyone who has observed the reactions of scholars when books are transferred to storage would be reluctant indeed to suggest that thousands of volumes be completely eliminated.

The report recommended, therefore, that we seek to preserve one copy of everything that is in research libraries, and that we preserve an original example of each work as long as we can, depending on film copies for ordinary use. In order to do this it recommended that a federally supported central agency be created to

> 1) undertake the centralized preservation of deteriorating records deposited by libraries; 2) coordinate its own preservation program with local programs of individual libraries to assure that all significant records are preserved while avoiding unwitting duplication; 3) assure the ready availability of microform or full size photocopies of deteriorating materials to all libraries; and 4) itself preserve, in the interest of textual preservation, economy, and

the the ready availability of copies, all microform masters made at its expense or deposited by others, and coordinate the preservation of microform masters made by other agencies. [28, p. 21]

In one sense, consideration of the problems of a central agency that has not yet been created may seem to take us a long way beyond the scope of a paper on "Deterioration of Library Collections Today"; but we are not here to discuss deterioration purely as an interesting natural phenomenon; we are concerned with what can be done, which means that we ought to examine the machinery proposed by Gordon Williams and approved by the ARL.

The agency would operate a central library that would "accept from other libraries and physically preserve, by deacidification and storage at the lowest practical temperature (or by improved techniques . . .), any example of an original written record," provided that another "example in equally good or better condition is not already adequately preserved," that it is catalogued or "part of an organized and coherent collection deposited in its entirety," and that it is complete or "as complete as any example known to exist" [28, p. 21]. Further:

In order to provide for the maximum availability to the nation of the text of the preserved books, the central library will, subject to copyright restrictions, make or cause to be made at its expense, a microform negative of any book in its collection whenever a library wants to buy or to borrow a copy of that book. It will lend to a library without charge a microform positive . . . and it will sell a microform positive or full size copy from its negative for the cost of the positive or copy alone. . . .

All negatives of preserved originals in the center will be retained by the center as master negatives, stored under optimum conditions for their longest possible retention (and physically separate from the preserved original), and used only to make positive prints for use. [28, p. 23]

It was easier to decide what such a central library ought to do than to agree on how libraries can be induced to deposit books in it. Their participation is essential, as the report explains:

the nation must depend upon libraries to provide the original books for preservation by depositing those from their own collections. Not only is it uneconomic to think of the central preservation library buying its own copies for this purpose, but many items that must be preserved are no longer available for purchase, and in any event it is a part of the responsibility of research libraries to help assure the continued availability of their books to their present and future patrons. The research libraries must therefore accept the positive responsibility to cooperate fully with the central agency. . . .

They must do this, first, by obligating themselves not to dispose of any catalogued book, or organized group of books, from their collections without first ascertaining whether or not an example as good as their own, or better, is already preserved. If . . . [not], then the library must deposit its example for preservation rather than dispose of it otherwise. This imposes no obligation on any library to deposit examples from its collection until it wishes, and in many cases libraries will naturally prefer to retain the original examples . . . for as long as possible. . . . But in order to assure the longest possible physical preservation it is desirable that the books be in as good condition as possible when preserved, rather than already deteriorated to the point of near unusability. . . . Any library may buy from the central agency a copy (micro or full size) of any preserved record for the cost of the print. . . . But in order to provide an inducement to libraries to deposit as early in the book's life as possible, the library first depositing a "usable" or "good" example of a record will be allowed to buy a positive microform copy of that book for half the cost of the print . . . immediately upon deposit . . . or at any time in the future. [28, pp. 24–25]

The report provides for the grading of copies deposited in order that published lists can indicate the condition of each item; thus, when considering a deposit, a library will be able to estimate whether the copy already being preserved is better than its own. The center will also encourage libraries to develop their own "preservation collections"

> by making microform copies of such locally preserved materials available for use under the same terms as if the material had been deposited for central preservation. In other words, the central agency will make when requested, or authorize to be made locally at its expense, a microform negative . . . and allow the library first preserving its usable or good example to buy a positive print for half the cost of the print. The central library agency will own and control this negative, insure that it is permanently retained as a master copy, and make prints from it readily available to any library. . . .
>
> Books preserved locally in this way, with the same chemical treatment, cold storage, and protection, as if in the central library, will be regarded as adequately preserved. They will be given the same bibliographic control as books preserved centrally, and except in unusual cases will not be duplicated in the central collection. [28, pp. 25–26]

The report also recommends the immediate acquisition and preservation of a copy of each new book published in the United States or acquired under the Farmington Plan or the provisions of Public Law 480. The center would build up a file of master negatives of works not yet deposited for preservation, and would make positive film copies available to libraries on a cooperative basis. Bibliographical control would be provided through the National Union Catalog by means of compact lists of preserved books which would simply refer to serial numbers in that catalog.

Alternative patterns of support by the federal government are considered in the final section of the report. Responsibility might be assigned to an existing agency such as the Library of Congress, to an independent bureau or commission, or, by contractual arrangement, to a nongovernmental agency. While I plan to make a suggestion on general strategy, this specific question of agencies is one on which the ARL committee did not make a firm recommendation, and neither shall I.

Indeed, while this is one of the questions that you might wish to debate as you review the comprehensive plan that I have tried to summarize, it may not be one on which members of this conference will have much that is new to contribute. Another such question is raised by the policy of accepting the selection of research materials that has already been made—that is, on the one hand, to preserve what is in research libraries without reappraisal but, on the other, to make no effort to gather in and preserve materials that these libraries have overlooked. No doubt there will always be some scholars and some librarians who question this policy, and it might be an interesting topic for debate; but, unless someone demonstrates that we now have relevant information that was not available five years ago, I suggest that we shall do better to concentrate on other matters.

In its recommendation that we preserve original books instead of depending entirely on film copies, as we do for newspapers, the report would seem to be on firmer ground now than it was when adopted in 1965. By this I mean that photographic reproduction has not grown any cheaper, while the prospects for inexpensive deacidification of books seem to be brighter than they were.

There are other questions that have troubled the ARL committee during its discussions of the past five years, and one of them seems to be especially appropriate for consideration at this conference. Do we know enough about the process of paper deterioration to prescribe conditions of optimum storage and to build storage facilities—either centrally on on our own campuses—that will fit the prescription? The Barrow findings emphasized temperature and concluded that we ought to keep our books very cool. Humidity, however, is a complicating factor to which somewhat less study has been devoted than to temperature, and there has been no thorough investigation of the effect of changes in environment such as those that will take place if books are kept in a very cold place from which they must be removed in order to be consulted.

In preservation, as in many other projects, we shall never do anything if we wait until we have all the information that might be desirable, but it does not follow that immediate action is always wise. The real question is whether it is likely that our planning of storage facilities would be modified substantially by the answers to specific questions that probably could be answered in a relatively short time—two or three years—if research were now begun. There are differences of opinion regarding this on the ARL committee, but the Council on Library Resources, by its continued support of work at the Barrow Laboratory, as well as by its recent grant to the Imperial College of Science and Technology in London [31], appears to support the view that investigation of optimum storage conditions is needed.

Since subsequent papers will deal with this, as well as with deacidification and other treatments designed to extend the life of books, with the preservation of film, and with binding practices, I should like to turn from these questions; when they are discussed, I hope we shall keep in mind the relation they have to the ARL proposal. Meanwhile, there is another family of problems that ought be be mentioned; these relate to organization and library cooperation.

Some work on these problems has been done since Gordon Williams completed his report. A grant from the Council on Library Resources enabled the ARL committee to sponsor a Pilot Preservation Project conducted at the Library of Congress in 1967 and 1968. This was an experiment in comparing copies of volumes in the Library of Congress brittle-book collection with copies of the same volumes in other libraries; costs of identifying such copies and of obtaining reports on their condition were investigated. As a base for the experiment, 1,085 titles—most of them extremely brittle and some of them lacking portions of text—were selected from a collection of 35,000 volumes that have been withdrawn from the general collection at the Library of Congress because of their brittle condition. Reports were received on 795 titles, and it was found that from one to three reports were usually sufficient to locate a copy that, while usually brittle, was complete and otherwise in excellent condition. Moreover, 15 percent were in a rare-book collection or were specially protected in some other way.

On the basis of the study, it was concluded that it is administratively feasible to establish a national preservation collection of materials now deteriorating in the nation's research libraries. This assessment, however, extends only to the identification of brittle or deteriorating materials in other libraries and to a determination of the physical condition of such materials. Although no special attempt was made to do so, the establishment of a central register of best copies appears to offer no particular problems. . . .

[The study did not investigate] the willingness of these libraries to contribute volumes to a national preservation collection; . . . their willingness to accept responsibility for preserving books in their own collections that have been designated as national preservation copies; . . . [or] the need for development of indemnification procedures. [*32*]

It has been seen that the plan of the ARL committee proposed certain inducements and indemnifications, but I think it is true that neither Gordon Williams nor those who approved his report would be willing to guarantee that these will be effective; experience, it has been assumed, may dictate modifications. It should also be noted that two persons who support the recommendations in every detail may still make distinctly different predictions. The plan provides for a central national preservation collection, but it also provides that each library may store on its own premises, under approved conditions, some of the books that have been "nationalized" as preservation copies. One of us, therefore, might envisage a future in which a single enormous preservation collection will contain one copy of nearly every book that has been acquired by any research library, the exceptions being a relatively few volumes of the kind that we shelter in our rare-book collections. Yet another advocate of the plan might envisage a future in which the central national collection will contain only the marginal and very infrequently used books that libraries gladly discarded, and the great bulk of the "national preservation collection" would be dispersed, housed in special "preservation stacks" of major research libraries.

Presumably the outcome will depend in part on the inducements that are offered and the organization that is created; moreover, regardless of which future one prefers, either is acceptable. When it comes to sources of financial support, however, there has appeared to be no alternative and there has been no difference of opinion—the problem of deterioration is too large, it is agreed, to be solved unless substantial federal funds are provided.

It will surprise me if anyone wishes to debate this conclusion of the ARL committee, but I should like to suggest that its implications have not been fully explored. If federal funds are to be obtained, presumably members of Congress will have be be convinced that deterioration is a serious and urgent problem. Scholars, of course, are the real victims of deterioration, and it seems unlikely that congressmen will be persuaded to appropriate funds unless scholars help to persuade them. Librarians generally—not just a few librarians in a few of the largest research libraries—must also be enlisted in the campaign.

As it is, few librarians have been particularly active, and not many scholars have volunteered. Librarians of the relatively new and small institutions are busy acquiring new books and reprints of old ones; their shelves are not filled with brittle books and, while they recognize that the old and enormous research libraries are national resources on which they must depend, they naturally regard deterioration as primarily a problem for those who are fortunate enough to have inherited great collections. With regard to the scholars, I think we should realize that the great majority are not directly and vitally concerned. Those scholars whose research is focused on contemporary materials—and they include most scientists—rarely encounter a book that is falling apart. It is historians, after all, who are menaced by deteriorating books. To be sure, every subject has its historians, but the percentage of scholars who are studying the past has clearly been decreasing during recent decades.

Yet the historians, if they had not been relatively apathetic, could have made themselves heard and could have convinced many of their colleagues on the faculty that something must be done. There seems to be a disparity between the alarming statements that have been published and the alarm that has been generated in individuals, even historians.

Perhaps this can be explained by a visit to the shelves. When one goes through the stacks of one of our venerable and enormous research libraries with a visitor—congressman, professor, or librarian—one does not find large numbers of volumes that have crumbled "literally into dust," as John Murray said his Bible was doing 146 years ago. If the library still has newspaper stacks, with bound volumes in them instead of microfilms, fairly dramatic instances of crumbling can be found, but it is hard to find genuinely shocking examples in our book stacks, even when one goes to the shelves on which some of the most brittle volumes have been segregated. (The number that have been segregated for this reason may seem surprisingly small—only 35,000, it has been seen, at the Library of Congress, representing a small fraction of 1 percent of its total holdings.)

As it is, when one tries to demonstrate the problem to a visitor, most of the volumes that are pulled from the shelves will appear at first glance to be in satisfactory condition, though the paper in many of them will be too brittle to bend very often or even very far without breaking. A few, in which leaves have broken loose, evidently ought to be rebound but cannot be. Even so—particularly if he observes that many of the books have not circulated for a decade or more—this is not likely to look like a crisis to the visitor.

Has the literature of deterioration exaggerated? We have never scientifically sampled and tested the holdings of a research library, but we have the Barrow findings, indicating that most of our books will soon be "in an unusable condition." Perhaps we must consider what *unusable* means.

The best of books are not strong enough to survive much rough and careless use. On the other hand, very few books—even among those in which the paper has deteriorated below the "one-fold" level—cannot survive very careful and gentle use. Glass, after all, is one of the most lasting substances; even the most fragile glass ornament will survive for centuries if it is not dropped or crushed, but it cannot be folded even a little way, even once. Like glass, much of our brittle paper may last a long while if it is not bent. If this were not so, we could hardly advocate the large-scale preservation of original books; we should have to film at once.

My point is that the distinction between *permanence* and *fragility* may sometimes have confused us, and is likely to complicate matters when we try to explain the problem of deterioration to congressmen and even to scholars. We know that some damage is inevitable, even in a rare-book reading room, to very fragile books. We know that books in our general stacks will not always be used carefully, that leaves will break loose from bindings, that some of these will be lost or bent again, and that portions of the text will be lost. It should be possible to explain this, but it may not be easy: essentially we are saying that millions of books in research libraries are unusable; yet thousands of them are in fact being used every day.

Such difficulties may help to explain the long history of unsuccessful efforts to spread the alarm from 1823 to 1957, as well as the fact that our current campaign has not been victorious thus far. It is not my conclusion that we are entitled to be sorry for ourselves or to give up. We have met to re-examine what we know and to decide what further investigation is needed. In addition I propose that our strategy be reconsidered.

Librarians, like members of many other groups, talk to one another so much that they often forget, when talking to "outsiders," that the library ideology and dialect may not be understood. No librarian needs to be reminded that we preserve books—just as we acquire them in the first place—in order that they can be used. We have to preserve if we are going to disseminate; but this may not be entirely self-evident to others. If we are honored by an attack from the anti-establishment forces, their epithet is not likely to be "pig"; more likely it will be "squirrel." Unfortunately there are those—conservative and moderate as well as radical—who regard us as misers, gloating over wealth that has been accumulated for its own sake.

The ARL committee is the Committee on the *Preservation* of Research Library Materials. Reviewing its history now, I fear I, as its secretary, have been culpable in not more vigorously and persuasively suggesting that *Dissemination* ought to be substituted for *Preservation*. Perhaps I was so busy preserving a record of its deliberations for the minutes that I failed to disseminate my opinion.

It would have been possible, without changing any feature of the plan formulated for the committee by Gordon Williams, to have presented it as a plan for dissemination—for making research library holdings of the nation increasingly accessible to scholars. In a document entitled "The Preservation of Deteriorating Books," however, access inevitably appears to be something of a by-product. It was not neglected, but a title role is a title role and top billing is top billing; preservation was the star in this show.

Would we not do better, at least whenever nonlibrarians may be listening, to speak of preservation as a by-product of accessibility and continued dissemination? A successful heart transplantation is not acclaimed because it keeps alive a heart that would otherwise have died with its original proprietor; our national plan will be acclaimed not because it keeps books from crumbling but because it contributes to the health of American scholarship. One approach is to ask the Congress for appropriations to protect property that has been amassed by major research libraries; the other is to demand that Congress meet the cost of opening up this national resource to all the country's scholars and of making sure that it will be kept open.

This should not be put down as merely a cynical public-relations ploy. It is not deceptive packaging. If we conclude that books need to be kept cold in order to preserve them, we are not going to call the whole plan a book-refrigeration project. Since preservation is no more our real objective than refrigeration is, I insist that it is a misleading label and the dissemination is the honest one.

As has been suggested, the ARL proposal could, without alteration, be given a better title. However, if it were rewritten to emphasize the objectives of dissemination and accessibility, it is possible that the reworking would suggest some modifications in the machinery that is recommended. Such modifications would not be desirable if they made the plan any less effective in insuring preservation. In theory it would be possible, though Gordon Williams made it clear that this would make no sense, to preserve merely in order to preserve—one could bury collections under a Greenland glacier. But clearly it is not possible to disseminate a text of which no copy remains in existence.

We have difficult and therefore very interesting problems to consider here, but let us not become so deeply engrossed in them that we fail to keep in mind and to state as clearly as possible why they must be solved.

REFERENCES

1. Walton, Robert P. "Paper Permanence." *Publishers' Weekly* 116 (September 7, 1929):979.
2. Grove, Lee E. "Paper Deterioration—An Old Story." *College and Research Libraries* 25 (September 1964):365–74.
3. "Frauds and Imperfections in Paper-making." *Annals of Philosophy* 6 (July 1823): 68.
4. Murray, J. Untitled letter. *Gentleman's Magazine* 93 (July 1823): 21–22.
5. Murray, John. *Observations and Experiments on the Bad Composition of Modern Paper.* London: Whittaker, 1824.
6. Murray, John. *Practical Remarks on Modern Paper.* Edinburgh: Blackwood; London: Cadell, 1829.
7. Grove, Lee E. "John Murray and Paper Deterioration." *Libri* 16 (1966):194–204.
8. Johnson, Rossiter. "Inferior Paper a Menace to the Permanency of Literature." *Library Journal* 16 (August 1891):241–42. Reprinted from the New York *World.*
9. Goldschmidt, Robert, and Otlet, Paul. "Sur une forme nouvelle du livre: le livre microphotographique." *Bulletin de l'Institut International de Bibliographie* 12 (1907):61–69.
10. MacAlister, J. Y. W. "The Durability of Modern Book Papers." *Library* 10 (September 1898):295–304.
11. "Report of the Committee on the Deterioration of Paper." *Journal of the Royal Society of Arts* 46 (May 20, 1898): 597–601.
12. "The Durability of Paper." *Report of the Librarian of Congress* [John Russell Young] *for the Fiscal Year Ended June 30, 1898.* Washington, D.C.: Government Printing Office, 1898.
13. Società Bibliografica Italiana, "Processi verbali delle adunanze pubbliche." *Revista delle Biblioteche e degli Archivi* 9 (October 1898):145–51.
14. Dauze, Pierre. "La question de la conservation du papier dans les bibliothèques publiques et privées et un moyen de la résoudre." In *Procès-verbaux et mémoires* of the Congrès international des bibliothécaires, Paris, August 20–23, 1900. Paris: Welter, 1901.
15. Davenport, Cyril. *The Book: Its History and Development.* London: Constable, 1907.
16. Wiley, Harvey Washington, and Merriam, C. Hart. *Durability and Economy in Papers for Permanent Records.* U.S. Department of Agriculture, Report no. 89. Washington, D.C.: Government Printing Office, 1909.
17. Scribner, B. W. "Report on Bureau of Standards Research on Preservation of Records." *Library Quarterly* 1 (October 1931):409-20.
18. Scribner, B. W. "The Preservation of Records in Libraries." *Library Quarterly* 4 (July 1934):371–83.
19. *Deterioration of Book Stock: Causes and Remedies: Two Studies on the Permanence of Book Paper.* Virginia State Li-

brary Publications, no. 10. Conducted by W. J. Barrow and edited by Randolph W. Church. Richmond: Virginia State Library, 1959.

20. Church, Randolph W., ed. *The Manufacture and Testing of Durable Book Papers.* Virginia State Library Publications, no. 13. Based on the investigations of W. J. Barrow. Richmond: Virginia State Library, 1960.
21. *Permanent/Durable Book Paper, Summary of a Conference Held in Washington, D.C., September 16, 1960.* Virginia State Library Publications, no. 16. Richmond: Virginia State Library, 1960.
22. W. J. Barrow Research Laboratory. *Permanence/Durability of the Book.* 5 vols. Richmond: Virginia State Library, 1963–67.
23. Minutes of the Fifty-fifth Meeting of the Association of Research Libraries, Montreal, June 18, 1960.
24. American Library Association, Committee on Resources, Subcommittee on Micropublishing Projects. "A Preliminary Report on a Proposal that There Be Established a Cooperative National Microfilm Deposit." Manuscript, May 20, 1959.
25. Simonton, Wesley. "The Bibliographical Control of Microforms." *Library Resources and Technical Services* 6 (Winter 1962):29–40.
26. Minutes of the Association of Research Libraries, Committee on the Preservation of Research Library Materials, Cambridge, Mass., September 21, 1960.
27. Williams, Edwin E. "Magnitude of the Paper-Deterioration Problem as Measured by a National Union Catalog Sample." *College and Research Libraries* 23 (November 1962):499, 543.
28. "The Preservation of Deteriorating Books: An Examination of the Problem with Recommendations for a Solution." Report of the ARL Committee on the Preservation of Research Library Materials. In Minutes of the Sixty-fifth Meeting of the Association of Research Libraries, Washington, D.C., January 24, 1965.
29. "The Preservation of Deteriorating Books." *Library Journal* 91 (January 1 and January 15, 1966):51–6, 189–94.
30. W. J. Barrow Research Laboratory. *Permanence/Durability of the Book.* Vol. 5. *Strength and Other Characteristics of Book Papers 1800–1899.* Richmond: Virginia State Library, 1967.
31. Council on Library Resources. "Recent Developments." News Release no. 271, February 22, 1969.
32. Shaffer, Norman J. "Library of Congress Pilot Preservation Project." *College and Research Libraries* 30 (January 1969): 5–11.

THE NATURE OF PAPER

B. L. BROWNING

DEFINITION AND ORIGIN

Paper is so ubiquitous in our daily lives that it is difficult to imagine effective functioning of our technological society without it. Indeed, we often measure the level of contemporary cultures by the amount of paper consumed. In the United States the amount is more than 500 pounds per capita annually and is rising year by year. The contributions of paper are not without drawbacks: a limited supply of fibrous source materials, problems of air and water pollution in manufacturing processes, and questions of disposal of the paper once it has served its intended purposes.

Paper has not always held so important a place in the human economy; the multitude of demands that paper now fills were necessarily satisfied by other materials. It is significant that the earliest use of paper was in written communication. In this, it was preceded by other less-abundant or less-appropriate materials; baked clay tablets in the Near East, sheets of papyrus in the Nile valley, parchment or vellum in the Near East and Europe, cloth or strips of wood and bamboo in China, and sheets of macerated barks in Oceania, Africa, and the early Americas.

The word "paper" is used to describe a felted sheet of fibers formed by passing a liquid suspension of the fibers through a fine screen. The liquid drains away to leave a mat of fibers which is removed from the screen and dried. The definition is general. The fibers commonly used are composed chiefly of cellulose, although paper can be and is made from fibers of many other types, including glass, asbestos, wool, metals, and synthetic polymers. The liquid is almost always water, although other liquids can be used. Water is inexpensive and plentiful, and its interaction with cellulose fibers contributes unique properties—in swelling of fibers during mechanical processing and in formation of the paper sheet, and in fiber-to-fiber bonding which occurs as the sheet is dried and which is responsible for the greater part of the mechanical strength of paper.

Paper is reported to have been in use in China before the Christian era, although *Hou Han Shu (Book of the Second Han Dynasty)* credits its invention in A.D. 105 to Ts'ai Lun, who is said to have made sheets of paper from macerated tree bark, hemp waste, old rags, and fishnets [1]. The craft soon spread to Korea and Japan, and found its way into Central Asia and Persia by the routes of the camel caravans. The Arabs began making paper about A.D. 750, and the art spread to Syria, Egypt, and Morocco. The Moors introduced paper into Spain about A.D. 1150. In 1268 a paper mill was established at Fabriano, Italy. Papermaking began in France and Germany in the fourteenth century and in England in the fifteenth. The first American paper mill was established in 1690 near Germantown, Pennsylvania, by William Riteenhouse, a Dutch papermaker.

Until the invention of the paper machine, paper was made by a laborious hand process. Common materials in Europe were cotton and linen rags, and hemp. The wet fibers were stamped or pounded by hand until they reached a condition suitable for papermaking, and then made into a dilute suspension in a large tank or vat. A portion of the suspension was dipped up into a rectangular mold fitted at the bottom with a wire screen, and the water was allowed to drain away while the papermaker gently shook the mold from side to side to ensure even formation of the sheet. The wet sheet was "couched" from the screen by pressing a felt or blotter against it, and a stack of felts and paper sheets was compacted in a screw press to flatten the sheets and to remove additional water. The stack was then separated and the sheets were allowed to dry in the air. The surface of the paper was smoothed or burnished by rubbing it with a polished stone, and sizings of animal glue or starch were applied to writing paper to prevent feathering of inks.

The invention of the printing press with movable type in the fifteenth century and the growing demand for printing and writing papers created increasing pressure on the supply and on the requisite raw materials. These needs were met by the paper machine and by the use of fibers from wood.

In 1798 the Fourdrinier machine was invented by Nicholas Louis Robert of France, and development by the Fourdrinier brothers in England followed soon thereafter. The paper machine forms, presses, and dries the sheet in one continuous operation. Machine-made papers were introduced in the early 1800s and rapidly found their way into newsprint, writing, and printing papers. Today, except for the making of some special art papers, the craft of hand papermaking in the United States is restricted to a few hobbyists. Handmade paper is still produced in Europe and the Far East.

As production of paper grew, an increasing scarcity of cotton fibers developed, and there was intense competition in the markets for used cotton clothing and rags. Cloth wrappings from Egyptian mummies were imported in large quantities in the early nineteenth century, sometimes over the violent opposition of many citizens who feared they might transmit disease. Other sources of fibers also proved inadequate, and attention was directed to wood. The first suggestion that paper could be produced from wood appears to have been made in 1719 by the naturalist Réamur, who observed the paperlike quality of wasps's nests made from wood. The idea was not reduced to practice, and only with the invention of chemical pulping processes with wood as an abundant raw material was the production of paper on a large scale made possible.

THE MATERIALS OF PAPER

FIBERS

Cellulose fibers are the chief source of fibrous materials for papermaking; only a few specialty papers include fibers of other compositions. Cellulose fibers from many sources are used. Fibers from the seed hair of cotton are the purest form of cellulose; raw cotton after dewaxing and a mild alkali cook is essentially pure cellulose.

Cellulose is a high polymer; that is, it is made up of many single, relatively simple units combined chemically into very large molecules. The individual units are composed of molecules of glucose (or grape sugar) combined, with loss of one molecule of water from each glucose unit added, into long linear chains. The structural form of glucose as drawn by the chemist is shown in figure 1; that of glucose units

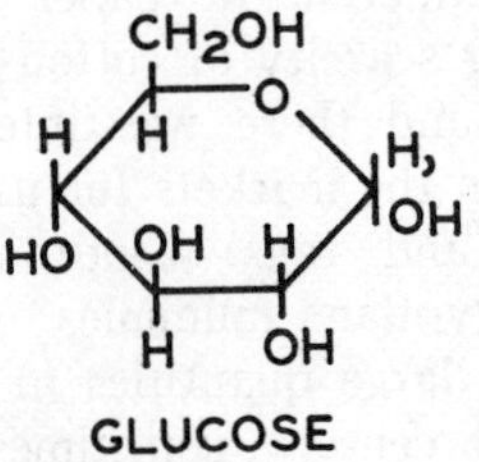

FIG. 1.—The chemical formula for glucose

[2]. Purification processes degrade and shorten the cellulose chains, which typically are composed of 500–1,500 units in common papermaking fibers. The length of the chain molecules can be visualized if one imagines that each glucose unit is one-eighth inch in length; a native cellulose chain then would be about 100 feet in length.

A cellulose fiber from wood is about one to seven millimeters in length (about one twenty-fifth to one-third inch) and twenty-five to fifty microns

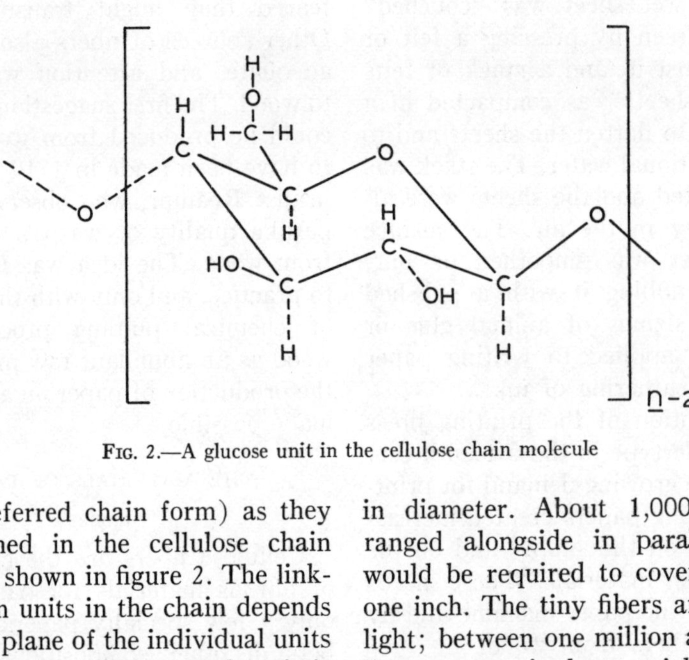

FIG. 2.—A glucose unit in the cellulose chain molecule

(in the preferred chain form) as they are combined in the cellulose chain molecule is shown in figure 2. The linkage between units in the chain depends on how the plane of the individual units are disposed. In cellulose, each unit is located at 180° to the plane of the adjacent units, and the glucose units are said to be β linked (fig. 2). Starch (the amylose portion) is identical with cellulose except that all glucose units are in the same relative positions in the chain and are described as being α linked.

The linear chains of glucose units in cellulose are very long. In native cellulose as grown in the plant, the chains are composed of 7,000–10,000 units in diameter. About 1,000 fibers arranged alongside in parallel fashion would be required to cover a span of one inch. The tiny fibers are also very light; between one million and ten million are required to weigh one gram (equivalent to one-thirtieth ounce).

Each fiber has a central cavity or lumen that contains the protoplasm in the growing cell. The lumen is collapsed in the processed fiber, which then commonly assumes a ribbonlike form. The chains of glucose units in the cellulose molecule are grouped in parallel fashion to form fibrils, which are arranged spirally around the axis of the fiber in concentric layers (fig. 3).

Wood is the major source of papermaking fibers; approximately 95 percent of the papermaking pulps produced in the United States are derived from wood. Other fiber sources include straws, bamboo, and sugarcane bagasse; these are important in countries in which they are available in quantity and which lack adequate wood resources. All these fibrous materials contain ligneous binding substances together with the group of carbohydrates which accompany cellulose in plants and are called the hemicelluloses. The fibers must be separated from the lignin and the major portion of the hemicelluloses by processes of chemical digestion and bleaching to yield fibrous pulps that are suitable for papermaking.

Pulps are manufactured from wood by several processes [see, for example, 3–5]. *Mechanical pulp* or *groundwood* is produced by grinding peeled bolts of wood against a rotating abrasive stone under a stream of water or by grinding chips in a disk-type mill. Properly prepared groundwood consists of separated fibers and fiber bundles; it contains all the components of the original wood except for the slight loss of water-soluble materials.

Chemical wood pulp is prepared by digesting wood chips with a cooking or pulping liquor at elevated temperatures (140°–180° C) under pressure. In the *acid sulfite* process, the cooking liquor contains calcium, sodium, or ammonium bisulfite with an excess of free sulfurous acid. The *bisulfite* process uses a less-acid liquor in which the chemical is magnesium or sodium bisulfite. In the *neutral sulfite* (or neutral sulfite semichemical—NSSC) process, the cooking liquor contains sodium sulfite plus sodium bicarbonate; the pulping reactions take place in a weakly alkaline solution. The oldest chemical pulping process is the *soda* process, in which the chips are cooked with a solution of caustic soda. This process produces a bulky pulp with good opacity and was in the past favored for manufacture of book papers, but production is now unimportant in comparison with other processes. Over 75 percent of the chemical wood pulp is now produced by the *sulfate* or *kraft* process, in which the cooking liquor contains sodium hydroxide (caustic soda) plus sodium sulfide. The spent

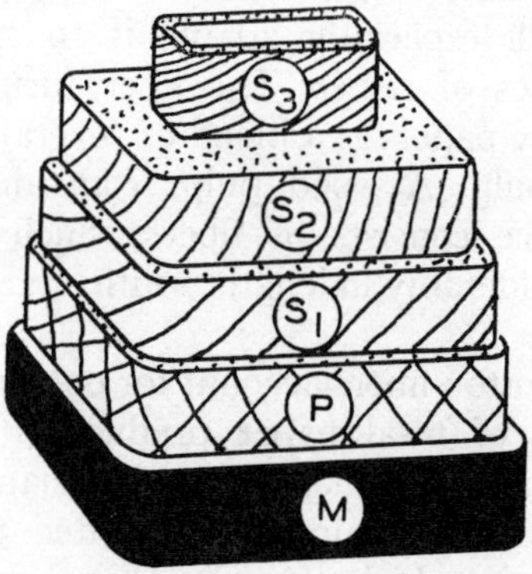

FIG. 3.—Schematic representation of the cell wall of a softwood fiber (after H. Meier). M = middle lamella; P = primary wall; S_1, S_2, S_3 = secondary wall.

liquor is concentrated and burned for recovery of inorganic chemicals; sodium sulfate (salt cake) is frequently used to make up chemical losses, accounting for the name "sulfate process."

Chemical pulps produced by any of these processes are tan to brown in color and contain residual lignin not removed by pulping. A white pulp is produced by a bleaching process to remove residual lignin and other organic impurities. Common bleaching agents are chlorine gas, hypochlorites, chlorine dioxide, and peroxides. These are applied in one or another sequence with washing or alkaline extraction between stages. Pulps for conversion to cellulose derivatives or for preparation of papermaking "alpha" pulps are given additional treatment with hot, dilute, caustic soda solutions, either at the end of the bleaching procedure or as an intermediate step in the bleaching sequence. Groundwood is bleached by application of peroxides or of sodium or zinc hydrosulfite; the process is one of "brightening" rather than bleaching, since little of the groundwood is dissolved during the process.

Pulps are made from both hardwoods and softwoods. Each has properties which especially adapts it to specific grades of paper. The fiber furnish of many papers is a blend of several types of pulp. A wood pulp from any one source consists of fibers which differ considerably in length, width, and structure.

Cotton fibers account for only a small part of total paper production; they are generally more expensive than wood pulps and their use is limited to papers in which they lend qualities not obtainable with wood pulp fibers. Many papers are manufactured from blends of cotton fibers with purified wood pulps; "rag content" papers are required to contain at least 25 percent cotton fibers. Cotton fibers are obtained from new and used rags, cotton wastes and cuttings, and cotton linters. Fine "rag content" papers are made almost entirely of new rags. The purification of cotton materials for papermaking is usually accomplished by an alkaline cook with soda ash or lime (or both) followed by bleaching. Cotton fibers are used principally for high-grade bond, writing, and ledger papers, where durability and permanence are important, and in drawing, index, onionskin, and technical papers, such as blueprint and direct line. These fibers are also used in the manufacture of blotting papers, saturating felts, and vulcanized fiber, where absorbency, fiber length, and fiber strength are necessary.

NONFIBROUS MATERIALS

A paper made of cellulose fibers alone has only limited applications. The extraordinary versatility of paper arises from the ease with which the basic sheet of fibers can be modified by addition of nonfibrous materials and the wide range of properties which can be achieved to meet the requirements of a multitude of end uses. The application of sizing, loading, coloring, coating, impregnating, and laminating materials illustrates only a few of the additives commonly employed. Fireproofing and flameproofing agents, antioxidants, microbiological control agents, insect and rodent repellents, wet-strength agents, internal adhesives, and many others are introduced for special purposes. Composite structures of paper with metal foil, wood veneer, plastic films, fabrics, asphalt, waxes, and others extend possible applications.

The grades of paper comprising writing, printing, and book papers are of particular interest in the fields of publishing, advertising, and communications. They cover a wide range of quality, depending on the intended use. These papers are always made of cellulose fibers, mostly derived from wood pulp and, in the more inexpensive papers, containing groundwood. The papers are normally internally sized with starch or rosin. Most printing and book papers are loaded; that is, inorganic white pigments or loading materials, such as clay or calcium carbonate, are introduced to improve opacity and printing quality. The printing and book grades are often coated with a composition containing a white pigment and an adhesive such as starch or casein in order to increase surface smoothness and printing quality. Practically all papers are colored, even white papers into which are introduced small quantities of tinting colors to increase apparent whiteness.

MANUFACTURE OF PAPER

The paper mill is designed to prepare fibrous and nonfibrous raw materials for papermaking and to manufacture paper by means of a paper machine [see, for example, 3, 4]. The first step is called "stock preparation"; the supply of fibrous pulps or blend of pulps (called the "furnish") is subjected to mechanical action in the presence of water by a process known as "beating" or "refining." In this process, the fibers are swollen in water, they are somewhat shortened, and, most important, they develop fraying and fibrillation at the surface so that the surface area is increased and bonding in the sheet is enhanced. Sizing, loading, coloring, and other nonfibrous materials may be added during the refining or before the paper sheet is formed.

The prepared fibrous stock is diluted with water and introduced onto the paper machine. The wet sheet is formed as the water is drained away through the moving wire screen, then pressed and dried by passage over a series of cylindrical, steam-heated driers. The present-day high-speed Fourdrinier paper machine is a costly and complex mechanism. It forms and dries the sheet, and in many cases introduces coatings or other surface treatments as a part of the operation. Some machines make a continuous web 360 or more inches wide; others operate at speeds of 5,000 or more feet per minute (about sixty miles per hour!). Recent modifications employ a method in which the sheet is formed between two moving wire screens so that the water is removed from both sides as the sheet is formed [6].

Another kind of paper machine is known as the cylinder machine, in which a wire screen–covered cylinder rotates in a vat containing the suspension of fibers. Suction applied inside the cylinder forms the mat of fibers on the screen; the wet sheet then is carried to presses and driers. The cylinder machine is used mostly in production of paperboard; it may comprise several cylinders, wet sheets from which are combined before pressing and drying.

Coatings and surface sizes may be introduced as a part of the machine operation; the treatment is applied to the partially dried sheet, and drying is completed through the remainder of the drying section. Many printing papers are manufactured in this way by the process known as "machine coating." The application of coatings and surface sizes is sometimes accomplished also as a separate operation after a "base sheet" has been dried.

Almost all paper is calendered to improve smoothness and gloss of its surface. The calender is a set or "stack" of horizontal cast-iron rolls with chilled, hardened surfaces, resting one on the other in a vertical bank at the end of the drier section of the paper machine; the paper is passed between all or part of the rolls [7]. Supercalendering is performed as an operation separate from the paper machine; it increases the density, smoothness, and gloss of the paper. The supercalender is a calender stack which has alternate chilled cast-iron and soft rolls of highly compressed cotton or paper. The effects of supercalendering are governed by the pressure, the water content of the sheet during the process, the temperature, and other factors.

Watermarks in handmade papers are produced by preparing raised lines to form a design on the wire screen. The mat of fibers is thinned in areas corresponding to the design so that the watermark is thrown in bold relief when the paper is viewed by transmitted light. Light-and-shade watermarks are produced by embossing the screen so that the design is formed by variations in thickness of the sheet. Watermarks in machine-made papers are produced by a "dandy roll," which is a screen-covered roll bearing a raised pattern and rotating above and in contact with the wet sheet as it passes under the roll on the paper-machine wire. "Laid" and "wove" marks in writing papers are made by use of a forming screen or dandy roll bearing the desired design. "Chemical watermarks" are formed by impregnation in areas corresponding to the design with a material which partially transparentizes the paper. (An extensive collection of watermarks, many exhibiting a high degree of artistry, may be seen at the Dard Hunter Museum, Institute of Paper Chemistry, Appleton, Wisconsin.)

MEASURABLE PROPERTIES OF PAPER

The properties of paper which are important to the user may be classified as physical, optical, and chemical. A prospective purchaser of paper may judge its quality by subjective observations, for example, color, opaqueness, smoothness, surface texture, stiffness or limpness, and water or oil repellency. For more dependable and objective evaluation of paper properties, and to provide specifications for sale or purchase, it is necessary to employ instrumental methods of measurement. Even these fail on occasion, and subtle differences that one can feel or detect often cause much agony in attempts to describe them instrumentally. Nevertheless, much effort has been devoted to standardization of methods for testing of paper, and considerable progress has been made. Standard methods have been established in the United States by the American Society for Testing and Materials (ASTM) and the Technical Association of the Pulp and Paper Industry (TAPPI) [8, 9], and internationally by the International Standards Organization (ISO).

Most of the physical tests are profoundly influenced by the moisture content of the paper at the time of test. Cellulose and paper are hygroscopic and maintain under normal conditions of relative humidity a water content amounting to several percentage points by weight. Typical sorption isotherms are shown in figure 4 (from [10]). Because of hysteresis, the desorption isotherm always lies above that for adsorption; that is, the amount of sorbed water at any relative humidity depends on whether the measurement is made after passing from a higher or a lower relative humidity. The desorption isotherm in figure 4 is that for a paper which is dried from the wet condition; a closed hysteresis loop is obtained only when the desorption isotherm is determined after the adsorption isotherm for the paper in an initially dry condition. Constant testing conditions and reproducible test values can be obtained only if the paper is properly conditioned and tested at a specified temperature and relative humidity to assure a standard moisture content; for example, according to the TAPPI Standard [9, *b*], a temperature of 23° ± 1° C and a relative humidity of 50 ± 2 percent.

As we have seen, paper is essentially a mat of fibers. We must now ask what holds the fibers together. What is the character of the fibers which lends to paper its remarkable strength? In brief, the mechanical properties of paper are determined by complex interactions of individual fiber properties and by the nature and extent of bonding between the fibers. The following are basic factors which establish paper strength: fiber dimensions, fiber strength, bonded area, bonding strength per unit bonded area, distribution of bonds (sheet formation), fiber conformability (flexibility), and stress distribution [11]. Many of these factors are influenced by chemical composition, mechanical treatment and degree of swelling of fibers during stock preparation, pressing of the wet sheet before and during drying, and the presence of additives (adhesives, sizing agents, fillers, etc.) in the furnish. No completely satisfactory theoretical treatment of paper strength has yet been achieved, although models based upon idealized fibrous structures

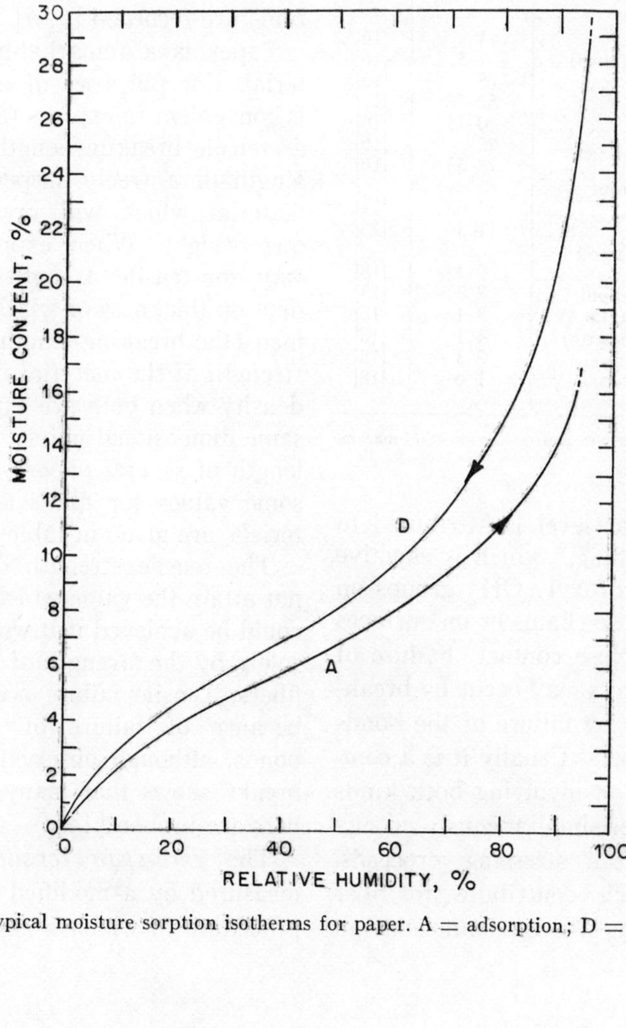

FIG. 4.—Typical moisture sorption isotherms for paper. A = adsorption; D = desorption.

have aided mathematical analysis (see, for example [12]).

The bonding between fibers depends largely upon the surface area in contact in the finished paper. This is established by the swelling and fibrillation of the fibers during stock preparation, the flexibility and compressibility of the wet fibers, the extent of wet pressing, and other factors. The bonding between fiber surfaces or fibrils at the molecular level is attributed to "hydrogen bonding," which is effective through the hydroxyl (OH) groups on adjacent cellulose chains or on surfaces in sufficiently close contact. Failure of paper under stress may occur by breaking of fibers or by failure of the bonds between the fibers. Usually it is a complex phenomenon involving both kinds of failure, either simultaneously or successively, as the stressing proceeds. Additives which contribute to fiber bonding, such as starch, mannogalactan gums, and several other high polymeric materials are known as "beater adhesives." They act as a cementing material between the fibers; they increase the strength properties and at the same time alter the contributions of fiber strength and bonding at failure caused by stress [13].

TABLE 1

TENSILE BREAKING LENGTH OF MATERIALS

Material	Breaking Length (kilometers)	Reference
Steel wire	41	[16]
Copper wire (hard drawn)	4.7–5.4	[16]
Rayon (acetate)	75	[16]
Hemp	52–58	[16]
Flax (Irish)	40–75	[16]
Silk	25	[16]
Cotton	18–53	[16]
Wood fibers (coniferous woods)	23–68	[17]
Wood (coniferous)	11–30	[16]
Greaseproof paper (wood pulp)	9.2*	[18]
Tracing paper (wood pulp)	8.7	[18]
Document paper (rag)	8.1	[18]
Duplicator paper (esparto)	4.1	[18]
Newsprint (wood pulp)	2.3	[18]
Blotting paper (cotton)	1.6	[18]

* Breaking lengths for papers are in the machine direction.

PHYSICAL PROPERTIES

The *tensile strength* of paper is measured by a "tensile testing machine." Strips of paper fifteen or twenty-five millimeters wide are stressed to failure [9, *c*, *n*]; the tensile strength at failure, the stretch, and sometimes the total work to failure (tensile energy absorption) are recorded [9, *n*].

Paper is a remarkably strong material. For purposes of comparison, it is convenient to express tensile strength as tensile breaking length, that is, the length of a freely suspended strip of material which will break under its own weight. When expressed in this way, the tensile strength is not dependent on thickness or width of the specimen (the breaking length is the tensile strength of the material divided by the density when both are expressed in the same dimensional units). The breaking length of several papers, together with some values for fibers and other materials, are given in table 1.

The tensile strength of paper does not attain the value which theoretically could be achieved if it were determined solely by the strength of the individual fibers. Tensile failure occurs primarily because of failure of the interfiber bonds, although observation of tensile breaks shows that many individual fibers are broken [14].

The *zero-span tensile strength* is measured by a modified tensile-testing procedure in which a strip of paper is held in two pairs of jaws which are in contact when initial tensile stress is applied [15]. The test provides a meaningful measure of average fiber strength; bonding between the fibers has little or no effect in the testing of most papers.

Resistance to tearing is an important property in many grades of paper. It is expressed as the force required to initiate and continue a tear [9, *d*], but the preferred approach defines the property as tearing energy, that is, the force times the distance through which the tear is continued. Most of the data on tearing "resistance" have been obtained by a procedure in which the force is exerted at a right angle to the paper; uncertainty arises when the tear does not occur cleanly across the sheet. In a recently developed method [19] known as the "in-plane" procedure, the tearing energy is measured by exerting a force in the plane of the sheet. The two methods do not always give comparable results because the nature of the tear is different.

The *folding endurance* is measured by an instrument (commonly the M.I.T. Tester) which subjects a strip of paper fifteen millimeters wide to folding through a total angle of 270° while it is held in jaws having a radius of curvature at the folding edge of 0.38 ± 0.005 millimeters [9, *p*]. The paper strip is held under a tension of one kilogram (or 0.5 kilogram) during the folding endurance test, so that the folding endurance measures the number of double folds which can be accomplished until the paper fails under the specified tension. The folding endurance test is especially important in papers which are subjected to folding during use, for example, record papers, map papers, currency papers, and book papers. The range of values for folding endurance is very large; some high-quality papers will endure, 1,000 or more double folds at one kilogram tension, whereas very weak or degraded papers may fail after one or two folds or may even break under an initial tension of 0.5 kilogram before any fold is made. Values of one or only a few folds are not usually considered significant. Unfortunately, the folding endurance test is less reproducible than most other physical tests, and a considerable scatter of values is commonly obtained even on relatively uniform machine-made papers.

Finish and smoothness are judged most reliably on the basis of printing quality, which at present is adequately determined only by making test prints with commercial equipment. There is a variety of smoothness tests, which are usually concerned with the printing quality of the paper. The gloss of some coated papers is measured with a "glossmeter" [9, *m*].

Absorption of water or oil is important in many sized papers, including those designed for writing, printing, and packaging. Resistance to absorption of water is measured by the time required for a drop of water of specified size to be absorbed into the paper or by the time required for penetration of liquid water into or through the sheet when one side is placed in contact with water [9, *g, i,*]. Resistance to absorption is contributed by sizing agents, such as, rosin, waxes, proteins, and fluorocarbons. Resistance to passage of liquids through the paper is important in applications such as filtering papers. Resistance to passage of gases and vapors [for example, 9, *l*] is important in filtering applications (for example, vacuum-cleaner bags), food-packaging materials, and many others.

OPTICAL PROPERTIES

Color is probably the first property of paper noted by an observer. A colored paper is produced by introduction of a dye or colored pigment during the papermaking process. Almost all papers are colored. Even "white" papers are colored by addition of a blue dye or pigment to make the paper appear whiter, although in fact it is made grayer.

The color of paper is determined by the extent to which light of various wavelengths is absorbed or reflected. Color is defined instrumentally by recording the percentage reflectance at wavelengths within the visible spectrum, that is, 400–700 millimicrons (mμ) or micrometers (μm). Typical reflectance plots for several papers are shown in figure 5 (from [20]).

Brightness is the most frequently measured and specified optical property. It is defined as the percentage reflectance at 457 mμ when measured by a carefully standardized procedure [9, *j*]. Since this wavelength is at the blue end of the spectrum, changes in brightness reflect increase or decrease in "yellowness" of white pulps or papers. Optical whiteners or brighteners are often added to make papers appear whiter; these are fluorescent dyes or pigments which absorb radiation in the ultraviolet region and reemit it in the blue region of the spectrum.

Opacity is especially important in printing papers to avoid "show-through" when the paper is printed on both sides. The relative opacity of papers can be judged easily in a subjective fashion by placing the sheets over a printed page. The property is measured instrumentally with an "opacity meter" or Opacimeter [9, *e*].

CHEMICAL PROPERTIES

The *composition* of paper is established by the fiber furnish, by the various sizing, filling, coating, coloring, and other nonfibrous materials added, and by impurities introduced from process water, mill equipment, or other sources. The analysis of paper is designed to detect the presence of or to determine the amount of various materials used in manufacture or present as impurities. The fiber composition of a paper is found by methods of "fiber analysis," in which the paper is disintegrated, the fibers are stained by an appropriate reagent, and the proportion of each kind of fiber is determined by counting with observation under the microscope [9, *a*]. Chemical analysis for any specific constituent is performed by suitable methods, many of which have been accepted as "standards" [8, 9]. A recent book gives a detailed description of procedures for detection and determination of the constituents of paper [20]. Methods for analysis of paper must include those for a wide range of components because of the extraordinary diversity of materials intentionally added during manufacture or present as impurities. Analysis frequently becomes a difficult undertaking because of the many components which may be present, the necessity for determining many substances present in small amounts or in traces, and the complex composition of many components which are commercial products and not pure compounds. Sometimes the analyst is presented with a still more perplexing problem—a paper is observed to have unusual properties, and he is required to deter-

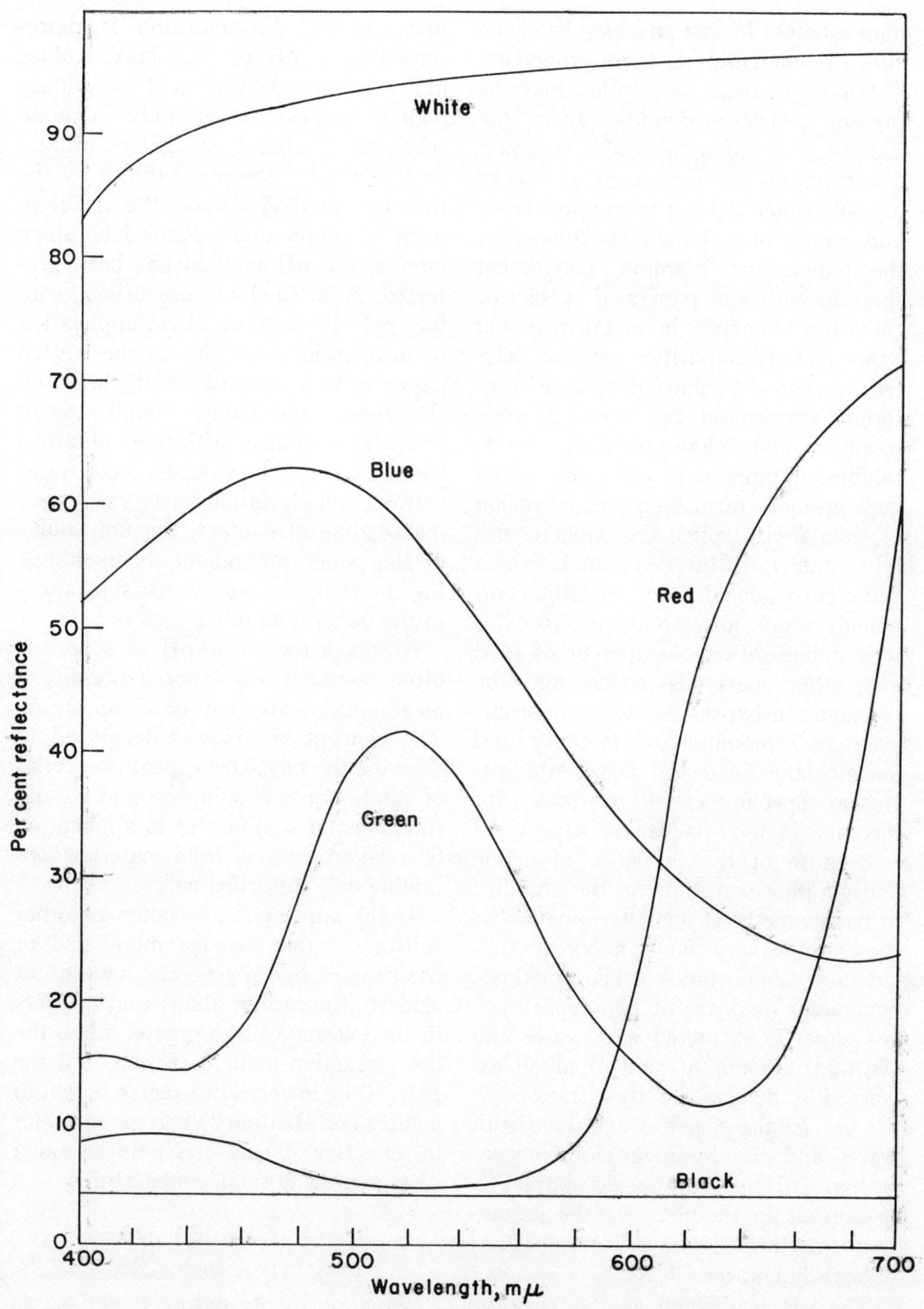

FIG. 5.—Typical reflectance spectra of papers

mine whether in fact *anything* has been added to contribute to these properties.

Minor or trace impurities may be present which profoundly affect the use properties of some grades of paper. These impurities may occur as specks or spots which detract from appearance and which may impair usefulness of the paper, for example, conducting spots in electrical papers or specks of corrosive materials in metal-wrapping papers. Other impurities may be deleterious even if they are distributed uniformly throughout the paper in very small amounts. Examples are water-soluble sulfates and chlorides which may promote tarnishing and corrosion of metals with which the paper comes into contact, sulfur compounds which cause corrosion of silver, metallic compounds which may contribute to catalytic deterioration of paper or of food and other materials which may be packaged in paper, and toxic materials such as compounds of mercury and arsenic (the Food and Drug Administration specifies zero tolerance for mercury in food-packaging papers).

Because of the influence of acidic and alkaline materials on the stability of paper, methods for determination of these substances have assumed considerable importance. The methods commonly used are of two types: (*a*) the paper is extracted with water and the total amount of acid or alkali extracted is determined by titration [9, *f*]; or (*b*) the paper is extracted with water and the hydrogen ion concentration (pH) of the water extract is measured. In method (*b*) the extraction is performed with cold water [9, *o*] or with hot water [9, *h*].

The pH is defined as the negative logarithm of the hydrogen ion concentration in moles (or equivalents) per liter. At 25° C, neutrality is represented by a pH of 7.0; lower values indicate increasingly acid solutions; higher values, increasingly alkaline solutions. Earlier investigators usually determined acidity or alkalinity by the titration method; since the development of simple and reliable laboratory meters, the pH method has been preferred. A method of measuring "contact pH" is based on direct application of measuring electrodes to the wetted paper or to a drop of water placed on the sheet; the values found are in essential agreement with those obtained by measuring the pH of the cold water extract, but deviations may result owing to time of contact, the uniformity of the paper throughout its thickness, the buffering capacity of substances in the paper, and other factors [21].

Although the term "pH of paper" is often used, it does not represent a meaningful statement of composition. The concept of pH was developed to describe the physicochemical properties of dilute aqueous solutions and has no fundamental significance in application to a heterogeneous solid material containing only adsorbed water.

If the paper contains alum or other substances that become more acid or basic upon hydrolysis, the amount of acid (in the case of alum) that appears in the extract will be greater when the hot extraction method is used, and the pH will be lower. The greater potential acidity (or alkalinity) may or may not be effective during the natural aging of papers at normal temperatures.

STABILITY OF PAPER

DURABILITY AND PERMANENCE

Paper is by its nature a perishable material. It can be burned, it decays, it can be attacked by insects and rodents, and it is degraded or destroyed by chemical reaction with many materials. Nevertheless, in the absence of seriously deteriorative influences, paper endures for many years or even for many centuries. Any paper product must last long enough to serve its intended function. Many uses of paper do not demand any great degree of permanence; once the use requirement has been satisfied, the paper has no further utility. On the other hand, in papers used for record keeping, legal documents, library books of permanent value, art works, and similar applications, it is vital that the paper retain its original character without alteration over periods of many decades or centuries.

The permanence of paper used for books and records has been a subject of concern for more than 200 years (see, for example [22]). The results of many observations and researches have been published; additional investigations are now underway in several laboratories. In 1962 the Cotton Fiber Paper Group of the Writing Paper Manufacturers Association established at the Institute of Paper Chemistry a research project on the permanence and durability of writing papers which is being continued currently. The objectives of this research have been primarily to study the validity of accelerated aging procedures for prediction of permanence and to establish the more important factors influencing permanence.

Paper is complex in composition and structure. The profound effects of source and nature of fibers, of the response of fibers during processing and stock preparation, of variables during the complicated processes of sheet forming, pressing, and drying on the paper machine, of the addition of sizing, filling, coating, and other additives, of the introduction of impurities from raw materials or in processing —all of these contribute to the fabrication of a product which cannot be described or evaluated simply. The sensitivity of measurable physical properties of paper to variations in moisture content, as well as to formation and relaxation of internal stresses which may be induced by mechanical treatment and by temperature or humidity cycling, contribute to difficulties in interpretation of test results. More research will surely be necessary to elucidate the behavior and properties of paper under various conditions of storage and use and to evaluate the relative contributions of factors which influence permanence.

Papermakers prefer to distinguish between the concepts of durability and permanence. Durability is the property of resisting deterioration by use, that is, the handling to which paper may be subjected, the hazards incident to heavy use of books in libraries, or the ability of sandpaper to hold together until the user finishes his work. Permanence, on the other hand, refers to the degree to which a paper retains its original qualities during storage [7]. In a sense, permanence may be defined as the retention of durability, whether the latter be small or great. A paper may be durable but not permanent that is, durability may be lost rapidly because the paper contains an excessive amount of acids), or it may be permanent but not durable.

The quality of durability is built into a paper when it is made, that is, by choice of fibers, conditions of manufacture, and the inclusion of additives which may enhance resistance to damage during use. Permanence is determined by the composition of the paper and by external conditions to which it is subjected during storage or use.

FACTORS INFLUENCING PERMANENCE

The factors which influence permanence may be divided into: (*a*) internal factors, which are established primarily by the composition of the paper; and (*b*) external factors, which are determined by conditions during storage and use, for example, temperature, relative humidity of the atmosphere (which controls the hygroscopic moisture content of the sheet), exposure to light, atmospheric contaminants (sulfur dioxide, nitrogen oxides, ozone), and the existence of biological hazards (decay by bacteria or fungi and attack by insects or rodents).

The control of internal factors is in the province of the manufacturer, who must choose the raw materials and processes which are requisite for production of paper having the necessary stability for intended uses. Control of external factors is the responsibility of the user. Methods for control of atmospheric contamination and biological deterioration are obvious and well known, even if burdensome. Hence, for any selected paper, the additional important conditions for maintaining stability available to the user are control of temperature and relative humidity.

Permanence of the fibers is governed largely by the resistance of cellulose to deterioration. Pure cellulose is a relatively stable organic compound; when stored under optimal conditions it can be preserved for centuries or millennia without severe deterioration. Nevertheless, it is subject to alteration by several types of chemical attack, of which the most important from the viewpoint of permanence are oxidation, hydrolysis, and photochemical reactions.

Cellulose is oxidized by atmospheric oxygen, although under normal conditions the rate of oxidation reactions is slow. Oxidation leads to formation of carbonyl (reducing) groups and of carboxyl (acidic) groups at one or more locations in the glucose units which comprise the cellulose chain molecule. Oxidation also results in formation of peroxides [23], which contribute to further oxidation and side reactions. Ozone in the atmosphere, even in minute concentrations, is a very active deteriorative reagent. The formation of oxidation products may be accompanied by immediate scission of the polymeric chain molecule, or it may result in a sensitivity to further deterioration by a variety of influences. The poor stability of "oxycellulose" has been abundantly established [24, pt. 1, chap. 3].

The hydrolysis of cellulose by acid attack leads to decrease in length of the polymeric chain molecule through random scission of the chains. The strength of the fiber is decreased; deterioration may proceed so far that the fiber becomes very weak and brittle and finally can be reduced to a fine powder. Hydrolysis may be caused by the presence of acids introduced into the paper during manufacture, for example, from the alum used in sizing or from some wet-strength resins. Oxidized cellulose or the acidic hemicelluloses associated with the cellulose in wood and wood pulps contain carboxyl (acid) groups which are a part of the polysaccharide chain molecules. Wood contains acetyl groups; hydrolysis of these groups in wood or in pulps from which they have not been removed introduces additional acidity. External sources of acids arise from the atmosphere of urban or industrial areas that may contain sulfur dioxide (which is readily oxidized to sulfuric acid) and oxides of nitrogen (which form nitric acid); these atmospheric sources contribute to acid deterioration.

The extent to which hydrolytic reactions proceed depends upon the amount (or concentration) of acidic substances originally present in the paper and upon the acids introduced later through oxidation of cellulose and hemicelluloses or through absorption of acidic gases arising from atmospheric contamination. The amount of acidic materials in paper introduced subsequent to manufacture may be large in comparison with that originally present. The contribution of such acids to deterioration is minimized if the paper contains buffering materials (a "buffer solution" is one which resists change in pH when acids or alkalies are added). Many papers exhibit a considerable buffering capacity; a high buffering capacity can contribute much to stability of paper during aging by partial neutralization of acidic substances formed or introduced.

Deterioration of cellulose by the chemical reactions of oxidation or hydrolysis proceeds more rapidly with increase in temperature. There is a rule-of-thumb (and useful approximation) among chemists that the rate of a reaction is doubled for each increase in temperature of 10° C. Many studies on aging of paper (for example [25]) have confirmed the profound effect of temperature and suggest the importance of this factor in the preservation of paper.

Hydrolysis and oxidation generally proceed more rapidly in the presence of moisture. Paper is hygroscopic and has a moisture content of 5–7 percent in equilibrium with relative humidities in the range of about 50 percent. The effect of moisture content during natural aging has not been well established, although it has been shown that aging reactions at temperatures in the range of 80°–120° C are much more rapid in the presence of moisture [25, 26]. Deterioration is promoted by the presence of many metallic salts, particularly those of iron and copper which are unavoidably introduced in small but measurable amounts during manufacturing processes.

Photochemical degradation, that is, the degradation produced by light, is not important in many uses of paper where prolonged exposure to strong light is not to be expected. Cellulose is degraded photochemically, but lignin is especially subject to deterioration from this source. Papers containing groundwood are observed to have poor stability upon exposure to light, particularly to strong ultraviolet sources.

PREDICTION OF PERMANENCE

The prediction of permanence is necessary in evaluation of papers for which this property is important. The manufacturer needs to determine the probable permanence of his product; the user wishes to know whether the paper meets his requirements [25]. Any practical predictive test must depend on some accelerated aging test. If accelerated aging is to have any predictive validity, it is necesary to demonstrate that there is a meaningful and reproducible relationship between such aging and aging under "normal" conditions.

An accelerated aging procedure based on heating the paper in an oven at circa 100° C was developed at the Swedish Government Testing Institute and at the U.S. Bureau of Standards in the period 1925–35 [27, 28]. Rasch and Scribner [29] considered the heating test (seventy-two hours at 100° C) as a valid means for estimating the relative aging quality of papers. Later investigators concluded that accelerated aging under these conditions is empirically equivalent to approximately twenty-five years (a range of about eighteen to forty-eight) aging at normal temperatures.

The oven aging test can be valid only if the reactions leading to deterioration are essentially identical at circa 100° C and at "normal" temperatures. The profound effect of moisture content on rate of aging [25, 26] suggests the necessity of taking this factor into account. In any case, the reactions in question can be only those whose rates are dependent on temperature; changes associated with photochemical effects, access to atmospheric contaminants, and other extraneous factors are not evaluated in oven aging.

It is necessary to establish that deteriorative reactions proceed in a regular and predictable way as a function of temperature. The relation of reaction rate to temperature has been determined for many systems; this is the scope of chemical kinetics. In the case of chemical reactions which can be studied in a fundamental way, it has been shown that a reaction rate is related to the temperature at which the rate is measured. The rate constant, k, at one temperature is described by an appropriate relationship which yields a linear plot of chemical composition versus time of reaction.

The rate constant, k, is then used to describe the temperature dependency of reaction rate according to the exponential form of the Arrhenius equation:

$$k = Ae^{-E/RT} ,$$

where $k =$ rate constant; $A =$ a frequency factor; $e =$ the base of the natural system of logarithms (2.71828...); $E =$ activation energy in kilocalories per mole; $R =$ the gas constant; $T =$ absolute temperature in degrees Kelvin (degrees centigrade + 273). The Arrhenius equation is usually used in its logarithmic form:

$$\log k = \log A - E/2.303RT .$$

For any specific reaction, log A and R are considered constant, and E is the activation energy which is constant if only one reaction occurs within the temperature range employed. Hence, a plot of logarithm of k versus $1/T$ will yield a straight line having a slope which is the activation energy E (fig. 6).

The changes of a paper property (for example, folding endurance or development of color) with time are not determined by any single chemical reaction whose effects can be isolated and controlled. Hence, applications of conventional kinetic treatment of aging data on paper are largely empirical. In any case, the results of kinetic treatment of data can be undertaken with confidence only if both the rate plots and the Arrhenius plots are linear.

The rate plots for loss of folding endurance are linear or nearly so for many papers if the reaction is treated as first order; that is, the logarithm of the property is plotted versus time of aging. However, many papers give nonlinear plots, and it is evident that not all papers exhibit the same type of behavior [25]. Other physical properties (for example, zero-span tensile strength, tearing energy) have also been plotted according to first-order kinetics; it appears that this is the most suitable general relationship for these tests, but again many rate plots are nonlinear [25]. The development of colored substances during aging is value of the measured property after any specified time of aging or determine, as in the case of folding endurance, the time for this to be reduced to one-half or other fraction of its original value. It has been shown that the Arrhenius plots for aging of paper are in fact approximately linear, but deviations are large enough that accurate

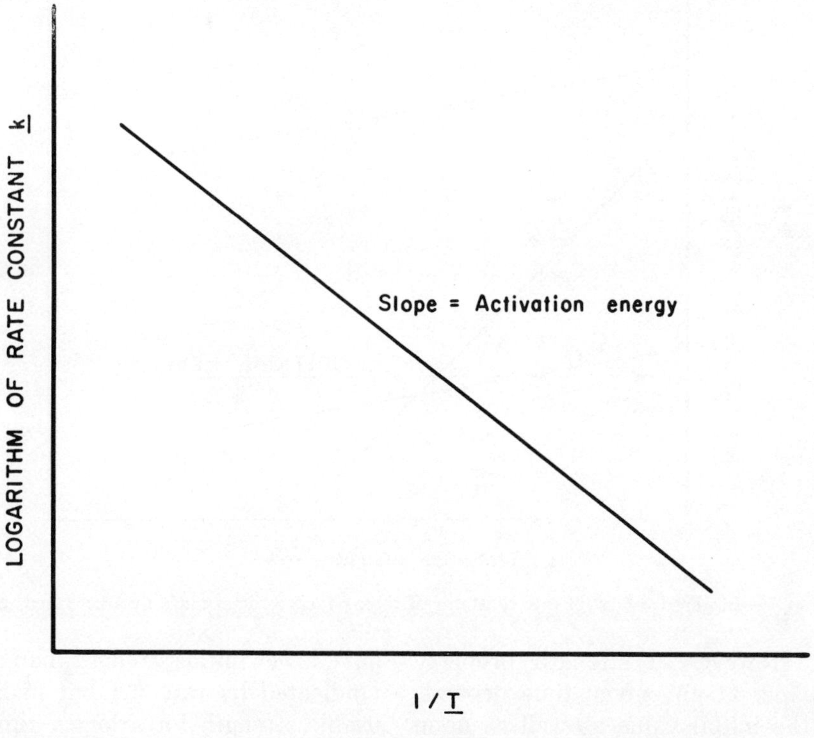

FIG. 6.—Relationship of the logarithm of the rate constant and the reciprocal of absolute temperature

shown by a plot of specific absorption coefficient versus time of aging; these plots are also linear for some papers and nonlinear for others.

If the Arrhenius plots (log k versus $1/T$) are linear, it becomes possible to extrapolate the relationship obtained upon aging at elevated temperatures and to determine the rate at a specified lower temperature, for example, 20° C or 70° F. One can then predict the predictions of changes taking place at lower temperatures can be established in only a very approximate manner. Nevertheless, the effect of temperature on aging rates is profound, and the relationship found, even if only an approximation, can be of great service in comparing stability of paper and in estimating rates of deterioration as a function of temperature during storage or aging [25]. Interpretation of aging data in this way assumes that all factors (including moisture content of the paper) other than temperature are held constant.

The relative stability of papers can be expressed by comparing the rates of change (rate constants k) in physical or other properties with time of aging. However, a strength property of a paper at any given time depends upon the initial value as well as upon the rate of change. For example, if two papers change at identical rates, indicated by rate constants k_1 and k_3 in figure 7 (from [20]) the one having the higher initial strength will maintain a higher strength throughout its life. Two papers may both have high initial strength values (designated by rates k_1 and k_2 in fig. 7), but the one having the higher rate of strength loss (k_2) will deteriorate more rapidly than the other (k_1). A high initial strength is desirable but alone is not sufficient; a paper (indicated by rate k_3) may have lower initial strength than another (indicated by rate k_2) but maintain a usable strength for a longer time. If it is possible to establish a critical level below which the paper loses its essential utility, the information furnished by the rate constants and by this critical level may serve for comparative evaluations of useful life.

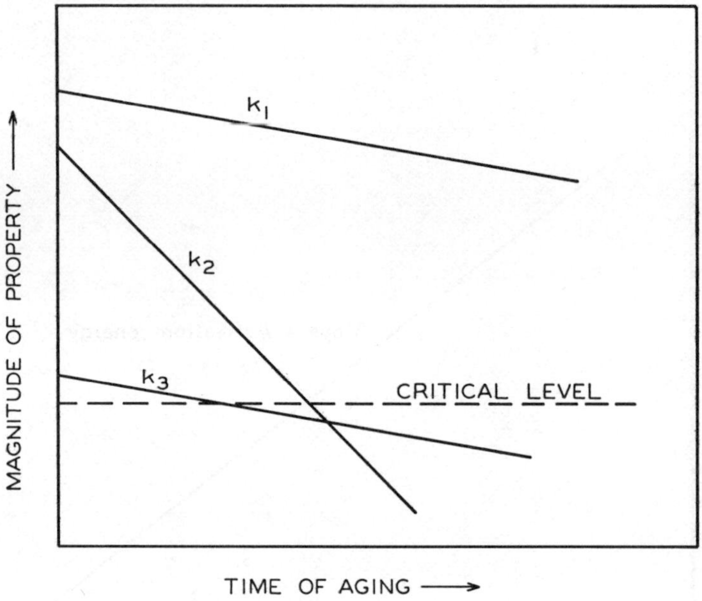

FIG. 7.—Idealized values for rate constants of three papers as determined by accelerated aging

REFERENCES

1. Hunter, D. *Papermaking: The History and Technique of an Ancient Craft.* New York: Alfred A. Knopf, 1943.
2. Timell, T. E. "Molecular Weight of Native Celluloses." *Svensk Papperstidning* 60 (November 30, 1957):836–42.
3. Libby, C. E., ed. *Pulp and Paper Science and Technology.* New York: McGraw-Hill Book Co., 1962.
4. Casey, J. P. *Pulp and Paper—Chemistry and Chemical Technology.* 2d ed. New York: Interscience Publications, 1961.

5. Rydholm, S. A. *Pulping Processes.* New York: Interscience Publications, 1965.
6. Wolfe, D. L. "Commercial Operation of the Twinverform." *TAPPI* 49 (December 1966):69A–72A.
7. American Paper and Pulp Association. *The Dictionary of Paper.* 3d ed. New York: American Paper and Pulp Association, 1965.
8. American Society for Testing and Materials. *1969 Book of A.S.T.M. Standards and Related Material.* Philadelphia: ASTM, 1969.
9. Technical Association of the Pulp and Paper Industry, *TAPPI Standards and Suggested Methods.* New York: TAPPI, n.d. (*a*) T401m-60, "Fiber Analysis of Paper and Paperboard," 1960; (*b*) T402m-49, "Conditioning Paper and Paperboard for Testing," September 1949; (*c*) T404ts-66, "Tensile Breaking Strength of Paper and Paperboard," 1966; (*d*) T414ts-65, "Internal Tearing Resistance of Paper (Elmendorf Tester)," 1965; (*e*) T425m-60, "Opacity of Paper," 1960; (*f*) T428su-67, "Hot Water Extractable Acidity or Alkalinity of Paper," 1967; (*g*) T433m-44, "Water Resistance of Paper and Paperboard (Dry-Indicator Method)," June, 1944; (*h*) T435su-68, "Hydrogen Ion Concentration (pH) of Paper Extracts—Hot Extraction Method," 1968; (*i*) T441m-60, "Water Absorptiveness of Nonbibulous Paper and Paperboard (Cobb Test)," 1960; (*j*) T452m-58, "Brightness of Paper and Paperboard," July 1958; (*k*) T453m-48, "Heat Test for Relative Stability of Paper," July 1948; (*l*) T460os-68, "Air Resistance of Paper," 1968; (*m*) T480-ts-65, "Specular Gloss of Paper and Paperboard at 75°," 1965; (*n*) T494su-64, "Tensile Energy Absorption of Paper," 1964; (*o*) T509su-68, "Hydrogen Ion Concentration (pH) of Paper Extracts—Cold Extraction Method," 1968; (*p*) T511, "Folding Endurance of Paper (M.I.T. Tester)," in press.
10. Wink, W. A. "The Effect of Relative Humidity and Temperature on Paper Properties." *TAPPI* 44 (June 1961): 171A–180A.
11. Swanson, J. W., and Jones, E. J. "Factors Which Affect Strength Properties of Paper." *Pulp and Paper Magazine of Canada* 63 (May 1962):T251–58.
12. Van den Akker, J. A. "Some Theoretical Considerations on the Mechanical Properties of Fibrous Structures." In *Transactions of the Symposium on Formation and Structure of Paper.* London: Technical Section, British Paper and Board Makers' Association, 1962.
13. Swanson, J. W. "The Science of Chemical Additives in Papermaking." *TAPPI* 44 (January 1961):142A–181A.
14. Van den Akker, J. A.; Lathrop, A. L.; Voelker, M. H.; and Dearth, L. R. "Importance of Fiber Strength to Sheet Strength." *TAPPI* 41 (August 1958): 416–25.
15. Wink, W. A., and Van Eperen, R. H. "The Development of an Improved Zero-Span Tensile Test." *TAPPI* 45 (January 1962):10–24.
16. Kollmann, F. F. P., and Cote, W. A., Jr. *Principles of Wood Science and Technology.* New York: Springer-Verlag, 1968.
17. Jayne, B. A. "Mechanical Properties of Wood Fibers." *TAPPI* 42 (June 1959): 461–67.
18. Meredith, R. *Mechanical Properties of Wood and Paper.* Amsterdam: North-Holland Publishing Co., 1953.
19. Van den Akker, J. A.; Wink, W. A.; and Van Eperen, R. H. "Instrumentation Studies LXXXIX. Tearing Strength of Paper. Tearing Resistance by the In-Plane Mode of Tear." *TAPPI* 50 (September 1967):466–70.
20. Browning, B. L. *Analysis of Paper.* New York: Marcel Dekker, Inc., 1969.
21. Smith, R. D. "A Comparison of Paper in Identical Copies of Books from the Lawrence University, the Newberry, and the New York Public Libraries." Unpublished report, June 24, 1969.
22. Smith, R. D. "Paper Impermanence as a Consequence of pH and Storage Conditions." *Library Quarterly* 39 (April 1969):153–95.
23. Marracinni, L. M., and Kleinert, T. N. "Aging and Color Reversion of Bleached Pulps. I. Peroxide Formation during Aging." *Svensk Papperstidning* 65 (February 28, 1962):126–31.
24. Ott, E.; Spurlin, H. M.; and Grafflin, M. W., eds. *Cellulose and Cellulose Derivatives.* 2d ed. New York: Interscience Publications, 1954.

25. Browning, B. L., and Wink, W. A. "Studies on the Permanence and Durability of Paper. I. The Prediction of Paper Permanence." *TAPPI* 51 (April 1968):156–63.
26. Richter, G. A., and Wells, F. L. "Influence of Moisture in Accelerated Aging of Cellulose." *TAPPI* 37 (August 1956): 603–8.
27. Hall, G. "Permanence of Paper." *Paper Trade Journal* 82 (April 8, 1926):52–58.
28. Rasch, R. H. "A Study of Purified Wood Fibers as a Papermaking Material." *Bureau of Standards Journal of Research* 3 (September 1929):469–506.
29. Rasch, R. H., and Scribner, B. W. "Comparison of Natural Aging of Paper with Accelerated Aging by Heating." *Bureau of Standards Journal of Research* 11 (December 1933):727–32.

ENVIRONMENTAL FACTORS AFFECTING THE PERMANENCE OF LIBRARY MATERIALS

CARL J. WESSEL[1]

I. INTRODUCTION AND OBJECTIVES

Protecting library materials against the dangers of environment is a critical problem. Inadvertent misguidance on the subject could hasten damage to valuable library materials. Most librarians realize this and agree on the need for deep study of the protection of library collections against deteriorative environments.

One of the more encouraging signs in the recent past is the Library of Congress brittle book project [1]. The recognition of the importance of the library materials deterioration problem at the level of the Library of Congress, the Association of Research Libraries, and the Council on Library Resources, places the matter at the echelon where adequate attention may be brought to it and the required national effort made to provide the restoration, conservation, and preventive measures required if we are to leave behind us library collections usable in the distant future.

[1] I acknowledge with thanks the kind cooperation and assistance of the following people in the preparation of this paper: Frazer G. Poole, Library of Congress; Verner W. Clapp and Melville J. Ruggles, Council on Library Resources; Charles Olin, William B. Walker, and Aleita Hogenson, National Portrait Gallery; Curtis L. Brown, Institute of Paper Chemistry; A. J. Haagen-Smit, California Institute of Technology; Arthur J. Broering, National Library of Medicine; Blanche L. Oliveri, National Agricultural Library; James Gear, National Archives; William K. Wilson and C. S. McCamy, National Bureau of Standards; Robert M. Organ, National Museum of History and Technology; Herbert C. S. Thom, U.S. Weather Bureau; Morton A. Bell, American Air Filter Company, Inc.; George Pettengill, American Institute of Architects; and Richard D. Smith and Howard W. Winger, Graduate Library School, University of Chicago.

This discussion will attempt to investigate environmental factors affecting the permanence of library materials and will try to draw some concepts from the information developed that will lengthen the life and usefulness of library collections. It is the objective of this paper to emphasize that deterioration of library materials can arise from inferior operating and storage conditions over both short-term and prolonged periods. It will review some pertinent evidence relating to deterioration originating with air pollution, heat and humidity, light, and biological agents. Focusing for the most part on the environments encountered in American urban research libraries, it will emphasize the effects of temperature, humidity, and such air pollutants as ozone, sulfur dioxide, and the nitrogen oxides. Since biological attack is not usually a widespread danger in these libraries, it will be discussed briefly. These points will lead to suggestions regarding how librarians may lengthen the useful life of library materials through environmental controls including some of the details of modern air-conditioning practices, criteria, and specifications.

II. ENVIRONMENTAL FACTORS IMPORTANT IN THE LIBRARY

A brief insight into the underlying causes of materials deterioration should prepare us to understand what happens to library materials when they are kept in hostile environments. The term "environment" is used these days in so many connotations that I shall define it as the physical, chemical, and biological elements which make up the space we live and work in and in which we carry out life and civilization as we know them. Usually these physical, chemical, and biological environmental factors bring their degrading effects to bear at a fairly slow rate. Some factors now included in our broadened concepts of environment damage our library heritage much more rapidly, such as riots, fire, and deliberate destruction.

TABLE 1

ENVIRONMENTAL FACTORS IMPORTANT TO MUSEUMS

a) The atmosphere (pollution)
b) Light (actinic effects)
c) Temperature (variations)
d) Humidity (variations)
e) Vibration
f) Parasites and saprophytes (insects, molds)
g) People (accidents, vandalism)
h) Acts of God (flood, fire)
i) Mechanical failure (of control systems)

SOURCE.—Cameron [2, p. 17].

The factors we are dealing with are energy forms—some of very high power, others of fairly low level. All are capable of bringing about physical or chemical reactions in materials. Usually the reactions are undesirable and decrease the stability of library materials. Obviously the reason we have libraries is to preserve man's historical records and his thoughts and intellectual creations. Some recorded material has little importance and it does not matter a great deal whether it lasts any longer than the people or events about which it is written. On the other hand, some recorded material has very great importance and should be preserved indefinitely. But often we cannot predict the importance of recorded material in advance. Thus, in the past, and even now, we have usually attempted to preserve all records for at least a moderate length of time, or as long as we practically are able, by utilizing the most stable materials known to the art and science of the times. Then we gamble that what is important will be recognized in time to take extra precautions to extend the useful life of the material on which it is recorded or of which it is made.

The materials on which we record events or print all manner of things vary greatly in properties and form. Some are rather fugitive in nature and even under good environmental conditions are soon unusable. Examples include some of the cheap papers. Other materials are extremely stable and even under rather undesirable environmental conditions will persist for long periods of time—as, for example, certain types of rock. But even the most stable materials are susceptible to some forms of environmental degradation. In the long run it becomes a matter of compromises—choices of materials of practical stability, available in amounts and at costs that can be afforded, and with properties that can be tolerated, and environments for use and storage which tend to reduce physical, chemical, and biological changes to a minimum.

The subject of this discussion is the factors of environment, their composition, the energy properties of environmental components, and the ability of these components to react advantageously or disadvantageously with the materials of our library collections. Included will be some examples of the effects of poor combinations of materials and environments on the valuable records of our civilization and history.

Duncan Cameron in 1968 [2] listed the environments he considers important to museums. These are shown in table 1. Table 2 shows Cameron's concepts of the ideal environment for the museum. His sanguine humor is undoubtedly shared from time to time by many librarians. The ideal environmental conditions for museums approximate those for libraries. If anything, museum people have to consider more environmental factors than librarians do because of the greater variety of objects and materials for which they are responsible. In addition, in many cases the museum objects are often much older and in an advanced condition of deterioration than is the case in libraries.

TABLE 2

THE IDEAL ENVIRONMENT FOR THE MUSEUM

a) Pollutant-free air
b) Total darkness
c) Constant temperature of 60°–68° F
d) Constant relative humidity of 50%–60%
e) Vibration-free structure and protection against shock and sound waves
f) Absence of all organisms (including humans)
g) A site on high land and a fireproof structure
h) Elaborate emergency back-up control systems
i) Cooperation of the Almighty

SOURCE.—Cameron [2, p. 17].

For the purposes of this paper the environmental factors of greatest importance to libraries are shown in table 3.

Atmospheric environments: Pollutants.—The atmosphere is commonly thought of as the gaseous envelope, that is, the air that surrounds the earth. Air has the properties of a mixture rather than those of a compound. A representative composite analysis of dry air is shown in table 4 [3]. The analysis of air is usually made after it has been freed of solids such as dust, spores and bacteria, and water vapor. Water vapor, or humidity, represents a very important constituent of atmosphere. It will be discussed in this paper as a separate topic because of its great independent influence on library materials. The composition of air varies with altitude and certain constituents such as ozone may vary considerably. The figures in table 4 may, however, be regarded as representative of the common components.

The atmosphere, especially in our industrialized urban areas, contains a host of other substances, termed pollutants. These pollutants are widespread because the United States is rapidly becoming almost completely urbanized. In 1920, less than one-half of the 106 million people of the United States lived in cities. In 1960, city-dwellers made up 70 percent of the 170 million total. By

TABLE 3

ENVIRONMENTAL FACTORS IMPORTANT IN LIBRARY DETERIORATION PROBLEMS

Atmospheric Factors
- Pollutants
  - Particulate Matter
    - Dust, dirt, etc.
  - Gases
    - Acidic Components
    - Oxidants
- Normal Constituents
  - Water

Radiant Energy
- Light
- Heat
- Other radiation effects

Biological Factors
- Microbiological Agents
  - Fungi, Bacteria, Actinomycetes
- Macrobiological Agents
  - Insects, Rodents

TABLE 4

COMPOSITION OF DRY AIR

Substance	Weight (%)	Volume (%)
Nitrogen	75.53	78.00
Oxygen	23.16	20.95
Argon	1.27	0.93
Carbon dioxide	0.033	0.03
Neon	....	0.0018
Helium	....	0.0005
Methane	....	0.0002
Krypton	....	0.0001
Nitrous oxide	....	0.00005
Hydrogen	....	0.00005
Xenon	....	0.000008
Ozone	....	0.000001

SOURCE.—Weaver [3, p. 25].

the year 2000, 95 percent of the population of 280 million will live in cities, according to an estimate of the U.S. Public Health Service [4]. Furthermore, the problem of permanence of library materials is made more serious since the largest library collections naturally tend to be concentrated in urban areas to serve the greatest concentrations of people.

TABLE 5

PRINCIPAL ATMOSPHERIC POLLUTANTS IN THE UNITED STATES

	Tons (Millions/ Year)	Percentage
By type:		
Carbon monoxide	65	52
Oxides of sulfur	23	18
Hydrocarbons	15	12
Particulate matter	12	10
Oxides of nitrogen	8	6
Other gases and vapors	2	2
Total	125	100
By source:		
Transportation	74.8	59.9
Manufacturing	23.4	18.7
Generation of electricity	15.7	12.5
Space heating	7.8	6.3
Refuse disposal	3.3	2.6
Total	125.0	100.0

SOURCE.—Committee on Pollution, Waste Management and Control [8, p. 11].

Most pollutants occur in very small concentrations compared with the "normal" atmospheric constituents. Even so, some of these abnormal constituents occur in concentrations high enough to pose serious problems. The subject of air pollutants has been widely documented, especially in the past few years because of the upsurge of governmental and public interest in the subject as it affects man, animals, crops, and materials of all kinds. Stern's 3-volume treatise on the subject of air pollution [5] is authoritative. A recent general review of the subject of pollution is that in *Chemical and Engineering News* [4]; an excellent review of technical information resources in the air pollution field is presented by Searle [6].

To provide an idea of the dimensions of the air pollution problem, the emissions of the principal pollutants into the atmosphere in the United States have been estimated by the National Research Council of the National Academy of Sciences to be about 125 million tons per year at the present time [7]. The amounts by types and sources are shown in table 5. Other estimates [4] are as high as 300 million tons per year. Some estimates of particulate matter are considerably higher than those shown in table 5. Haagen-Smit [9] quotes figures for the United States as high as one million tons of pollen, thirty million tons of natural dust, five million tons of smoke (carbon), and ten million tons of industrial dust and ash. Haagen-Smit quotes other interesting figures pertaining to the magnitude of the air pollution problem. For example, he states [10] that dustfall per month per square mile in Los Angeles amounts to twenty to thirty tons, although Los Angeles is considered to be a comparatively clean city in this respect; other highly industrialized cities receive several times this amount. Carbon monoxide, produced in automobile traffic, reaches concentrations of ten to thirty ppm (parts per million) (vol/vol) and on heavily traveled streets 100 ppm is normal [10]. The worldwide emission of sulfur dioxide from smelters, refineries, and fuel burners would require one million tank trucks of twenty-ton capacity to transport. This procession would stretch twice around the earth [10].

A complete listing of all substances found as contaminants or pollutants in the atmosphere would require several pages. The *Guide and Data Book* of the

American Society of Heating, Refrigerating, and Air-Conditioning Engineers (ASHRAE) [11, 12] provides an excellent listing of the various air pollutants as well as a wide discussion of the problem of air contaminants in general. Table 6 presents a partial listing of pollutants. Those representing the greatest known hazard to library materials for the most part are those which are either acidic or oxidizing. Notable deleterious substances in the library and museum fields are sulfur dioxide, the oxides of nitrogen, and ozone. These substances play roles in a rather complicated system of photochemical atmospheric pollutants which are seriously damaging to man, animals, vegetation, and materials.

The subject of photochemical air pollutants has been reviewed by a number of investigators. For example, Jaffe [13] and Haagen-Smit [9, 10] provide helpful summaries of a very extensive literature on the subject. Sulfur dioxide, or pollutants containing sulfur dioxide derived from coal burning, has been recognized for more than six hundred years as a damaging pollutant in the atmosphere [14]. Photochemical air pollution is a fairly recently recognized phenomenon, first recognized about twenty-five years ago because of its effect in causing cracking of rubber products and damage to plant species.

One of the symptoms of photochemical pollution is the presence of high concentrations of oxidizing substances in the air. Photochemical smog consists of mixtures of gaseous and particulate (aerosol) products resulting from atmospheric photochemical reactions of gases evolved primarily from the combustion of organic fuels [13]. Ultraviolet radiation from sunlight is responsible for the initiation of a series of atmospheric reactions between the oxides of nitrogen and such photochemically reactive substances as olefins, aromatic hydrocarbons, aldehydes, and, to a limited extent, some paraffins [13].

The photochemical oxidants consist of a dynamic complex of oxidizing substances which are not yet completely defined chemically. Because of the practical difficulty of measuring the various oxidizing substances separately, they are usually measured as total oxidant values in the atmosphere. Total oxidant values as high as 100 parts per hundred million or one part per million have been reported in dense photochemical smog [13].

TABLE 6

ATMOSPHERIC SUBSTANCES CONSIDERED AS POLLUTANTS

Particulate Matter (Aerosols)	Gases
Dust, dirt, smoke	Carbon monoxide
Coal and coke dust	Nitric oxide
Fly ash	Nitrous oxide
Salt particles	Sulfur dioxide
Calcium and ammonium sulfates	Ozone
Nitrates	Olefins
Chlorides	Aromatic hydrocarbons
Solid oxides	Aldehydes
Soot	Paraffins
Tars	Hydrogen sulfide
Spores	Halogen compounds
Bacteria	Ammonia

Although it is not a purpose of this discussion to become involved in the detailed chemistry of atmospheric oxidants, it is interesting to note a few aspects of present knowledge on the subject. Jaffe's review explains that a number of products are formed in the photochemical smog-forming process through the initiating photo-dissociation of nitrogen dioxide with the concomitant formation of atomic oxygen. This permits ozone formation, already present normally to some extent in the atmosphere, and known to be a principal oxidizer. In addition, there is formation of the strong oxidants, the organic peroxides, of which the peroxyacyl nitrates have been identified. These comprise a homologous series of organic peroxide nitrogen compounds which have been designated as PaNs compounds; to distinguish the originally discovered peroxyacetyl nitrate (PAN) from the series, the group designation is now commonly PaNs. In addition to the foregoing, other unidentified oxidants are formed, oxygenated compounds such as carbonyl compounds (aldehydes and ketones) and certain degradation products, such as carbon monoxide and carbon dioxide. Thus the principal identifiable photochemical atmospheric pollutants are thought to be ozone, the PaNs, and the oxides of nitrogen, chiefly nitrogen dioxide. The latter, comprising usually about 10 percent of total oxidants, are relatively weak oxidants.

Tables 7 and 8 are taken from Jaffe [13]. In these compilations, he presents summaries of values measuring the total oxidizing power of polluted atmospheres in a number of the larger industrialized cities of the United States. Also shown

TABLE 7

1965 PPM TOTAL OXIDANT CONCENTRATIONS, YEARLY SUMMARY CAMP* DATA†

City	No. Days Valid	Year Mean	Maximum Month	Maximum Day	Maximum Hour	Maximum 5 Minutes
Chicago	275	0.02	0.05	0.08	0.13	0.19
Cincinnati	310	0.03	0.04	0.1	0.17	0.19
Denver (February–December)	285	0.03	0.05	0.08	0.25	0.29
Los Angeles (LACAPCD)‡	365	0.038	0.06	0.14	0.58	0.65
Philadelphia (no data May–June)	266	0.03	0.07	0.23	0.33	0.35
San Francisco (BAAPCD)§	348	0.02	0.03	0.09	0.18	0.21
Saint Louis	329	0.03	0.04	0.07	0.35	0.62
Washington, D.C.	284	0.03	0.05	0.08	0.21	0.23

SOURCE.—Jaffe [13, p. 788].

* Continuous Air Monitoring Program.

† Total oxidant values corrected for sulfur dioxide interferences.

‡ Los Angeles County Air Pollution Control District.

§ Mission Street Station, Bay Area Air Pollution Control District. The downtown location of this station generally shows lower oxidant levels than other stations in this air pollution control district.

TABLE 8

FREQUENCY OF DAYS WITH OXIDANT CONCENTRATION FOR VARIOUS CITIES IN 1965
(Data from CAMP and Cooperating Stations)

CITY	0.15 PPM		0.1 PPM		0.05 PPM		DAYS OF VALID DATA
	No.	%	No.	%	No.	%	
Chicago	0	0	9	3	120	44	275
Cincinnati	5	1.5	19	6	182	59	310
Denver (February–December)	14	5	51	18	226	79	285
Los Angeles (LACAPCD)	121	33	185	51	275	75	365
Philadelphia (no data May–June)	4	1.5	23	9	109	41	266
San Francisco (BAAPCD)	4	1	15	4	107	31	348
Saint Louis	8	2.5	33	10	206	63	329
Washington, D.C.	3	1	25	9	150	53	284

SOURCE.—Jaffe [13, p. 788].

are the number of days in these cities when the concentrations of total oxidants reach the values shown.

A seemingly anomalous phenomenon in the air pollution field should be noted. It is especially interesting to the librarian because of the importance of the acidic sulfur dioxide to the degradation of paper. Sulfur dioxide is a reducing substance, while the photochemical air pollutants we have been discussing are oxidizing substances. Ordinarily, one might expect that such oxidants as ozone and sulfur dioxide would react with each other until there is an excess of one or the other. The extreme dilution of these pollutants in the atmosphere, however, permits them to coexist, and one may note oxidizing and reducing degradation phenomena simultaneously. The situation is rather easily understood when one considers reaction rates in relation to the small concentrations of reactants. Whereas in fairly high concentrations, a reaction would proceed in perhaps a few thousandths of a second, in the extremely low concentrations of air pollutants a similar reaction might require an hour [10].

Atmospheric factors: humidity.—Water occurs in all the normal states of matter—solid, liquid, and gas. It also takes many forms—ice, snow, glaze, sleet or hail, ice fog, liquid water, rain, water in the aerosol form of fog or mist, and finally water vapor. Water vapor is water in the gaseous phase and is usually referred to in terms of humidity. For the consideration of the librarian, water vapor is the most important form of water. The materials of the librarian—his buildings, his collections, and practically all that he works with, are protected, for the most part, against all forms of water except water vapor. The following discussion considers water only in the vapor form and will omit the less usual albeit devastating damage which may come about from such phenomena as floods or water damage caused by sprinkler systems and the like.

Humidity measurements include absolute and relative humidity. Absolute humidity is measured in terms of the mass of water vapor per unit volume of natural air. Relative humidity expresses the ratio of the actual water vapor content of the air to its total capacity at a given temperature. The warmer the air, the greater amount of water vapor it is capable of holding. When air holds as much water vapor as it is capable of holding at that temperature, it is said to be saturated, and is at its dew point.

TABLE 9

Temperature		Absolute Humidity (g/kg)		
°C	°F	RH=20%	RH=60%	RH=100%
0	32	0.38	2.28	3.82
20	68	1.43	8.69	14.61
40	104	4.55	28.30	48.64
60	140	12.50	83.55	152.45

Source.—Plenderleith and Philippot [15, pp. 243-89].

An enlightening way of showing the relations between temperature, relative humidity, and absolute humidity is that of table 9 taken from Plenderleith and Philippot [15]. This shows how the actual amount of water in the atmosphere increases, for a given relative humidity, as the temperature rises.

The effect of humidity on library materials is more important than on library workers or patrons. Nonetheless, because temperature and humidity conditions in libraries are usually chosen with both materials and people in mind, a few remarks should be made about factors of human comfort. Cold air with high humidity feels colder than dry air of the same temperature. On the other hand, hot air with high relative humidity feels warmer than it actually is. These effects are due to a combination of heat conduction from the body at the temperatures and humidities involved as well as the cooling effect on the body brought about by evaporation of water from body surfaces. The feeling of comfort or discomfort experienced by man is then a result of both temperature and humidity. The U.S. Weather Bureau has developed a temperature-humidity or comfort index which gives values in the 70–80-range, reflecting outdoor atmospheric conditions of temperature and humidity as a measure of comfort or discomfort in warm weather. This index, *I*th, is measured as follows:

$$I\text{th} = 0.4 \text{ (dry bulb temp. F}^\circ + \text{wet bulb temp. F}^\circ) + 15.$$

When this index value is 70 most people feel comfortable; at 75 about half the population is satisfied; at 80 most people are uncomfortable. Without unnecessarily oversimplifying a subject which is complex at best, man is an aqueous creature. In order to exist in his most healthy state he must maintain a proper water balance with his surroundings. This may sometimes require humidity conditions which would be considered a bit on the uncomfortable side. He cannot suffer dehydration of any magnitude for more than short time periods without serious physiological effects.

The various materials the librarian is dealing with daily also must remain in equilibrium with the proper humidity in order to retain their most desirable properties and endure for long periods of time. These conditions are not necessarily the same for all library materials. It stands to reason that conditions must be chosen so that most materials involved are in or near some reasonably favorable range of humidity.

When considering the matter of humidity and temperature with reference to the possible damaging effects of the heat and water on objects (books, manuscripts, museum items, etc.), it is very important to remember that it is the temperature and humidity conditions of the object which control deterioration reactions. These conditions are not always the same as the measured ambient or atmospheric conditions, except when they are under constant control. For example, in a library, if an object such as a book is at a temperature higher or lower than that of the air in the library, the relative humidity of the layer of air close to the book will differ considerably from that of the ambient room air. This has given rise to the term "object humidity" [12], which, of course, refers to the relative humidity of the thin film of air in closest contact with the surface of the book. If the temperature conditions in a library vary greatly over the period of a day, relative humidities thought to be in the safe range of perhaps 45–55 percent can rise to much higher humidities conducive to mildew or other damage to books, paper, leather, and other objects.

The nature of water makes it important both as a chemical agent and as a physical agent. Often it acts in both roles simultaneously. For example, when water dissolves carbon dioxide, a small amount of the water actually reacts chemically to form the compound H_2CO_3. Most of the water, however, plays the physical role of acting as a solvent medium for ionization and the production of hydrogen ions, responsible for the acidic properties of the solution. Water may be regarded as extremely active in promoting reactions between other substances, entering into chemical reactions itself, and serving as the medium for the interaction of numerous otherwise inert substances.

Among its most important roles, water is required for the hydration of many substances in everyday life. Some of these roles are not completely understood, and often not sufficiently appreciated. The role of water as a plasticizer for certain materials such as nylon is important in preserving the properties of the substance over long periods. The maintenance of proper water levels in paper, wood, and leather, to mention a few materials, is absolutely required to prevent drying out with consequent brittleness and eventual disintegration. The discovery of ancient records or historical and art objects usually poses severe restoration problems; at least partial rehydration must occur before the objects can be handled to any great extent or studied and exhibited. Although the objects have endured because they were dry and undisturbed, to be of practical value they must (if possible) be restored to a water content consonant with usable properties.

On the other hand, the presence of excessive water in materials can bring about destruction. Some constituents of materials such as dyes and adhesives may be dissolved out. Other components may become hydrated to the point of becoming pulp as in the case of cellulosic materials in paper. Excess water may cause some materials to act as adhesives, causing pages of paper to stick together almost beyond separation.

Excessive water may also bring about the completely different problem of biological attack. This is usually manifested as the growth of fungi or mildew, and is accompanied by the characteristic musty odor, but more importantly by staining of paper, leather, and other materials. Weakening or even destruction of the materials results if the organisms are permitted to progress too far.

To provide some idea of the relative humidity, precipitation, and temperature in typical cities in the United States, table 10 is included. These data are adapted in part from an earlier publication [16]. The cities included are Chicago, Cincinnati, Denver, Los Angeles, Philadelphia, San Francisco, Saint Louis, and Washington, D.C., to provide data on the same cities as in tables 7 and 8. Table 11 summarizes the mean relative humidity conditions for these cities.

The data in these tables should be viewed only as generally indicative. A more complete set of data would also include values for the saturated vapor pressure, for vapor pressure, for depression of wet bulb, and for dew point. The original reference should be consulted for those data. There are many other factors which play a part in determining the real significance of the climatic environment of a given location. Elements which are important include local variations in conditions. For example, we all know that rainfall is measured at relatively few spots for a given city. In large cities it may simultaneously be raining in some sections but not in other sections. Humidity and temperature conditions may vary from place to place depending upon such factors as existence of local bodies of water, vegetation, and protection from sun. Daily ranges vary from spot to spot. In extreme climates, such as in the desert, precipitation values may not have much significance. For example, there may be long periods of no rainfall at all. Suddenly the area may receive a two-inch rain. This could give an average value of perhaps 0.17 inch per year—a meaningless figure. Wind also can influence conditions significantly and may vary

TABLE 10

RELATIVE HUMIDITY, PRECIPITATION, AND TEMPERATURE IN TYPICAL CITIES OF THE UNITED STATES

City and Month	Temperature (° F)	RH (%)	Precipitation (inches)
Chicago:			
January	25.0	77	1.96
February	26.8	75	1.87
March	36.2	72	2.70
April	47.2	68	2.84
May	57.6	68	3.58
June	67.6	70	3.62
July	73.3	68	3.18
August	72.1	71	3.13
September	65.3	72	3.15
October	54.1	70	2.55
November	40.1	73	2.35
December	29.1	77	2.01
Cincinnati:			
January	32.7	77	3.48
February	34.4	74	2.88
March	43.3	70	3.90
April	53.8	66	3.28
May	64.1	70	3.59
June	73.1	73	3.90
July	77.1	72	3.54
August	75.3	74	3.31
September	68.8	74	2.66
October	57.3	74	2.40
November	44.6	74	2.92
December	35.2	76	2.89
Denver:			
January	30.6	56	0.46
February	33.0	58	0.54
March	39.2	54	1.08
April	47.8	54	2.03
May	56.7	56	2.32
June	66.7	53	1.39
July	72.5	50	1.57
August	71.4	49	1.36
September	62.9	49	1.00
October	51.7	49	1.00
November	40.2	51	0.62
December	32.7	53	0.63
Los Angeles (Civic Center):			
January	55.8	58	3.07
February	57.1	62	3.33
March	59.4	63	2.26
April	61.8	65	1.17
May	64.8	67	0.16
June	68.0	70	0.06
July	73.0	68	Trace
August	73.1	69	0.04
September	71.9	65	0.23
October	67.4	65	0.41
November	62.7	54	1.08
December	58.2	55	2.87

City and Month	Temperature (° F)	RH (%)	Precipitation (inches)
Philadelphia (International Airport):			
January	32.3	67	3.32
February	33.2	64	2.80
March	41.0	64	3.80
April	52.0	61	3.40
May	62.6	65	3.74
June	71.0	67	4.05
July	75.6	69	4.16
August	73.6	70	4.63
September	66.7	72	3.46
October	55.7	70	2.78
November	44.3	67	3.40
December	33.9	67	2.94
San Francisco:			
January	47.7	77	3.59
February	50.4	78	3.37
March	53.0	75	2.85
April	54.4	78	1.20
May	56.8	78	0.37
June	59.7	77	0.13
July	60.8	79	0.01
August	60.9	80	0.01
September	61.9	76	0.09
October	59.5	76	0.76
November	54.2	76	1.51
December	49.5	80	3.79
Saint Louis:			
January	32.4	72	2.32
February	35.0	70	2.41
March	44.8	67	3.51
April	56.2	65	3.77
May	66.2	66	4.43
June	75.3	67	4.42
July	79.8	63	3.47
August	77.9	66	3.57
September	70.8	68	3.23
October	59.5	65	2.87
November	45.7	68	2.81
December	35.8	72	2.46
Washington, D.C.:			
January	34.6	66	3.42
February	35.7	63	3.02
March	43.9	61	3.64
April	53.9	59	3.26
May	64.6	65	3.68
June	73.0	69	3.93
July	77.2	71	4.44
August	75.1	72	4.33
September	68.7	73	3.67
October	57.4	71	2.95
November	46.2	67	2.62
December	36.9	66	3.06

SOURCE.—Adapted from Herbert Thom's data in Greathouse and Wessel [16, pp. 26, 33, 35, 37, 43]. Values for Los Angeles and Philadelphia are from Herbert Thom, Environmental Sciences Services Administration, U.S. Department of Commerce, 1968.

NOTE.—All values are mean values.

greatly from spot to spot and from one time to another.

The relationship between absolute and relative humidity must also be kept in mind. Trewartha [17] makes the interesting observation that in comparison with air at Madison, Wisconsin, air at Yuma, Arizona, contains nearly as much moisture in July and twice as much moisture in January. Yet the relative humidity figures for Yuma are only two-thirds to one-half the magnitude of those for Madison. Evaporation rate, which is dependent not upon actual amounts of moisture in the air but rather upon relative humidity, is high in the desert, which accounts in a large part for the dryness of the climate.

Nonetheless these data will give an idea of the mean conditions for the cities listed and some insight into the conditions of humidity faced over the year by their library collections.

Radiant energy.—Of all of the chemical and physical agents of deterioration, sunlight probably accounts for the most widespread destruction of materials *outdoors*. Materials used mainly indoors for the most part are protected from the powerful effects of solar radiation. Nonetheless, they are subject to damage by the radiant energy of natural light entering the building via windows, skylights, and doors, and by artificial sources of illumination. Thus, although light is not regarded as being as damaging to library collections as some other deteriorative factors, it is certainly worthy of considerable attention. The effectiveness of radiant energy as an agent of deterioration is explained by the fact that some portions of the electromagnetic radiation spectrum are able to bring about photochemical reactions with the materials being irradiated either alone or in the presence of other agents like moisture or oxygen.

TABLE 11

MEAN RELATIVE HUMIDITY FOR SEVERAL CITIES

Month	Chicago	Cincinnati	Denver	Los Angeles	Philadelphia	San Francisco	Saint Louis	Washington, D.C.
January	77	77	56	58	67	77	72	66
February	75	74	58	62	64	78	70	63
March	72	70	54	63	64	75	67	61
April	68	66	54	65	61	78	65	59
May	68	70	56	67	65	78	66	65
June	70	73	50	70	67	77	67	69
July	68	72	53	68	69	79	63	71
August	71	74	49	69	70	80	66	72
September	72	74	49	65	72	76	68	73
October	70	74	49	65	70	76	65	71
November	73	74	51	54	67	76	68	67
December	77	76	53	55	67	80	72	66

For details of the photochemical phenomena which are involved in materials deterioration the reader is referred to earlier reviews [16, 18]. The barest details are mentioned here to provide a generalized discussion. Sunlight, or solar radiation, and certain sources of artificial light are important in photochemical and photosensitized reactions because they are the sources of the radiant energy which make the reactions possible. In nonphotochemical reactions, the energy is provided by heat.

Solar radiations comprise wavelengths from about 1,500 to 1,200,000

Angstrom units (A) in the electromagnetic spectrum. Figure 1 illustrates the electromagnetic spectrum [19]. Radiation is classified according to wavelengths, the shortest of which are as low as 10^{-14} cm and the longest are measured in km. The shortest are known as cosmic rays, followed by gamma radiation, X-rays, ultraviolet rays, visible light, infrared rays, radio waves, and radiations from power lines, the last having wavelengths measured in kilometers.

energy of this quantum unit is expressed by the term $h\nu$, where h is Planck's constant or approximately 6.6×10^{-27} erg sec and ν is the frequency of the particular light. The energy of quanta in long wavelength radiation ranges (low frequency radiation) such as infrared, is much lower than that in the short wavelength (high frequency) radiation ranges, such as ultraviolet.

We can now relate to the energy required for chemical reactions to proceed. Most chemical reactions which

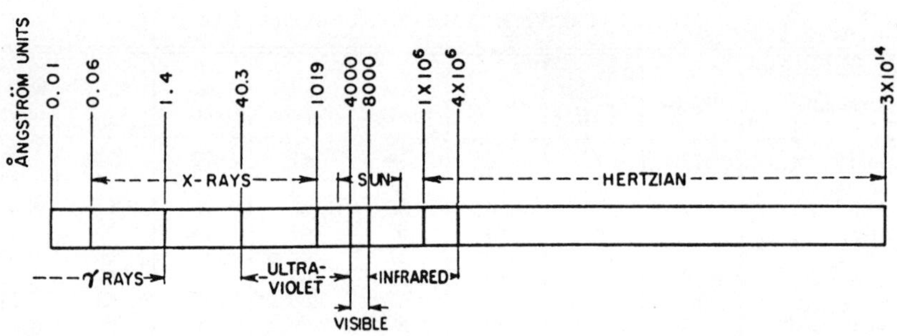

FIG. 1.—The electromagnetic spectrum. From Greathouse, Glenn A., and Wessel, Carl J., *Deterioration of Materials: Causes and Preventive Techniques* (New York: Reinhold Publishing Corporation, 1954). By permission of Van Nostrand Reinhold Company.

Of solar radiations, about 99 percent of the energy lies between wavelengths of 1,500 and 40,000 A. About half the energy is in the visible region between 3,800 and 7,700 A, and the other half in the invisible ultraviolet and infrared regions.

Two fundamental laws of photochemistry are at work in photochemical reactions. The first law states that light must be absorbed by the reacting atoms or molecules; the second law states that one molecule of a reacting substance may be activated by the absorption of one light quantum. A light quantum is the smallest amount of energy that can be removed from a beam of light by any material system. Whereas a molecule can absorb multiples of quanta it cannot absorb less than one. The power or

proceed with reasonably slow rates at room temperature require about 25 kilocalories (kcal) per gram-molecule for activation. Those reactions which go on only at very high temperatures may require as much as 100 kcal per gram molecule or even more. For the breaking of bonds between atoms such as carbon-carbon and carbon-hydrogen bonds, 84 and 100 kcal, respectively, are required [18]. Table 12 [20] shows why radiation in the short wavelength regions such as blue green to ultraviolet are required to activate the majority of photochemical reactions, and why these wavelengths are so important to the materials deterioration problem. In the longer wavelength (low frequency) ranges of the solar spectrum, as with infrared, the energy of quanta is relatively small. In this range, quanta can influence vibrations and rotation and thus heat molecules, but they cannot provide enough energy to overcome the forces which hold atoms of the molecules together. In the visible and especially the ultraviolet ranges of the spectrum, chemical bonds can be broken. These reactions are limited in the atmosphere only by the ozone layer in the upper atmosphere which does not permit radiation of wavelengths below 2,900 A to reach the earth's surface [18].

An informative example of the comparative damaging effect and the luminosity of radiant energy is provided in table 13. This is taken from a report by the National Bureau of Standards [21], describing work done in connection with preservation of the Declaration of Independence and the Constitution of United States. The sample used in their experiments was of a low-grade paper and is used only for illustration. Animal parchment deterioration under light is not as rapid as is the case with this sample of paper. The influence of wavelength of the radiation on ability to destroy the paper is clearly demonstrated.

TABLE 12

ENERGY IN VARIOUS TYPES OF RADIATION

Description	Wavelength (A)	Frequency	Calory/ Einstein
X-rays	1	3×10^{18}	2.84×10^{8}
Ultraviolet	1,000	3×10^{15}	284,500
Ultraviolet	2,000	1.5×10^{15}	142,300
Ultraviolet	3,000	1×10^{15}	94,840
Visible (violet)	4,000	7.5×10^{14}	71,120
Visible (blue green)	5,000	6×10^{14}	57,000
Visible (orange)	6,000	5×10^{14}	47,400
Visible (red)	7,000	4.3×10^{14}	40,600
Visible (red)	8,000	3.7×10^{14}	35,500
Near infrared	10,000	3×10^{14}	28,450
Infrared	100,000	3×10^{13}	2,845
Far infrared	1,000,000	3×10^{12}	284

SOURCE.—Duggar [20].

In summary, in photochemical reactions the energy supplied by radiation must first be absorbed and may result in displacement of electrons in the reactants. If the energy of electronic excitation displaces atoms within a molecule, chemical reaction may take place. If the atomic displacement is large enough the molecule may dissociate. If atoms are displaced, but not enough to be expelled, molecular reactions may occur. The energy of the particular radiation must be at least as great as or greater than the energy of activation of the reaction. Whether activation and reaction occur depends not upon the total amount of energy in a beam of radiation but rather upon the intensity of the radiation, that is, the amount of energy per quantum.

TABLE 13

COMPARISON OF DAMAGE AND USEFULNESS FACTORS OF RADIANT ENERGY

Wavelength ($m\mu$)	Relative Damage Factors	Relative Luminosity Factors (Usefulness)
360	145	0.0000
380	107	0.0000
400	66	0.0004
420	37	0.0040
440	20	0.023
460	12	0.060
480	6.5	0.139
500	3.7	0.323
520	2.1	0.710
540	1.2	0.954
560	0.7	0.995
580	0.4	0.870
600	0.2	0.631
620	0.1	0.381
640	0.05	0.175
660	0	0.061
680	0	0.017
700	0	0.004
720	0	0.001

SOURCE.—National Bureau of Standards [21, p. 6].

Radiant energy: heat.—Heat is an environmental factor. It is difficult to visualize any phenomena in the material world which does not involve heat or cold in some way, for the complete absence of heat would be that point at which there is no molecular motion—absolute zero or 0° K. Heat is the energy a body possesses because its molecules are in motion. Except at absolute zero, there is always some heat in a body, and for our purposes we should think in terms of how much heat is available rather than whether or not there is heat in a body. Heat, and its correlative, cold, or the absence of heat, act as powerful agents of chemical and physical deterioration for two basic reasons. First, the physical properties of almost all materials are greatly influenced by changes in temperature, and second, the rates of almost all chemical reactions are greatly affected by the temperature of the reactants.

The concepts of heat and temperature are often confused. Temperature, or the degree of heat content of a body, is a function of the speed of motion of the molecules in the body. Heat depends upon both the speed of motion and the number of molecules.

Thermodynamically, heat is defined as energy in transmission because of a temperature gradient. Heat then may be viewed as the energy which passes from one body to another because of differences in temperature. These bodies may be gases, liquids, or solids, or any combination of these states of matter.

There are three modes of transmission of heat—convection, conduction, and radiation. All three affect the permanence of library materials. Convection is the process of transmitting heat by means of the movement of heated matter from one place to another, and takes place in liquids and gases. The heating of a building with a hot air furnace is a good example of convection. The air heated by the furnace expands, becomes less dense than the cold air above it, rises, and thus causes movement of heat throughout the building by currents of heated air.

Conduction is the process of transferring heat from one molecule to another. An example of this is heating a bar of metal in a flame. As the molecules nearest the heat of the flame are heated and move more rapidly from the heat, they strike adjacent molecules. These in turn strike more molecules and the heat is transmitted throughout the bar of metal.

Radiant energy was discussed briefly in the section on light. Heat is also transmitted by radiation. Whereas in the cases of convection and conduction, heat is transmitted via material media, radiant energy may be transmitted through space in the form of waves. This radiant energy, falling upon a body causes molecular motion with the resultant heating of the body.

As in the case of most other environmental factors, heat rarely acts alone. Its deleterious effects are usually accompanied by other factors such as humidity, sunlight, pollutants, biological agents, and the like. Changes in temperature are often very damaging to materials because of expansion or contraction of the materials with consequent cracking. The action of heat in driving off water, or other solvents and plasticizers, and the consequent brittleness often destroys paper, leather, some plastics, and other materials. Heat plays a very important part in affecting the speed of chemical reactions. An increase of 10° F roughly doubles the rate of many chemical reactions. Included in these may be reactions with air pollutants. Holding materials at low temperatures is often an acceptable method of prolonging useful life.

The influence of heat on the water

content of materials and of the atmosphere is important in the problem of permanence. With a given water content of the atmosphere, a sudden drop in temperature will bring about a rise in relative humidity. If the rise of humidity is sufficient, condensation of the water in the air can occur, covering surfaces with liquid water. If this occurs often enough or for a sufficient time, water damage to susceptible materials can result. Condensation due to temperature changes in air-cooled buildings is discussed in considerable detail by Verrall [22]. This article is recommended especially for study by those responsible for libraries in older buildings or in small wooden buildings and buildings with crawl spaces. Specific recommendations are made for the storage of photographic film.

Finally, the influence of heat in combination with biological agents cannot be overlooked. Although humidity is a much more important environmental factor in occurrence of and damage by microbiological agents, heat does play a part even with these organisms. Heat plays an even more important part with the macrobiological agents—insects and rodents.

Biological agents.—Biological agents do not cause great damage in the majority of urban libraries in the United States. However, this should not be misunderstood to mean that the biological deterioration problem no longer exists in any urban libraries or is not a serious source of trouble in some libraries throughout the world. The problem of deterioration of books and archival materials caused by biological agents often becomes of great importance in some countries. Certainly if one includes museums along with libraries, biological agents assume tremendous importance in damaging historic and artistic cultural works. Museums, of course, commonly include in their collections many materials rarely (if ever) found in libraries; many of these are particularly susceptible to damage by biological agents. It is of the greatest importance to be aware of infestations of certain microbiological and biological agents when newly discovered materials are brought into museums and/or libraries. It is essential that such materials be treated to destroy the organisms before they enter the collections. Although many of our modern urban libraries do not have large rare book collections, it is nonetheless essential that newly introduced materials of often uncertain history and composition be examined and treated adequately before acceptance.

The subject of biological agents with reference to libraries and museums has been reviewed many times with considerable authority [16, 23, 24, 25, 26]. Fungi, bacteria, and actinomycetes are the organisms referred to as microbiological agents in libraries and museums. In small numbers, they are usually too small to be studied by the naked eye. In sufficiently large numbers their colonies are, of course, visible. Theoretically, the bacteria could be of importance to libraries. However, few (if any) cases of bacteria damage have been recorded, although there are bacteria which can attack cellulosic materials such as in paper and do considerable damage. Library environmental conditions are not conducive to such attack. There are a few cases of actinomycetes being found in libraries [16, 23, 27, 28].

The fungi constitute the most important of the microbiological agents to the librarian, for the most part because, compared with bacteria, they thrive best in relatively dry conditions. That is to say, although fungi require high relative humidities, they do not thrive well in the presence of liquid water. Bacteria, on the other hand, require comparatively aqueous conditions for growth and multiplication.

The fungi are extremely numerous in genera and species and are ubiquitous. Spores of fungi are to be found just about anywhere under, on, and above the earth, and await only the proper conditions of moisture, temperature, and sometimes light, to vegetate, grow, and reproduce. It is perfectly safe to state that every library in the world is liberally seeded with perhaps hundreds of genera and species of fungi. Thus, the important idea in control of fungi is to maintain temperature and humidity conditions at levels not conducive to growth of the microorganisms. This does not mean that cleanliness and removal of dust and dirt do not assist in reduction of the fungal problem, but it does mean that cleanliness is only part of the story.

There are numerous genera and species of fungi. Table 14 presents only a very approximate idea of the various genera which have been identified on materials in libraries, chiefly on paper. These data have been gathered together from a few of the very large number of references on the subject [16, 24, 26–37], but probably the most important genera of fungi which endanger libraries are represented.

The growth and reproduction of fungi are influenced by a number of environmental factors—temperature, relative humidity, light, oxygen, and nutrients. Fungi are more tolerant of relatively wide temperature ranges than they are of wide ranges in other environmental factors. That is, they may be expected to be viable at unexpectedly low and unexpectedly high temperatures. Three temperatures are important to growth and reproduction—the temperature below which growth and reproduction do not occur, the temperature range at which most rapid growth takes place, and the temperature above which no growth occurs. Fungi have been found to grow at temperatures near freezing as well as those as high as 50°–55° C. Low temperature growth of

TABLE 14

MICROBIOLOGICAL AGENTS OF DETERIORATION

Genera of Fungi		Materials Attacked	References
Alternaria	*Dematium*	These organisms may not necessarily attack paper but may damage it by staining or foxing. Some can destroy cellulose, can cause staining of bookbindings, and damage to glue, pastes, and other adhesives and to binding cords, and leather, parchment, artificial leather, and plastics	16, 24, 26–37
Monilia	*Cladosporium*		
Aspergillus	*Stysanus*		
Penicillium	*Stephanoma*		
Mucor	*Botryotrichum*		
Stemphylium	*Haplographium*		
Hormodendrum	*Trichoderma*		
Fusarium	*Trichothecium*		
Chaetomium	*Sporotrichum*		
Myxotrichum	*Sporodesmium*		
Eidamella	*Rhizopus*		
Acrostalagmus	*Streptomyces*		
Spicaria	*Epicoccum*		
Cephalothecium	*Scopulariopsis*		
Torula	*Monosporium*		
Stachybotrys	*Acrothecium*		
Gymnoascus	*Paecilomyces*		
Cephalosporium			

fungi is common as witness events which often occur in your refrigerator. The temperature range for optimal growth and reproduction is variable, depending upon genera and species of fungi but are approximately 15°–35° C or about 59°–95° F. The average optimum temperature is about 86° F, when the relative humidity is 95–100 percent. The absence of growth and reproduction at low temperature does not signify the death of fungal spores. Many species will withstand prolonged periods of freezing or subfreezing temperatures and, upon restoration to favorable temperatures, they are able again to grow and reproduce. However, alternation of below-freezing and above-freezing temperatures is not tolerated well by most species. High temperatures—especially high temperatures combined with moist conditions—will kill most fungi and fungal spores. In order to consistently kill fungal spores, steam pressure at 15 pounds per square inch, or 250° F, for 15 minutes is required.

Relative humidity is very important to growth of fungi. Generally it is believed that below 70 percent relative humidity (RH) there is little opportunity for growth. At 80–95 percent RH most forms grow well; above 95 percent RH growth is luxurious. However, the combination of temperature and relative humidity is important. Optimum humidity at 86° F is between 95 and 100 percent RH. Optimum temperature at close to 100 percent RH is about 100° F. Optimum temperature at lower humidities, for example, 70 percent RH, is considerably lower.

Light does not appear to be an essential requirement for most fungi. Generally, fungi will grow either in the light or dark. Certain band-widths of ultraviolet light are injurious or even lethal to fungi. Other parts of the electromagnetic spectrum (X-rays) are capable of causing mutations in fungal organisms, giving rise to new species which may have considerably different characteristics such as nutrient requirements. The characteristics of light in libraries do not appear, therefore, to be of any consequence to the fungal problem. Certain workers have attempted to use portions of the electromagnetic spectrum to control organisms in libraries as witness the work of Belyakova with gamma radiation on fungi in the Lenin State Library [36].

Although there are many bacteria which can thrive under anaerobic conditions, most fungi require oxygen for growth. This requirement has no influence on the library problem. Fungi require several nutrients, some of which do have an influence on growth in libraries. Required are carbon, hydrogen, nitrogen, sulfur, potassium, magnesium, and phosphorus. Some trace elements may also be required such as iron, zinc, copper, manganese, and in some cases calcium. Certain of the vitamins are also needed. These nutrients may be provided in many forms; for example carbon may be provided in the form of carbohydrate. The inorganic requirements may be in the form of salts of metallic elements. Nitrogen is essential, in the reduced form of ammonium ion, as oxidized nitrate, or in organic form of amino acids or proteins.

The fungal nutrient problem is interesting to the librarian for several reasons. Certain fungi will consume cellulose and can therefore do irreparable damage to paper. Others thrive on the nutrients in leather, glues, pastes, and other adhesives, or on binding threads. Some, though not consuming constituents of books or other library materials, stain surfaces because of metabolic products, such as the red water-soluble dye produced by *Gymnoascus setosus* [35].

As noted in the section on air pollutants, many of the constituents of polluted atmospheres, especially the particulate matter, are the salts and organic matter needed by fungi. It is important to control air pollution, not only to prevent soiling or even chemical reaction with library materials, but also to reduce provision of microbiological nutrients.

Numerous orders, families, genera, and species of insects are dangerous to libraries. Like the microbiological agents, insects are not considered to be a major problem in most urban American libraries. Cleanliness, awareness, and periodic inspections rather easily control insects, and they can be eradicated by fumigation or by the application of insecticides. But they should not be ignored as potential problems. Insects can be brought in by careless patrons and many thoughtless library users leave insect attractants, such as uneaten food, candy wrappers and similar materials in books. The danger of introducing insect infestations into libraries through acquisitions of old collections from poorly kept quarters makes it mandatory to sterilize such materials before adding them to shelves or storage areas. Table 15 indicates the varieties of insects which, from time to time, have been encountered in various libraries around the world. Also shown are types of materials which may be attacked.

No effort will be made to discuss the

TABLE 15

INSECT AGENTS OF DETERIORATION

Insects	Materials Attacked	References
Thysanurans: (silverfish, bristletails, fishmoths, firebrats)	Starchy material, blue, bookbindings, photographs, labels, paper sizings, onionskin paper, cellophane, wax paper, slick magazine paper	16, 23, 24, 30, 33, 38–41
Termites: *Reticulotermes* *Calotermes* *Heterotermes*	Books, paper, pasteboard, blueprints, documents, labels, cardboard boxes. Termite damage is often accidental	16, 23, 24, 41, 42
Cockroaches: German, small tan American, large brown Oriental, large black Australian cockroach, smoky-brown cockroach, brown banded cockroach, surinam cockroach, wood cockroach	Bindings, leaves of books, magazines, paper boxes, parchment, leather, fabrics	16, 23, 24, 33, 41
"Bookworms": Sitodrepo panicea Anobiidae of genera: *Catorama* *Dorcatoma* *Stegobium* *Gastrallus*	Consume or damage all types of materials in books, paper, paste, bindings, cover, etc.	16, 23, 24, 33, 43
Stegobium paniceum (bread beetle)		30
Death-watch beetle		30
Furniture beetle		30
Booklice: Psocids	Starch, glue, bindings	16, 41, 43
Cerambycidae:		
Longhorned beetle	Various library materials	30
Dermestidae: *Anthreni*	Books, leather or silk bindings	30, 33
Clothes moths	Many book materials	30

environmental, respiratory, or nutritional requirements of these many insects. Since these factors vary widely, suffice it to say that insects are found under numerous combinations of climatic conditions and occurrence of nutritional factors, from extremely dry to hot and humid. Low temperatures, however, discourage most insects.

III. THE EFFECTS OF IMPORTANT ENVIRONMENTS

Atmospheric pollutants.—Atmospheric pollutants are important to the librarian not only because of their physiological effects on himself and his clients but because of their deteriorating effects on the materials in his collections and the great trouble and costs required to protect against them. Thomson [44] recently reviewed the subject of air pollution as it pertains to conservation chemists. This article is recommended for review by all librarians and museum curators interested in protecting their collections.

The public as well as government officials in the United States have been awakened to the fact that the air pollution problem is of vast importance to all aspects of American life and far-reaching programs have already begun to alleviate the problem. However, the problem is still with us and we must be aware of the damage which has already been done and continues to occur.

Particulate matter in the air is one problem. Even though some programs successfully reduce or eliminate the emission of particulate matter by industrial emitters such as chimneys and stacks, common dust, dirt, sand, and other finely divided particulates are caught up from streets, buildings, fields, and other sources and blown about by winds. Thus, librarians must always be prepared either to clean up such materials from library collections by dusting or use of vacuum cleaners or they must prevent the particulates from entering buildings by using high efficiency filters.

A glance at table 6 reminds us of the types of particulate matter. Although much flying dust and dirt is quite dry—that is why it is so easily picked up by the wind—it can still soil surfaces such as book pages and bindings. If conditions are moist, such dirt can stain the materials and be difficult to remove. If it comprises nutrients for fungi, and if conditions are moist, such dirt can result in the growth of mildew with consequent staining and discoloration of paper or other materials. The abrasive action of dust and dirt on paper and other library materials such as leather is also a serious deterioration problem.

If dust or dirt carries acidic or alkaline substances and conditions are moist, it can alter the pH of paper or other materials and cause deterioration.

One of the most important deterioration problems facing librarians today and well into the future is the deterioration of book paper as a consequence of improper acid content. This is not solely an environmental problem, since it has arisen primarily from methods of manufacture of the papers which have gone into books all over the world for a very considerable time. Yet, part of the problem is environmental and thus a proper subject for inclusion in this discussion. That is to say, part of the library deterioration problem which occurs today, and has for the past several hundred years, is caused by the presence of acidic components in the atmosphere, especially sulfur dioxide. The contemporary nitrogen oxide problem in the polluted atmosphere of many of our cities gives rise to some nitric acid. This too adds to the hydrolytic degradation of paper. This part of the discussion will pertain chiefly to the effects of sulfur dioxide and to the acid—sulfuric acid—which arises through oxidation and solvation from sulfur dioxide.

The subject of permanence of paper, as well as of many other materials of interest to the librarian, has a very large literature. There are, of course, many reviews and texts on the subject which should be consulted [16, 24, 25, 26, 45, 46, 47, 48, 49, 50, 51, 52, 53, 54, 55]. Some of these works are on the general subject of "aging" and include much more than the effects of acid, such as heat aging, light effects, biological damage, the effect of paper composition, and miscellaneous causes of deterioration of paper, other library materials, and even museum collections.

The subject of paper impermanence due to high acid content is treated authoritatively by Smith in a recent review [45]. There does not appear to be any question that high acidity causes paper impermanence. There have been numerous investigations of the subject and the evidence is overwhelming. The deterioration which occurs is characterized as hydrolytic and is chiefly an attack, catalyzed by the hydronium ions produced from acid substances, on the cellulose which comprises the chief fibrous ingredient of paper. The rate of deterioration increases with hydronium ion concentration, that is, with a lowering of the pH values of the paper as measured on a water extract. The deterioration is manifested by a decrease in the strength (tear-resistance) of the paper and loss of flexibility (folding endurance).

A very considerable portion of the acidity in papers can come from the materials used in manufacturing, chiefly the alum-rosin sizing. This is discussed in some depth by Smith [45], who cites the outstanding works on the subject. Among others, the reader is referred to the extensive work of Barrow [56, 57, 58, 59, 60, 61, 62, 63]. Barrow was one of the first modern research workers to recognize in an effective way that the acidity which was really built into the paper as a consequence of the constituents used in the manufacturing process is more important than the acidity of polluted atmospheres. Some earlier workers had, of course, discussed the matter. According to Smith, at the turn of the twentieth century, experts thought that a minimum pH of 4.0 for a hot water extract from first-class, permanent book paper was acceptable. We now know that this is much too acid and that paper with this acid content will embrittle quickly with time.

The opinions about the pH value required for stable permanent papers altered as time passed. Smith points out that, by 1928, workers claimed that the pH of hot water extracts should be at least 4.5 and preferably above 4.7. By 1936, it was recognized that hot water extracts with a pH of less than 5.0 was a major cause of deterioration in even the best classes of paper. According to Smith, in 1937, Grant claimed a minimum hot water pH of 6.0 to be necessary for permanent printing papers. Lewis [64] in 1959 reported on a test commenced in 1934 in which the hot water extract pH of the three good papers used were 6.4, 6.3, and 5.7. Smith further discusses the most desirable hydrogen-ion conditions for permanent paper and leaves the impression that hot water pH extract values should approximate neutrality, that is pH 7.0, or even be on the alkaline side of neutrality.[2]

Although acidic components of paper

[2] Other considerations in addition to permanence pertain to the pH problem and are discussed by other speakers of this conference.

play a major role in paper hydrolysis and deterioration, the acidic components of polluted atmospheres cannot be dismissed. There is excellent evidence that atmospheres containing SO_2 can lower paper-folding endurance as much as 15 percent in ten days, when the SO_2 concentrations approximate what might be expected in badly polluted cities. Slow oxidation of the carbohydrates of paper with the production of carboxylic acids and an accompanying production of hydronium ions or decrease in pH occurs in accelerated aging of papers and presumably in natural aging.

Acidity due to sulfur emissions is usually produced by sulfur dioxide. This oxide forms sulfurous acid when in contact with water. In order to form sulfuric acid, a much stronger acid and oxidizing agent than sulfurous acid, it is necessary for sulfur dioxide to be oxidized to sulfur trioxide. When sulfur dioxide is emitted from stacks or chimneys, for example, it is almost immediately oxidized to sulfur trioxide, probably catalyzed by ash constituents [5]. The sulfuric acid formed from sulfur trioxide in the presence of water is largely responsible for the bluish smokes typical of what is called "sulfur dioxide" emissions [5]. In areas where strongly oxidizing materials, such as nitrogen dioxide, ozone, peroxides, and the peroxy-free radicals are present, more rapid oxidation of sulfur dioxide to sulfur trioxide may be expected. Automobile exhaust and also olefins in the presence of nitrogen oxides also appear to cause more rapid sulfur dioxide oxidation by the photochemically produced oxidants [5]. The presence of iron and manganese salts also materially increases SO_2 oxidation to SO_3 [5].

For some time, there was some question whether sulfur dioxide pollution of the atmosphere could cause paper deterioration in books. Smith [45] quotes from Jarrell, Hankins, and Veitch who demonstrated, however, that all kinds of paper in books will pick up enough acidity by SO_2 penetration throughout an exposed book to have devastating effects on permanence. Although the position of the page in the book and the distance from the edge of the page has an influence, no parts of the paper appear to escape deteriorating effects.

Hudson [65], using a flat glass electrode and a small amount of water for each sample, was able to measure the pH of samples of twenty-five books, varying from 150 to 350 years of age. His results confirmed that atmospheric pollution is one of the causes of low pH values, particularly at the edges of pages. His nondestructive method of pH measurement is easily applied and should be considered by anyone interested in the acidity of the book papers in his library collection.

Hudson and his co-workers [51, 66] developed a method for measuring the affinity of sulfur dioxide for paper and for examining the effects of such variables as temperature and humidity on this affinity. The method uses sulfur dioxide containing radioactive sulfur (S^{35}) so that its presence and migration may be detected and measured easily. They found that even good quality papers easily pick up sulfur dioxide, at concentrations which can be expected in the atmosphere of any normal city. The moisture content of the paper is closely related to the rate of sulfur dioxide pickup and this rate is increased by storage under damp conditions. High pickup is also favored by high ambient temperatures. They point out that conditions in books would be different than their tests with single sheets, since the paper in books is protected by the edges. Other studies have shown, however, that there is diffusion of acid into the body of books. Still other investigations have shown that chemicals can migrate from one page to another or from one document to another [67].

Langwell [50, 52] in his investigations of a simple and effective test for sulfur dioxide, and development of methods for protecting books and other library materials against it, stated that SO_2 itself is not damaging to paper. But it combines readily, in the presence of metallic impurities, to form sulfuric acid, which is seriously detrimental. These metallic impurities occur in most modern papers and in many papers made after the middle of the eighteenth century. Parchments, vellums, and papers made before or about 1750, may usually be regarded as immune to this attack.

The role of the nitrogen oxides in the deterioration of paper and other library materials has not been investigated as extensively as that of the sulfur oxides. In addition to the role of helping oxidize sulfur dioxide to sulfur trioxide, the nitrogen oxides can themselves play an important part in deterioration. This deterioration extends beyond paper and into the realm of other polymeric materials used in libraries such as rubber adhesives, and synthetic elastomers used as fabrics, threads, and adhesives. The nitrogen oxides are being investigated extensively in modern air pollution problems and it is hoped that they will be investigated at greater length in library problems.

Although it is not properly a subject in this discussion for detailed presentation, there are suitable methods for the deacidification of paper. This material has been covered in publications of Barrow [61] and recent papers of Smith [68, 69].

Sulfur acids also play an important part in the deterioration of leather [16, 33, 70]. Many old leathers are more acidic than fresh leathers. What has been referred to as "red rot" is actually an acidic deterioration. Sulfur dioxide, from polluted atmospheres, catalyzed at the leather surface to sulfur trioxide, subsequently converted to sulfuric acid, is thought to be the degrading agent. This form of deterioration is very damaging to the leather and can cause its complete destruction. The leather becomes dry, reddish brown, porous, and tends to peel or powder. The leather is easily scratched, corners wear easily, and cracks appear.

Smith reviewed the subject of preservation of leather bookbindings from sulfuric acid deterioration. This is an excellent review of the literature, with an extensive list of references on all aspects of the subject. He summarized his findings thus [33, p. 55]:

1. Sulfuric acid is a prime cause of leather bookbinding deterioration.
2. Sulfuric acid is introduced into leather directly during certain steps of the tanning process and indirectly by adsorption and oxidation of sulfur dioxide from the atmosphere.
3. The chemical mechanism of deterioration by sulfuric acid on leather is hydrolysis.
4. The critical point of leather deterioration by sulfuric acid is approximately a pH of 3.
5. The addition of grease does not protect leather from deterioration by sulfuric acid.
6. Leather bookbindings can be protected to a limited degree by addition of certain salts.
7. Ideal protection for leather bookbindings would consist of isolating leather bookbindings from contamination by sulfuric acid and requiring storage in air-conditioned areas.

Temperature and humidity.—There appears to be a close relationship between the chemical and physical deterioration caused in paper by light, heat, and moisture. All three environmental factors occur simultaneously to some extent in library stacks, storage, and reading areas and are grouped together as "aging." The concepts of stability, permanence, and durability of paper are often grouped under the term "aging." Wilson and Hebert [54] discussed this matter succinctly in a recent paper. They stated that permanence is basically a function of the chemical stability of paper. Durability on the other hand, they say, is primarily a function of the physical properties of the fibers and the way they are compounded to form a sheet of paper. A paper which is intended to receive rough treatment for a short lifetime must be durable but not necessarily permanent. There is obviously a relationship between permanence and durability and the proper balance must be achieved.

The phenomena which occur in paper as time passes and which are somehow involved in demonstrating durability and permanence can be classed together as aging. Librarians are more interested in permanence than in durability. Many properties of paper seem to be involved during the aging process and the determination of these properties gives some idea of how papers measure up to expectations. Some of these measurements are reflectance (color and brightness); pH (acidity); folding endurance (brittleness); tear, burst, and tensile (strength) measurements. The commonest measures of permanence are folding endurance and pH.

It is not my intention to explore property analysis methods but only to mention them briefly, as terms which will be used from time to time in discussing deterioration. It is appropriate to mention in passing that Hebert, Tryon, and Wilson [71] have added a new method—differential thermal analysis—to those available for investigators and find it appears to be promising as a technique for evaluating stability. There appears to be high correlation with pH values. In another study, however, Wilson and Hebert [54] did not find high correlation between pH and the rate of deterioration of physical properties of paper.

High temperature exposures of paper, even for short periods, cause yellowing and brittleness. Moderate heat over long periods has a slow aging effect on paper. Low temperatures are regarded as preservative to paper. A combination of moderate to high temperature and low humidity will cause paper to dry out and become brittle. The moisture content which is in equilibrium with 30 percent RH represents about as low as is safe for paper; if humidity is held above 75 percent RH for long periods mildewing will occur. Generally, it is recommended that temperature be about 70°–80° F and relative humidity 45–55 percent for effective preservation of paper [16, 72]. James Gear (personal communication, May 1969) at the National Archives states that they maintain temperature at 74° ± 4° F and relative humidity at 50 percent ± 4 percent.

Werner [73] recommends for archival materials—chiefly paper and parchment—that the atmospheric humidity should be controlled between 50–60 percent relative humidity at a temperature of 60°–75° F. As will be recalled from an earlier part of the discussion, the new National Agricultural Library at Beltsville, Maryland was built to specifications equivalent to 50–60 percent RH, in the temperature range of 74°–78° F. At the same time, Werner gives 68 percent RH as the critical value, above which mildew and mold growth will occur. Plenderleith [25] also states that 68 percent RH is the absolute danger limit in the temperature range of 60°–75° F. In actual practice, he states that 65 percent RH is preferable as the permissible upper limit of relative humidity to guard against mildew.

In view of the importance of "object humidity" as discussed elsewhere in this paper, a permissible value of 68 percent appears to be a bit high. Further, the recommendation of permitting ambient humidities as high as 60 percent RH seems to be skirting the danger zone; somewhat lower relative humidity values, perhaps 45–55 percent, appear to be safer for library materials.

Launer and Wilson [74] found that a temperature of 100° C for three days will cause extensive damage to paper. Mild heating will cause yellowing of paper made from new-rag, refined sulfite, old-rag soda-sulfite, and newsprint pulps, especially those bleached by light. They found that the yellow color caused by heating could be bleached out by light and the bleaching caused by light could be nullified by heating, depending upon which process predominated.

The effects of heat on paper vary greatly depending upon the quality of the paper and the nature of the various constituents used as fillers. Shaw and O'Leary [75] found that rag papers characterized as good book paper were not appreciably affected in heat tests. Purified wood pulp also produced a fairly stable paper. Paper made from a mixture of sulfite and soda pulp was less stable than those made from the purer fibers. There was a close relationship between the purity of the cellulosic fibers used and the stability of unsized papers made from them, but only a small amount of alum and no rosin size was used. In other tests, the acidity of the paper has had a great bearing on ability to withstand heat.

In his review on paper permanence associated with acidity and storage conditions, Smith [45] makes several good points with respect to the effects of heat. He points out that a good deal of our past history shows deplorable lack of interest in the effects of high heat on books and paper. Several cases of extremely high storage temperatures are cited which must have resulted in greatly abbreviating the useful life of the books. Smith observed that we should not be surprised that many of our books are useless, but rather that the majority of books in libraries can still be used. And it is probably true that today many libraries and book storage areas still have excessively high temperature conditions, especially in the summer. Temperatures of 135°–140° F are normal in the summertime in warehouses and boxcars.

Values taken from Barrow [59] are of interest in that they show the effect of temperature on a paper's rate of deterioration. Folding endurance was measured on new book paper after heat-aging at 120° C, 100° C, 80° C, and 60° C and the data plotted as regression lines for each temperature. The values obtained in the Barrow study indicated that it takes 7.5 times longer to reduce this paper's folding endurance to a given value for each drop of 20° C in temperature. The times required to reduce the paper from 219 folds to sixty-five folds by heating at temperatures from 120° C to 60° C, and by extrapolation, the times required to produce the same result at temperatures below 60° C are shown in table 16.

Smith [45] adapts the data of Browning and Wink [76], using calculations with the Arrhenius equation[3] to develop

[3] The logarithmic form of the Arrhenius equation is as follows:

$$\log_{10} \frac{k_2}{k_1} = \frac{E_a}{2.303R} \cdot \frac{T_2 - T_1}{T_2 \cdot T_1},$$

where $\log_{10} k_2/k_1$ is the ratio of the rates of reaction k_2 at the higher temperature (60° C) and a table showing the effect of storage temperature on paper impermanence. This approach utilizes the concept of paper half-life, an idea similar to the concept of half-life in the decay of radioactive elements. Thus, for example, a paper with an original fold value of 100 folds would, after expenditure of its half-life, have a fold value of 50, after the second half-life a fold value of 25, and so on. The ideal, high quality paper, is defined as one with a folding endurance half-life of one year when stored at 60° C (140° F). The values obtained are shown in table 17. The accuracy of the prediction increases at the higher temperatures or as the temperature of the experiment is approached. The low temperature predictions would be low because the reaction rates caused by water would be reduced.

TABLE 16

EFFECT OF TEMPERATURE ON PAPER DETERIORATION

Temperature (° C)	Time* (Days)	Temperature (° C)	Time (Estimated Years)
120........	0.4	40	3.5
100........	3.0	20	26
80........	22.5	0	195
60........	169	−20	1,463
		−40	10,973

SOURCE.—Barrow [59, p. 21].

* Time required to reduce folding endurance from 219 to 65 folds.

Luner [53], in a recent article on paper permanence, also discusses the Browning and Wink application of the Arrhenius equation for developing values for predicting paper aging. He points out that there are a number of difficulties inherent in the use of the Arrhenius equation which are not readily apparent. Further, the characteristics of the various papers have a strong influence on the results. More information is needed on the chemical and physical reactions which contribute to loss of paper permanence over a temperature range before the Arrhenius relationship can be used with confidence to predict paper permanence. Nonetheless, the equation appears to be a very useful tool in studies of paper permanence properties in libraries.

TABLE 17

EFFECT OF STORAGE TEMPERATURE ON PAPER IMPERMANENCE

Average Storage Temperature: ° F	Diff. from 68° F (in ° F)	Paper Half-Life (in Years)*	Average Storage Temperature: ° C	Diff. from 20° C (in ° C)
140......	+72	1	60	+40
122......	+54	4.1	50	+30
104......	+36	18	40	+20
95......	+27	40	35	+15
86......	+18	88	30	+10
77......	+ 9	204	25	+ 5
72.5....	+ 4.5	320	22.5	+ 2.5
68......	......	490	20	....
63.5....	− 4.5	760	17.5	− 2.5
59......	− 9	1,200	15	− 5
50......	−18	3,100	10	−10
41......	−27	7,900	5	−15
32......	−36	21,000	0	−20
14......	−54	170,000	−10	−30
− 4......	−72	1,700,000	−20	−40

SOURCE.—Smith [45, p. 185].

* One folding endurance half-life is defined as one year at 60° C (140° F) for purposes of estimating half-life at lower temperatures.

Smith brings together the effects of both temperature and acidity on paper permanence, using considerations similar to those he used with reference to storage temperature. For this purpose, he defined a paper as having a half-life of 100 years at a pH of 6.0 and a temperature of 68° F (20° C). He then varied the pH and temperature to ob-

k_1 at the lower temperature (20° C); E_a is the energy of activation estimated at 30,000 calories per mole; R is the gas constant, 1.986 calories at 1° C per mole; T_2 is the higher temperature and T_1 is the lower temperature in degrees Kelvin.

tain values of half-life. The effect of pH change on half-life was estimated at 53.2 percent and 10.0 percent half-life retention for an increase in acidity of 1 hot and 1 cold water extraction pH unit, respectively. The effect of temperature change on half-life was estimated as he did in the previous example. Table 18 provides his results. Smith discusses the situation with its several variables in details which should be sought in the original article. In any case, the method of prediction indicates that both pH and storage temperature have had strong influences in producing the deteriorated condition of books in many libraries.

TABLE 18

ACTION OF pH AND TEMPERATURE ON PAPER HALF-LIFE (IN YEARS)

TEMPERATURE (° F)	pH 6.0	pH 5.0	pH 4.0
	Hot Water pH		
68	100	53	28
72.5	65	35	18
77	42	22	12
86	18	10	5.1
95	8.2	4.6	2.4
104	3.7	1.9	1.0
	Cold Water pH		
68	100	10	365*
72.5	65	6.5	240
77	42	4.2	150
86	18	1.8	66
95	8.2	0.82	30
104	3.7	0.37	17

SOURCE.—Smith [45, p. 189].

* Figures in this portion of column are given in days and were computed by extrapolating the cold water pH line.

Smith [45] rates humidity, or rather the water contained in paper, as the third most important factor in paper deterioration in libraries, after pH and storage temperature. While excessive dryness will cause paper to become brittle and excessive wetness is conducive to mildew or fungal growth, apparently the role of moisture is not that easily dismissed. Some water in paper, as in many materials, is in a bound form—not easily freed to enter into or catalyze chemical reactions as free water.

Water in paper in equilibrium with 50 percent RH has been reported by Browning and Wink [76] to hasten the rate of deterioration during accelerated aging by ten times that of a bone-dry paper.

Smith cautions that our usual present-day recommendations of a relative humidity of 50 percent for storage and for library stack and reading room values may emphasize current physical properties of a paper at the expense of its future properties. However, it is very difficult to recommend the optimum value when sufficient definitive information is unavailable today, particularly for values below 50 percent RH. He suggests that paper permanence should improve with reduction of relative humidity but also admits that costs for achieving low relative humidities with air-conditioning systems are high.

The effect of relative humidity and temperature on paper is discussed at some length by Wink [77], who shows that properties such as folding endurance are extremely dependent upon humidity control. Mason [78], in discussing the effects of low humidity climates on brittleness in paper, suggests that water should be added to the atmosphere since for every 10 percent rise in relative humidity, the folding strength of paper doubles. Obviously, this curve levels off fairly rapidly. In making recommendations for rare book collections, Mason [78] suggests a separate air-conditioning machine—a system capable of maintaining a constant temperature of 70° F (or lower if personnel can stand it) and 50 percent relative humidity. This would introduce costs, however, which many libraries might not be able to afford. Storm [79], making recommendations for preserving rare book collections, stipulates 68°–75° F and 45–50 percent RH. Storm states, however, that 65° F would be better for books of all ages and kinds, but is a little chilly for people.

Noblecourt [80] suggests the following relative humidities for storage of library materials at temperatures of 60°–75° F: 45 to 63 percent RH for newspapers, leather, buckram, printed books, maps, music, manuscripts, parchment, engravings, prints, and drawings; and 50 to 63 percent RH for postage stamps, adhesive labels, and acetate and celluloid base photographic films.

Raistrick [81] emphasized the effects of heat and moisture on leather, stating that a common cause of deterioration is the combined action of these factors. Such damage is manifested in loss of strength and hardening of the leather. Storage at temperatures about 40° C (104° F) and 100 percent RH results in a considerable loss of strength in most types of leather. Increased stiffness and cracking, loss in area, and fall in shrinkage temperature are also reported. In tests Raistrick performed, all leathers tested lost about 50 percent strength after five weeks at 60° C (140° F) and 100 percent RH.

Light.—Recalling the admonitions of the many people who have written on the subject of materials deterioration by light, Stolow [82, p. 302] summed up the matter succinctly for museum curators as follows:

> The deteriorating effects of light on museum collections depend on the intensity of the radiation; the time of exposure; the spectral characteristics of the radiation; and the intrinsic capacity of individual materials to absorb and be affected by the radiant energy. External factors also influence the rate of deterioration —humidity, temperature, and active gases in the atmosphere. We know we cannot consider light as a single danger; high temperature, high humidity, and the presence of oxygen usually speed up the process of deterioration. Essentially, we must take into consideration: the characteristics of the radiation, the materials exposed, and the condition of their exposure. Until laboratory tests prove to the contrary, any museum curator must assume that the extent of photochemical damage will be reduced in direct proportion to the reduction of the intensity of illumination or the time of exposure—no matter what the light source. He must also remember the important factor of temperature: for with a ten-degree rise in temperature the rate of chemical change can double. Depriving an object of oxygen . . . can also serve to minimize photochemical change in that oxygen is often necessary to propagate intermediate steps in photochemical reactions.

Although, if anything, the photochemical deterioration problems of the museum curator are more severe than those of the librarian, Stolow's remarks also hit close to home for library collections. Practically speaking, librarians usually cannot provide the special environments for their collections that curators can for unusual objects. But for rare library items, the situations are much the same for the two types of institutions. Although the deteriorating effect of light is not considered so serious for library materials as is that of such factors as pH, temperature, and humidity, it warrants attention and has been known to assume serious dimensions under some circumstances.

The effects of light and the need for adequate lighting in libraries, archival depositories, and museum collections have been reported on and reviewed a great many times. Several of the references available to the reader are provided at the end of this paper [16, 26, 47–48, 72, 74, 82–96]. Of the various materials found in libraries in large quantities, paper represents the material most affected by light. Other library materials subject to deterioration by light [16] include textile (cotton) binding materials, binding cords and thread, parchment, and various types of plastics, rubbers, and adhesives, inks [97] and many dyes [87, 89].

The effect of sunlight on inks was investigated by Barrow [97]. He found, for example, that the iron-gall inks of the colonial period in America, have either remained black, turned rusty brown, or faded out completely. His tests indicated that sunlight decomposes the tannic acid in the ink, causing the writing to turn brown or fade.

The basic material in paper which undergoes degradation is the polymer, cellulose, the structure of which is shown in figure 2. Cellulose itself does not absorb visible radiation. Thus one might expect that it would not be degraded by wavelengths longer than about 400 millimicrons. But several investigators have shown it to be affected by wavelengths as high as 460 millimicrons. Feller [91] suggested that perhaps some components of paper other than cellulose—glue, rosin, or other constituents—absorb the visible violet and blue and sensitize the paper to deterioration.

Although the exact mode of action of sunlight on cellulose is not completely known, there appear to be roles played in addition to that of light, by oxygen or ozone, by moisture, and possibly by other reactants. The cellulose structure is considered to be made up of glucose residues united by linkages known as 1,4-glycosidic linkages of the beta type. All the potential reducing groups, except that on one terminating unit in each chain, are involved in these glycosidic linkages. Each glucose unit, except those terminating chains, has one primary and two secondary hydroxyl

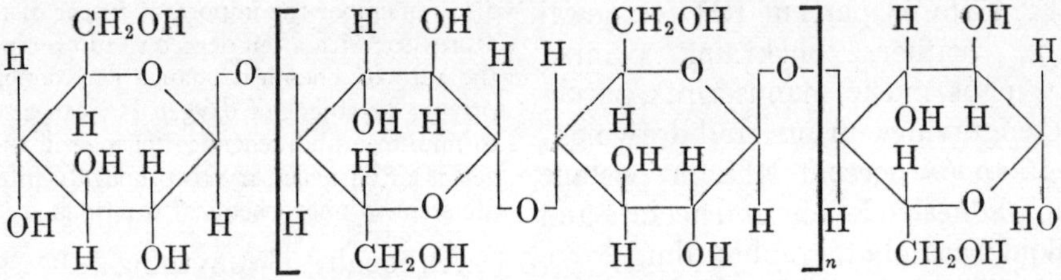

FIG. 2.—Cellulose molecule. From Greathouse, Glenn A., and Wessel, Carl J., *Deterioration of Materials: Causes and Preventive Techniques* (New York: Reinhold Publishing Corporation, 1954). By permission of Van Nostrand Reinhold Company.

groups. The main reactions of the molecule are those of the hydroxyls and of the glycosidic linkages. Any oxidation of the cellulose molecule by atmospheric oxygen will be a complex reaction with several possibilities. For example, the primary hydroxyls may be oxidized to aldehydes, which may be further oxidized to carboxyls; the secondary hydroxyls may be oxidized to ketones; oxidative action may cause opening of the ring with aldehyde groups formed; glycosidic linkages may be attacked; and secondary valency forces between individual chains may be broken [98].

The action of ultraviolet light upon cellulose leads to the formation of oxycellulose. Photochemical degradation of cellulose is apparently due to oxidation of cellulose by atmospheric oxygen, ozone, or other atmospheric oxidants (see the section on pollution, above). The reaction is accelerated by water vapor, and is preceded by absorption of ultraviolet light [98, 99].

Tests used for detecting the degradation of paper by light include measurement of copper number, of the amount of alpha-cellulose, of the viscosity in cuprammonium solution, of the folding endurance, and of the bursting and tensile strengths. Folding endurance is a measurement of brittleness. Bursting and tensile strength tests measure overall paper strength. The alpha-cellulose measurement, which determines the amount of cellulose insoluble in a solution of 17.5 percent sodium hydroxide, is a measure of the amount of reducing materials present. A high copper number is a measure of either low grade paper or deteriorated paper. Cuprammonium viscosity is a measure of degradation, a low viscosity indicating broken cellulosic chains.

Carboxyl groups (-COOH) may be measured by titration, by liberation of carbon dioxide, and other methods. An increase in carboxyl content may indicate oxidation of aldehyde groups or primary hydroxyls, but differentiation between the two is difficult. For further discussion of measurement of carboxyl and aldehyde groups the reader is referred to investigations of Wilson and co-workers [100, 101].

It is fairly well agreed that the sunlight resistance of paper in general depends to a large extent on the composition of the paper and on the kind of cellulosic material present. Yet, all papers are susceptible to damage by sunlight. Launer and Wilson [74] found that photochemical stability of papers is related to the kind and source of materials used in manufacture and they rated different papers in the following decreasing order of resistance: new rag, refined sulfite, old rag, soda-sulfite, and newsprint. The presence of rosin, glue, alum, iron, lignin, or other substances, whether included accidentally or purposely, has a strong bearing on degradation of paper by light.

Although there is no question that unfiltered sunlight is a strong degrader of almost all organic materials, and all kinds of paper are certainly included in that category, the problem of light deterioration of paper of most concern to librarians, archivists, and museum curators is not that caused by unfiltered sunlight. Rather, it is that caused by the light which enters the building through windows or skylights, and the artificial light used for illuminating the premises.

Studies of the degradation of cellulose products by radiation have shown that the greatest damage is caused by ultraviolet energy of wavelengths shorter than 360 millimicrons. However, damage is still appreciable for wavelengths up to 500 millimicrons. This includes all the violet and blue part of the visible spectrum [16, 102]. Launer and Wilson [74], however, demonstrated that the light usually affecting papers is in the range of 330–440 millimicrons. They pointed out that direct sunlight, light from the quartz-mercury arc, and from the unfiltered carbon arc all fail to represent the kind of light to which record papers are normally subjected in libraries and archives. They noted that exposure in these places is limited to indirect sunlight transmitted by window glass, or to that from the tungsten incandescent lamp.

Launer and Wilson [74] used a light source for a series of tests filtered to eliminate all infrared, as well as the ultraviolet shorter than 330 millimicrons. Thus they had a light source with wavelengths of approximately 330–750 millimicrons with a strong band at 389 millimicrons. In these tests, they showed that discoloration of paper is a combined effect of light and heat. The yellowing of delignified paper, commonly ascribed to light, is due to heat or age. When heat effects were eliminated during irradiation by control of temperature of the experiment, the papers actually bleached, and even lignified paper bleached when irradiated in an oxygen-free nitrogen atmosphere. The two apparently opposite effects—bleaching and yellowing—may occur simultaneously. If a white paper turns yellow when irradiated, reactions other than photochemical ones may be involved. Papers containing lignin will, however, yellow in air or oxygen even in the absence of heat effects. Paper scorched brown at high temperatures, or yellowed at 100° C, as well as a 250-year-old yellowed paper, all were bleached by light.

TABLE 19

PROBABLE RELATIVE DAMAGE

Wavelength ($m\mu$)	Probable Relative Damage
300	775
320	450
340	263
360	145
380	107
540	1.2

SOURCE.—Adapted from Judd [86] (Judd's values × 100).

Launer and Wilson [74] also showed that water vapor accelerates the effect of light on paper made of cotton cellulose, but has the reverse effect on paper made from wood pulp. Free rosin and sulfuric acid increase the effect of light on cotton, rag, and purified woodpulp papers much more than on inferior papers.

Work done by the National Bureau of Standards in connection with the preservation of the Declaration of Independence and the U.S. Constitution shows the connection between the wavelengths of light and damage to paper and parchment exposed to this light. Reference is made to table 13 previously shown.

The National Bureau of Standards also did studies to extend the range shown in table 13 to 300 millimicrons. Some of these values are adapted from Judd [86] and shown in table 19. Here we can see how rapidly relative damage increases as we get deeper into the shorter wavelengths.

Judd [86, p. 4] makes the statement:

> The probable rate of damage from radiation continues to rise with decreasing wavelengths below 300 millimicrons; but this is of no interest in museum lighting because none of the light sources available emits appreciably at wavelengths below the band, 290 to 310 millimicrons, characterized by the value of probable rate of damage at 300 millimicrons. Similarly, the probable rate of damage from radiation continues to fall with increasing wavelength above 640 millimicrons and is known not to reach zero short of 1100 millimicrons (note that the infrared can be photographed to about this wavelength), but these small probable rates of damage to the average museum object are negligible compared to those associated with the shorter-wave energy emitted by all light sources suitable for museums.

What Judd says about museum light sources and damage can generally be considered to hold true for libraries.

Judd's study [86] of the radiation hazard of museum light sources contains valuable information for librarians seeking advice on the protection of their collections from light. Harrison's report on the deteriorating effects of modern light sources [87] should also be consulted for valuable information. Our review does not permit us to include many of the details in these two reports but some indicative material should be mentioned. It should be recognized, of course, that the museum curator's lighting problem is somewhat different from that of the librarian. Museum objects of historical or artistic value vary greatly in their material nature. Also there is always a problem of exhibiting these objects to the best artistic advantage to permit the viewer to see them as the original artist intended. Many of these objects already have suffered considerable deterioration. Many more of the objects in museums and art galleries must be displayed to the best color advantages, as for example paintings.

TABLE 20

RECOMMENDED MINIMUM ILLUMINATION VALUES IN FOOTCANDLES

	1931	1932	1937	1938	1941	1947	1949	1952	1956
Reading rooms	10	7.5–10	20	30	30	25	20	30–50	30–50
Workrooms	......	7.5–10	30	20	30	25	20	30	30
Periodical room	......	7.5–10	20	......	......	25	20	......	......
Card catalog	8	......	......	10	25	25	......	30	30
Stacks	1.5	......	10	5	10–15	25	......	10–30	10–30
Corridors	3	3–4	5	5	5	5	......	......	5–10
Lavatories	5	......	......	......	10	10	......	......	10

SOURCE.—White [88, p. 301]. Original sources of values provided by White.

Judd brings out clearly the dilemma of the museum curator [86, p. 4]:

> From the estimate of probable relative rate of damage of museum objects from radiation[4] it may be seen that every light source giving good color rendition (radiant emittance well distributed throughout the visible range, 380 to 760 millimicrons) is necessarily associated with appreciable radiation hazard. . . . The directors of museums have therefore to make a difficult choice for each museum object. Either they can display the treasure by a light source yielding a good approximation to the color rendition of natural daylight, thereby eventually destroying it by photochemical decomposition; or they can seal the treasure in a vault screened from all radiation and filled with an inert gas, thereby preserving it indefinitely but also preventing anybody from ever seeing it; or they can adopt some compromise between these two.

By comparison, the librarian's problems of illumination are simpler. He wishes chiefly to provide suitable light by which clients may read or study, albeit often for extended time periods, without doing damage either to his clients' eyes or to the items in his collections.

Studies of damage by radiation to museum collections are quite applicable to library problems. For example, White [88], in discussing library lighting standards, brings out the fact that recommendations for illumination in libraries has increased considerably over the period of 1931–56. Table 20 shows the recommended values. White also points out that some libraries (Kent State Library and Davenport Public Library) have already gone to levels of 70–100 footcandles in reading rooms. Blackwell [93] reports on the lighting requirements for sample library tasks. His data ranges from 0.9 footcandle required for very easily read print to 141.0 footcandles for reading difficult spirit-duplicated samples. Some of his recommended lighting standards for libraries range considerably higher than those reported on by White.

Judd's report on museum lighting [86] provides interesting data both from the standpoint of relative damaging effects per footcandle for a large number of different light sources and for consideration against the increasing levels of illumination being recommend-

[4] Radiation values provided in Judd's tables.

ed for libraries. Judd's data are shown in table 21. He reported on six light sources—an incandescent lamp of color temperature 2,854° K; a daylight fluorescent lamp of 8,000° K; a warm-white deluxe fluorescent of 2,900° K; a cool-white deluxe fluorescent of 4,300° K; natural sunlight with sun at 30° altitude and air mass of 2 with 5,300° K; and the zenith sky equivalent to 11,000° K.[5] He made combinations of these sources with no filter and with four different filters, including window glass, to give a total of thirty combinations. His figures were calculated and expressed as the probable rate of damage per footcandle. Judd [86, p. 7] states: "It is believed that these computed results indicate reliably the relative rates of photochemical decomposition of cellulose by these light sources. Furthermore, these computed results are the best estimates of radiation hazard for museum objects generally that we can make from presently available information. These esti-

[5] Feller [84] points out that zenith sky has the greatest proportion of ultraviolet and blue light per lumen of any source of illumination under consideration in museum lighting.

TABLE 21

PROBABLE RATE OF DAMAGE PER FOOTCANDLE FOR THIRTY LIGHT SOURCES EXPRESSED IN PERCENTAGE RELATIVE TO ZENITH SKY

Light Source	Filter	Probable Rate of Damage/ Ft-C Relative to Zenith Sky (%)
Zenith sky	None	100.0
Zenith sky	Kingsport water white	70.4
Zenith sky	Window glass	32.9
Sun at altitude 30°	None	16.5
Sun at altitude 30°	Kingsport water white	12.9
Cool-white deluxe	None	11.5
Zenith sky	Greenish nultra	11.3
Cool-white deluxe	Kingsport water white	9.6
Warm-white deluxe	None	9.2
Sun at altitude 30°	Window glass	8.9
Daylight fluorescent	None	8.4
Daylight fluorescent	Kingsport water white	8.2
Daylight fluorescent	Window glass	7.5
Zenith sky	Noviol 0	7.0
Warm-white deluxe	Kingsport water white	6.9
Cool-white deluxe	Window glass	6.1
Daylight fluorescent	Greenish nultra	5.5
Sun at altitude 30°	Greenish nultra	4.7
Warm-white deluxe	Window glass	4.4
Daylight fluorescent	Noviol 0	4.1
Cool-white deluxe	Greenish nultra	3.4
Sun at altitude 30°	Noviol 0	3.3
Incandescent	None	2.8
Incandescent	Kingsport water white	2.7
Cool-white deluxe	Noviol 0	2.5
Incandescent	Window glass	2.2
Warm-white deluxe	Greenish nultra	2.1
Incandescent	Greenish nultra	1.4
Warm-white deluxe	Noviol 0	1.4
Incandescent	Noviol 0	1.1

SOURCE.—Judd [86].

NOTE.—Sources arranged in order of probable rate of damage.

mates are submitted as guides in the selection of light sources for museums."

I do not wish to draw any quantitative conclusions by combining White's and Judd's reports; rather I wish simply to draw attention to the manner in which increasing values of illumination bring with them increasing probabilities of deterioration.

IV. ENVIRONMENTAL CONTROLS

Because we know the effects of improper environmental conditions on the materials in library collections, we are in a position to reduce deterioration by adjusting conditions to desirable levels. The adjustment of temperature and humidity, the removal of particulate matter such as dust and dirt, and the elimination of damaging air pollutants such as sulfur dioxide, nitrogen oxides, and ozone are properly the responsibility of the air-conditioning expert. Adjusting these factors to optimum levels for permanence of library materials helps to insure that the present library collections will remain useful into the far future. Although air-conditioning will not repair the damage of past deterioration, it will appreciably reduce any further damage. Restoration experts can apply their talents to returning the materials to a useful condition in many cases.

It is the responsibility, not of the air-conditioning expert, but rather of library materials research people, to inform the air-conditioning engineers of the environmental conditions required to keep books in the physical-chemical states most conducive to long life. As will be evident from earlier discussions in this paper, we have fairly good knowledge of temperature and humidity requirements. We know that dust and dirt should be held to a minimum. But we do not yet have definitive knowledge of criteria for gaseous air pollutants. It is quite important that we develop such knowledge, because the criteria that must be met determine the cost of providing the service. With costs rising so rapidly today, many library budgets cannot stand extravagant air-conditioning costs and the end result could be a return to improper environmental conditions.

Although this discussion pertains mostly to long life for books, the air-conditioning problem reaches into the human comfort area. Fortunately, the most desirable ranges for both considerations coincide approximately. If anything, the most desirable temperature conditions for books are somewhat lower than for people. It appears that Americans make more of this problem than do Europeans. Europeans appear more willing to dress warmer to be able to utilize libraries at lower temperatures than Americans do.

The subject of heating, ventilating, and air-conditioning libraries is discussed for the layman in Metcalf's book [83] on planning library buildings. It provides a fine discourse on the general aspects of the subject, chiefly from the standpoint of patron and staff comfort. Some hints on collection preservation are included, however, such as the importance of humidity regulation when moisture conditions are low. For example, in areas where outside temperatures may be very low, perhaps —20° or 30° F, heating of the same air indoors to 70° F will lower relative humidity to perhaps 10 percent. While people may adjust to these undesirable conditions, albeit with discomfort, books, papers, and old leather bindings will deteriorate. Among numerous other aspects, Metcalf also discusses the problems associated with addition of moisture to library atmospheres, and the filtering of air to remove particulate matter. He provides a summary of at least five alternatives the librarian is faced with in deciding upon what type of environmental control his library should have. These are shown in table 22.

The technical aspects of air-conditioning are discussed in a number of recent works. Among these are Merritt's

TABLE 22

ALTERNATIVE ENVIRONMENTAL SYSTEMS

a) Heating only, not recommended for most libraries
b) Minimum recommended installation: heating and ventilating with air filtration
c) Comfort installation: heating, ventilation, air filtration, and cooling. This is recommended if the library is open to the public during long hot and humid periods
d) Conditioned installation: heating, ventilation, air filtration, cooling and humidity control. This is recommended for situations noted in [3] if the collections have rare and irreplaceable books and manuscripts
e) The ideal installation: heating, ventilation, air filtration, cooling and humidity control, all within certain specified narrow limits in order to maintain ideal conditions of temperature and humidity the year around, regardless of outside conditions

SOURCE.—Metcalf [83, p. 198].

Building Construction Handbook [103] and the guide and data books of the American Society of Heating, Refrigerating, and Air-Conditioning Engineers [11, 12, 104]. The latter provide both theoretical discussions of all phases involved in the field, as well as practical applications. The general subject of public buildings, specifically libraries and museums, is discussed in detail. Any librarian seriously interested in introducing air-conditioning into his present facilities, or responsible for assisting in the design of new air-conditioned facilities, would do well to familiarize himself with these guide and data books. The composition of air, the numerous pollutants or contaminants which can be expected, the relationships of temperature and humidity, design of systems, criteria for environmental factors, and some discussion of the effects of the various environmental factors on library and museum materials are included.

Earlier in this paper, the statement was made that the environmental problems of libraries and museums are reasonably parallel. The literature indicates, however, that museum curators and research people have devoted themselves more deeply to studying the details of environmental control by means of air-conditioning systems. I was somewhat disappointed to find relatively few discussions or reviews particularly directed to air-conditioning of libraries. A similar statement can be made regarding the scarcity of criteria and specifications on temperature, humidity, particulate matter, aerosol air pollutants, gaseous air pollutants which developed in discussions with librarians, government officials and government engineers responsible for public buildings. There appears to be a general opinion among these people, however, that such specifications are badly needed, but suitable criteria upon which to base them have not yet been stated clearly. Library materials research groups should make a renewed effort to develop the information upon which such clear criteria could be based.

Some of the results obtained in the studies made by museum research people are applicable to library situations and are recommended for study by librarians [14, 15, 105–110]. Some of the references found pertain specifically to libraries [12, 78, 104, 111] and some to document preservation [112, 113].

In order to control the growth of fungi by adjusting environmental conditions, most authorities feel it is necessary to maintain relative humidity below 70 percent. The specifications for the proper conditions of relative humidity necessary to prevent the growth and reproduction of fungi vary considerably. It is probably safe to say that a constant relative humidity of 60–65 percent or lower will control the organisms. However, if any considerable variations of temperature occur, so that local conditions of humidity rise above 70 percent, there will be danger of vegetation and growth. After all, the humidity condition important in preserving library materials is that at the surface of the paper or book where the fungal spores are. If the measured RH of the room is 60 or 65, but the RH at the surface rises to 80 or so due to a drop in temperature, the local condition would allow fungal growth. Thus, temperatures and humidities should be held fairly constant or within a narrow range which precludes sudden rises of RH or even condensation of water.

Niuksha [32] states that optimum storage conditions for preventing fungal damage to books are 16°–20° C and 45–60 percent RH. Beljakova [30] states that, for the Lenin State Library, temperature in the stack rooms is kept at 16°–18° C, ±2° C (61°–64° F) and relative humidity at 50–60 ± 5 percent. Generally speaking, relative humidities approximating 50 percent are sought to keep fungal damage to a minimum. Even this statement must, however, be oriented to other factors which bear on relative humidity requirements in libraries—human comfort, cost, machinery available, temperature loads of the specific local climate, and many others.

The recommendations of Noblecourt [80], cited in an earlier part of this paper, for relative humidity and temperature values for the storage of various library materials should be recalled. It is felt that Noblecourt considered not only the prevention of mildew but also other moisture requirements of the materials in question.

The specifications for the new National Agricultural Library at Beltsville, Maryland [114] call for dry-bulb temperatures of not over 78° F and not less than 74° F, with a wet-bulb temperature not over 65° F. These conditions would correspond to relative humidity conditions of about 50–60 percent.

The ASHRAE *Guide and Data Book* [11, 12, 104] presents a fairly concise and definitive discussion of air-conditioning for libraries. Depending upon the type of library, the air-conditioning requirements, chiefly with regard to people, may amount to sixteen hours per day, or about 5,000 hours per year. However, the ambient temperature and relative humidity should not be subject to variation and should be maintained twenty-four hours per day. Stolow of the National Gallery of Canada, agrees with this wholeheartedly [110, p. 183] stating, "It is difficult to understand the logic of air-conditioning during the hours of public entry and turning it off when the museum is closed. The focus should be on the materials in the collection and what happens to them in their environment. The particular relative humidity selected depends on climate, on human comfort, and on budget. But whatever the setting is to be, control at this level must be continuous. If control is not continuous, the resulting environment can be worse than an utterly uncontrolled one."

The ASHRAE [104] recommendations for design criteria are: A dry-bulb temperature of 70°–74° F and 40–50 percent RH. For rare book, document, and manuscript storage rooms, the recommended temperature is 70°–72° F and 45 percent RH the year around. The ASHRAE recommendations for dust and dirt suggest 85 percent efficiency filters. For acidic fumes, ASHRAE suggests the use of water sprays at pH 8.5–9.0 incorporated into the conditioning apparatus. However, alkaline water sprays are not always used. For example, although the U.S. National Archives washes its air in water, the use of alkaline washes was stopped in 1941 (James Gear, personal communication). On the other hand, Robert M. Organ of the U.S. Museum of History and Technology (personal communication, 1969) recommends alkaline wash water for acidic fumes, and filtering with oiled fiber glass filters for particulate matter. ASHRAE also recommends four to six air changes per hour in stack areas.

Grad and Greenberg [111] in discussing air-conditioning for books and people state that there is very little information on criteria for air-conditioning. Their recommendations of 76° F and 50 percent RH fall in the same range as most others. In the John M. Olin library of the Washington University (Saint Louis), they state that temperature limits are 72° F in the winter and 78° in summer. They further state that to maintain 76° F during the summer, an optimum for both people and books, would require an increase of 12 percent in refrigeration tonnage. Relative humidity is controlled at 50 percent ±5 percent and stack areas are air-conditioned twenty-four hours per day.

According to Grad and Greenberg [111], one of the biggest problems is keeping books clean. Even in air-conditioned libraries, layers of dust due to inadequate filtering are found on books and other surfaces. Many other authors have commented on the same point. The particulate matter problem is made serious by the dust and dirt brought into libraries by patrons and staff on shoes and other items. About 80 percent filter efficiency is adequate for cleanliness and economy. This may be improved, however, by addition of 35 percent efficiency prefilters.

One of the most effective methods of removing dust and dirt from the air is by electrostatic precipitators. The efficiency of these machines in removing aerosol particles is higher than all but the finest fabric filters [44]. However, the electrostatic precipitator characteristically produces ozone in sufficient amounts to be damaging to organic materials and is thereby not recommended for removal of particulate matter in museums and archival storage areas. These machines also produce some nitrogen oxides, which also deteriorate organic materials.

The relative importance of heat, humidity, air pollutants, light, and biological agents will vary according to the person making the comparison. The cost of providing environmental control of these factors appears to be only partially documented in easily accessible sources. For example, I have found no specific discussions of the cost of providing control of temperature, humidity, and gaseous pollutants in libraries. The ASHRAE guide and data books furnish helpful hints for calculating costs of providing temperature and humidity controls for buildings in general in terms of owning and operating costs for 1961 [12]. However, a very helpful discourse on the cost of furnishing clean air is provided by Bell [115]. Furthermore, the evaluation of air cleaners is treated definitively by Whitby and his associates [116].

Bell states that the cost of air filtration systems is usually second only to energy costs in mechanical air-conditioning system operating budgets of commercial or industrial structures. It is assumed that Bell's study applies approximately to providing the same type of air-cleaning service to libraries in the same types of urban areas.

Without attempting to provide all details of Bell's analysis of clean air costs, certain of his findings are presented to acquaint librarians with the more important factors involved in insuring clean air in their libraries. For actual application to a specific case, reference should be made to the original article and the assistance of an expert obtained.

Bell assumes a typical system which delivers 45,000 cubic feet per minute to the air-conditioning system in an office building in New York City. The efficiency level of the filters is assumed to be in the 80–90 percent range, as determined by a National Bureau of Standards test. The cooling system provides 20 percent outside air in appropriate weather. The fan of the system operates approximately 4,400 hours per year.

The so-called owning-operating cost analysis chart developed by Bell is presented in table 23. The three types of filters listed with their characteristics[6]

TABLE 23

OWNING-OPERATING COST ANALYSIS CHART*

Item	Type of Filter: Category A	Category B	Category C
1. Air volume per system (cfm)	45,000	45,000	45,000
2. Size of filter bank	5×5	12–114	10–104
3. Resistance (in., w.g.):			
Initial	0.32	0.35	0.55
Final	1.00	0.45	1.00
Average	0.66	0.40	0.78
4. Average efficiency (%):			
NBS (Dust Spot)	80–85	90	95–97
5. Filter life (hours)	3,615	3,200	9,600
6. Replacement time (man-hours)	11.8	16.1	15.2
7. Cost of one complete set of replacement media ($)	941	147	1,020
8. Installation cost ($):			
Equipment	960	6,130	6,875
Labor	155	265	310
Wiring	....	305	165
Plumbing	....	....	....
Miscellaneous	....	....	....
Total cost to owner	1,115	6,700	7,350
9. Annual operating cost ($):			
Material	1,078	203	467
Labor ($7/hour)	83	113	106
Fan power	386	231	455
Miscellaneous	....	....	....
Total cost to owner	1,547	547	1,028
10. Fixed charges (amortized at 15% of total cost to owner)	167	1,005	1,103
11. Total owning and operating cost ($)	1,714	1,552	2,131

SOURCE.—From Bell [115, p. 41].

NOTE.—Cfm = Cubic feet per minute, w.g. = weight gain; NBS = National Bureau of Standards.

* Job: XYZ Building; location: New York City; date: July 1968; operating hours per year: 4,400.

[6] The study by Bell was not made with reference to libraries, archives, or museums. The filters of categories A, B, and C are included for comparison purposes only and are not to be considered as recommendations.

are (1) Category A—Replaceable cartridge filter with an average National Bureau of Standards (NBS) efficiency of 80–85 percent on atmospheric dust; (2) Category B—Automatic renewable media/electronic agglomerator combination, NBS efficiency of 90 percent on atmospheric dust; (3) Category C—Replaceable cartridge/electronic agglomerator combination with an NBS efficiency of 95–97 percent on atmospheric dust.

The single factor in any filter cost study that can have the greatest effect on final results is the filter life. Table 24 shows Bell's data for various filter types and combinations which apply to New York City, where dirt concentrations average 0.08 gr. per 1,000 cubic feet of air. Table 25 provides the multipliers for a number of other cities in the United States to convert the New York City values.

There are additional factors which must be considered in cost analysis, such as proximity of air intake to ground level where the greatest amount of dirt is brought in, amount of outside air introduced, and use of more filtering than is required. Bell provides factors which may be applied to these and other considerations in analyzing the cost of

TABLE 24

LIFE EXPECTANCY OF VARIOUS FILTERS AND FILTER COMBINATIONS IN NEW YORK CITY

Type of Filter	Efficiency (%)		Resistance at Rated Capacity		Media Base Life (Hours)*
	AFI	NBS	Initial	Final	
Throwaway	78	10–15	0.10	0.35	480
Cleanable	73	8–10	0.10	0.50	600
Replaceable pad	78	10–15	0.10	0.50	600
Automatic renewable media	80–85	20–25	0.40	0.40	3,750†
Cartridge	....	50–55	0.30	0.80	5,500
Cartridge	....	80–85	0.37	1.00	4,000
Cartridge	....	93–97	0.48	1.00	2,500
Cartridge‡	....	50–55	0.47§	1.00	9,000
Cartridge‡	....	80–85	0.54§	1.25	5,500
Cartridge‡	....	93–97	0.65§	1.25	3,500
Cartridge‖	....	50–55	0.70	1.25	10,000
Cartridge‖	....	80–85	0.77	1.50	6,000
Cartridge‖	....	93–97	0.88	1.50	4,000
Replaceable media	85	30	0.12	0.50	600
Replaceable media‡	85	30	0.22	0.75	1,000
Electronic Agglomerator with automatic renewable media storage section	....	90	0.45	0.45	4,000†
Electronic Agglomerator with replaceable cartridge storage section (93%–97% efficiency)	....	97	0.55	1.00	12,000

SOURCE.—From Bell [115, p. 43] (American Air Filter Co., New York, by permission).

NOTE.—AFI = American Filter Institute, NBS = National Bureau of Standards, fpm = feet per minute.

* Values based on operating data from a single brand. Verify life expectancy with specific manufacturer.

† Life expectancy based on 10 feet of media exposed to airstream. Smaller footage yields longer life; larger footage, shorter life.

‡ Replaceable prefilter.

§ Initial resistance of replaceable pad filter is 0.17 inches, w.g. when used as prefilter at 500 fpm media velocity.

‖ Automatic renewable prefilter.

purchase and operation of a variety of air-filtering systems for providing clean air.

Table 23 is self-explanatory in providing the various factors and costs associated with the attainment of the parameters specified in the study.

The cost of humidity control is not discussed specifically in the literature for libraries. Stolow of the National Gallery of Canada [110] makes some cogent remarks about museums which are applicable to some library situations. For example, he states [110, p. 184]:

> The cost of humidity control depends on a number of variables. The most expensive is total control throughout a structure. If this expense is prohibitive, it is often feasible to supply controlled environment to a particularly sensitive area or even an object, and to provide lesser humidity control to the rest of the exhibition rooms. Local control can be arranged within glass cases or similar containers. . . . Relative humidity in a small room can be controlled by portable humidifiers of the spray type. To be fully effective, windows should be tightly sealed and doorways installed with automatically closing doors. Untreated water used in such portable humidifiers can result in a fine salt-like deposit forming over surfaces in the room. The use of demineralized water eliminates this objectionable dust. The small wick-type humidifiers with a three to five-gallon capacity are virtually useless in winter, unless a sufficient number are operated continuously to full capacity to achieve a relative humidity of 45 percent or more.

Stolow also describes some of the various types of instruments which are used in making measurements of humidity, from the most simple to some of the more elaborate. He quotes approximate costs of these instruments which may be adjusted upward to account for higher prices since 1966, but which enable the librarian to estimate costs when making needed measurements.

One of the most important cases in which a highly controlled special environment was developed for documents of a highly revered nature, and which are irreplaceable, is that of the original copies of the Declaration of Independence and of the Constitution of the United States. The sealed receptacle developed for these documents (of animal parchment) is described in a report of the National Bureau of Standards [102]. In this specially designed case in the National Archives, the atmosphere provided is the inert gas, helium, with moisture added to maintain a relative humidity of 25–35 percent at room temperature (the temperature changes with the seasons of the year). Purity of the atmosphere was insured by use of high purity helium (less than 0.01 percent impurities) and flushing out the case until all air was removed. Protection against the damaging effects of radiation, chiefly light, is provided by the

TABLE 25

MULTIPLIER TO ADJUST MEDIA BASE LIFE VALUES FROM TABLE 23 TO OTHER LOCALITIES

City	Factor
Atlanta, Ga.	1.6
Baltimore	1.2
Boston	1.2
Charlotte, N.C.	1.5
Chicago	1.1
Cincinnati	1.2
Dallas	1.6
Denver	1.3
Des Moines, Iowa	1.3
Detroit	1.0
Hartford, Conn.	1.6
Kansas City, Mo.	1.3
Los Angeles	1.0
Memphis, Tenn.	1.5
Miami, Fla.	2.0
Philadelphia, Pa.	1.0
Pittsburgh	1.1
Saint Louis	1.2
San Francisco	2.0
Syracuse, N.Y.	1.3
Tulsa, Okla.	1.8
Washington, D.C.	1.7

SOURCE.—From Bell [115, p. 43] (American Air Filter Co., New York, by permission).

use of filters which remove practically all damaging wavelengths, but permit adequate illumination for display purposes.

The subject of climatology and conservation is treated thoroughly by Plenderleith and Philippot [15]. Their discussions of hygrometry, or the measurement of the amount of moisture in the air, of the instruments for measuring atmospheric moisture, and of the various equipments for humidifying and dehumidifying the atmosphere, are especially recommended for any librarian wishing to become more knowledgeable in control of his collection environment. Modern air-conditioning equipment, that is, for controlling temperature and humidity, are discussed. The matter of cost of environmental control is discussed in terms of its importance in the overall budget of a museum, and the comparative costs of different approaches. Helpful suggestions are made for consideration of numerous aspects of the environmental problem; some can eliminate need for extensive environmental control and some give very practical common-sense solutions to problems.

Pollak [112, 113] discusses the several methods in common use for reducing humidity as a method of preventing document deterioration. These vary from the simple method of reducing relative humidity by heating; to the absorption of water vapor out of the air by using substances such as silica gel; to the use of the heat pump type of equipment. A common example of the heat pump is the refrigerator. This type of equipment operates by removal of water through condensation brought about by lowering the temperature of the air. The temperature of the newly dried air is then restored to the desired level, in some cases utilizing heat generated in the process, and returned to the areas controlled. Although Pollak does not provide any specific costs in terms of dollars, he discusses the economics of the various dehumidification methods.

Amdur [107] introduces a novel idea for humidity control in museums in his "isolated area plan." This plan appears to be most applicable to buildings in climates with very cold winters. Here one meets the problem of condensation and frosting on windows when an effort is made to keep relative humidity at a safe level for museum objects. The same observation would hold true for libraries, since the relative humidity requirements are similar. Amdur's idea is to prepare a building within a building and to utilize the intermediate air insulation layer to buffer the temperature differences between the outside and inside.

The subject of equipment and costs for removal of the gaseous air pollutants is not well documented. As mentioned earlier, ASHRAE does recommend an alkaline wash of the air at pH 8.5–9.0, but this recommendation is not always followed. Thomson [44] discusses removal of sulfur dioxide and oxidants briefly. He mentions that water washes alone can sometimes remove as much as 95–97 percent of the sulfur dioxide, but cautions against depending upon this efficiency. He quotes studies in which all sulfur dioxide is removed as pH values of 8.6 or better, but states that pH values of more than 9.0 could cause damage to metals. Some efforts to control sulfur dioxide by absorbents are mentioned but not prominently.

The removal of oxidant gases such as ozone, nitrogen dioxide, hydrogen peroxide, and a variety of organic ozonides is also discussed briefly by Thomson [44]. Recommendations in this area are quite vague. We must look to further research to develop methods for removing these damaging pollutants from museum and library atmospheres. Haagen-Smit [10] reports, however, that activated charcoal filters will destroy ozone and plant-damaging peracylnitrates. As we know by the damage caused by ozone to unsaturated organic materials, ozone is strongly absorbed by such substances. Thomson [44] asks why we should not develop cheap and effective ozone absorbers using such materials—a reasonable and logical question. Buck [108] also suggests activated charcoal for gaseous pollutants, including ozone.

One of the few articles found reporting on the effectiveness of air-conditioning systems in removing acidic pollutants is that of Waller [14]. He presents figures for removal of smoke, sulfur dioxide, and acid droplets by the equipment at the National Gallery in London. Table 26 is adapted from Waller and shows figures for sulfur dioxide and acid droplets. The removal of the acid components was quite incidental, according to Waller, and evidently was accomplished by the water in the humidifier tank. As will be noted, the system was effective in reducing sulfur dioxide by about 96 percent.

V. CONCLUSIONS AND RECOMMENDATIONS

There does not appear to be any question that library materials are subject to serious deterioration now, have been subject ever since the first document was made, and probably will suffer deterioration to some extent as long as men record matters on materials as we know them. It appears to be a part of the nature of materials to revert to more stable states. These stable states of matter are usually not the most desirable states that man wants for recording history. The process of reverting to these more stable states is known as deterioration.

Deterioration of materials can be brought about by a number of circumstances. Two of these are the composition of the materials and the environmental conditions under which these materials exist. It has been the objective of this discussion to examine some of the environmental factors which cause deterioration of library materials.

TABLE 26

POLLUTION INSIDE AND OUTSIDE THE NATIONAL GALLERY, LONDON, 1959

MONTH	SO_2 ($\mu g/m^3$)			ACID (as H_2SO_4) ($\mu g/m^3$)		
	A	B	C	A	B	C
February..........	809	34	927	29	3	17
March............	363	0	180	2	1	3
April..............	295	3	206	3	1	7
September.........	123	29	140	....	....	....
Mean (4 months).	398	16	363	11	2	9

SOURCE.—Waller [14, p. 67].

NOTE.—Site A = plant room (outside air); site B = gallery 19 (air-conditioned); site C = Duveen room (natural ventilation).

The environmental factors are various forms of energy, all of which seem bent on changing materials into other materials we do not want. Among the environmental factors examined have been those making up the atmosphere—both the normal constituents, including water, and the abnormal constituents, including pollutants; radiant energy and heat; and the deteriorative biological agents. Something of the nature of these environmental factors and the effects they actually have on materials have been shown. Emphasis has been placed on ways librarians might reduce deterioration of materials in their collections by seeking environmental conditions conducive to long life and avoidance of deleterious conditions. Finally, some of the criteria and specifications for environmental control available to librarians have been examined.

Attention has been focused mainly on the more common materials in libraries, chiefly paper and leather, with brief mention of a few other materials. This was necessitated more by the time limits of the article rather than by the lack of problems and information. Of necessity then, discussion was avoided of some of the more recently recognized environments such as forms of radiation which affect the storage of magnetic tapes—certainly a form of storage becoming quite common and very important. Furthermore, it was necessary to omit discussion of the effects of the common environments on the many types of new materials such as photographic and microfilms, magnetic tapes in general, plastics, rubbers, and adhesives.

In conclusion, it is recommended that more attention be paid to library deterioration problems. The criteria for safe usage, and short- and long-term storage of library materials could be investigated in much greater depth and clarified considerably. The preparation of more acceptable specifications for library environments safe for library materials is sorely needed. These specifications should cover not only temperature and humidity but all forms of pollutants—particulate matter of all kinds and the gaseous acidic and oxidizing pollutants as well. Finally, the specifications should provide practical guidance for the librarian in choosing the proper illumination so that both his clients and his collection will be adequately protected.

REFERENCES

1. Schaffer, Norman J. "Library of Congress Pilot Preservation Project." *College and Research Libraries* 30 (January 1969): 5–11.
2. Cameron, Duncan. "Environmental Control: A Theoretical Solution." *Museum News* 46 (May 1968): 17–21.
3. Weaver, Elbert C. "Air." In *The Encyclopedia of Chemistry*, edited by George L. Clark and Gessner G. Hawley. New York: Reinhold Publishing Corp., 1957.
4. "Pollution: Causes, Costs, Controls." *Chemical and Engineering News* 47 (June 9, 1969): 33–68.
5. Stern, Arthur C. *Air Pollution.* 3 vols. New York: Academic Press, 1962.
6. Searle, Victor C. "Technical Information Resources in the Air Pollution Field." *Journal of the Air Pollution Control Association* 19 (March 1969): 137–41.
7. Hanks, James J., and Kube, Harold D. "Industry Action to Combat Pollution." *Harvard Business Review* 44 (September–October 1966): 49–62.
8. Committee on Pollution. *Waste Management and Control.* Washington, D.C.: National Academy of Sciences Publication 1400, 1966.
9. Haagen-Smit, A. J. "Air Conservation." *Scientia* 103 (May–June 1968): 1–20.
10. Haagen-Smith, A. J. "The Chemistry of Atmospheric Pollution." In *Museum Climatology*, edited by G. Thomson. London: International Institute of Conservation, 1967.
11. American Society of Heating, Refrigerating and Air-Conditioning Engineers. *ASHRAE Guide and Data Book, Fundamentals and Equipment.* New York: ASHRAE, 1963.
12. American Society of Heating, Refrigerating and Air-Conditioning Engineers. *ASHRAE Guide and Data Book, Applications.* New York: ASHRAE, 1964.
13. Jaffe, Louis S. "Photochemical Air Pollutants and Their Effects on Men and Animals: I. General Characteristics and Community Concentrations." *Archive of Environmental Health* 15 (December 1967): 782–91.
14. Waller, R. E. "Studies on the Nature of Urban Air Pollution." In *Museum Climatology*, edited by G. Thomson.

London: International Institute of Conservation, 1967.

15. Plenderleith, H. J., and Philippot, P. "Climatology and Conservation in Museums." *Museum* 13 (1960): 243–89.
16. Greathouse, Glenn A., and Wessel, Carl J., eds. *Deterioration of Materials, Causes and Preventive Techniques.* New York: Reinhold Publishing Corp., 1954.
17. Trewartha, Glenn T. *An Introduction to Weather and Climate.* 2d ed. New York: McGraw-Hill Book Co., 1943.
18. Haagen-Smit, A. J. "Reactions in the Atmosphere." In *Air Pollution*, edited by Arthur C. Stern. Vol. 1. New York: Academic Press, 1962.
19. Ellis, Carleton; Wells, Alfred A.; and Heyroth, Francis F. *The Chemical Action of Ultraviolet Rays.* New York: Reinhold Publishing Corp., 1941.
20. Duggar, Benjamin M., ed. *Biological Effects of Radiation.* Vol. 1. New York: McGraw-Hill Book Co., 1936.
21. "Protective Display Lighting of Historical Documents: A Report by the National Bureau of Standards to the Library of Congress." Circular 538. Washington, D.C.: National Bureau of Standards, April 1, 1953.
22. Verrall, A. F. "Condensation in Air-Cooled Buildings." *Forest Products Journal* 12 (1962): 531–36.
23. Gallo, Fausta. "Biological Agents Which Damage Paper Materials in Libraries and Archives." In *Recent Advances in Conservation; Contributors to the IIC Rome Conference*, 1961, edited by G. Thomson. London: Butterworth & Co., 1963.
24. *The Conservation of Cultural Property With Special Reference to Tropical Conditions.* Museums and Monuments, no. 11. Prepared in cooperation with the International Centre for the Study of the Preservation and Restoration of Cultural Property, Rome, Italy. Paris: UNESCO, 1968.
25. Plenderleith, H. J. *The Conservation of Antiquities and Works of Art: Treatment, Repair, and Restoration.* London: Oxford University Press, 1956.
26. Flyate, D. M., ed. "Preservaton of Documents and Papers." Translated from Russian by J. Schmorak. Available from U.S. Department of Commerce, Springfield, Va., 1968.
27. Kowalik, R., and Sadurska, I. "Microorganisms Destroying Paper, Leather and Wax Seals in the Air of Archives." *Acta Microbiologica Polonica* 5 (1956): 227–84.
28. Niuksha, U. P. "A Taxonomic Survey of Fungi Dwelling On Paper, Books and Pulp." *Botanicheski Zhurnal* 46 (January 1961): 70–79.
29. Kowalik, R., and Sadurska, I. "Microorganisms Destroying Leather Bookbindings." *Acta Microbiologica Polonica* 5 (1956): 285–90.
30. Beljakova, L. A., and Kozulina, O. V. "Book Preservation in USSR Libraries." *UNESCO Bulletin of Libraries* 15 (July-August 1961): 198–202.
31. Armitage, F. D. *The Cause of Mildew on Books and Methods of Prevention.* Bulletin 8. Leatherhead, England: Printing, Packaging and Allied Trades Research Association, 1949.
32. Niuksha, U. P. "Mycoflora of Books and Paper." *Botanicheski Zhurnal* 41 (June 1956): 797–809.
33. Smith, Richard D. "The Preservation of Leather Bookbindings from Sulfuric Acid Deterioration." Master's paper, University of Denver, 1964.
34. Wälchli, O. "Paper-damaging Pests in Libraries and Archives." *Textil-Rundschau* 17 (February 1962): 63–76.
35. Niuksha, U. P. "A Microscopic Study of Paper Pigmented by the *Gymnoascus Setosus* Fungus." *Mikrobiologiya* 29 (January–February 1960): 133–36.
36. Belyakova, L. A. "Gamma-Radiation as a Disinfecting Agent for Books Infected with Mold Spores." *Mikrobiologiya* 29 (September–October 1960): 762–65.
37. Flieder, F. "Etude des blanchiments chimiques des taches des papiers anciens." *Association Technique de l'Industrie Papetière*, Bulletin No. 4 (1960): 173–84.
38. Metcalf, Clell Lee, and Flint, Wesley P. *Destructive and Useful Insects; Their Habits and Control.* New York: McGraw-Hill Book Co., 1928.
39. Mallis, Arnold. "Preliminary Experiments on the Silverfish *Ctenolepisma urbani* Slabaugh." *Journal of Economic Entomology* 34 (1941): 787–91.
40. Brett, Charles H. "Thysanurans: Damage by and Control of Silverfish and Firebrats." *Pest Control* 30 (October 1962): 75–78.
41. Kathpalia, Y. P. "Deterioration and Con-

servation of Paper. I. Biological Deterioration." *Indian Pulp and Paper* 15 (July 1960): 117–25.

42. Snyder, Thomas E. *Our Enemy the Termite.* Rev. ed. Ithaca, N. Y.: Comstock Publishing Co., 1948.
43. Evans, Dorothy M. *The Protection of Books Against Insects: A Short Review of Existing Methods.* Bulletin 9. Leatherhead, England: Printing, Packaging and Allied Trades Research Association, 1949.
44. Thomson, Garry. "Air Pollution—A Review for Conservation Chemists." *Studies in Conservation* 10 (November 1965): 147–67.
45. Smith, Richard D. "Paper Impermanence as a Consequence of pH and Storage Conditions." *Library Quarterly* 39 (April 1969): 153–95.
46. Thomson, G., ed. *Recent Advances in Conservation; Contributors to the IIC Rome Conference, 1961.* London: Butterworth & Co., 1963.
47. Byrne, Jerry, and Weiner, Jack. *Permanence.* Bibliographic Series no. 213. Appleton, Wis.: Institute of Paper Chemistry, 1964.
48. Kantrowitz, Morris S.; Spencer, Ernst W.; and Simmons, Robert H. *Permanence and Durability of Paper: An Annotated Bibliography of the Technical Literature from 1885 AD to 1939 AD.* Washington, D.C.: U. S. Government Printing Office, 1940.
49. Banks, Paul N. *An Annotated Reading List of the Most Important Current Material on the Chemical Deterioration and the Chemical and Physical Preservation of Paper.* Chicago: Newberry Library, 1965.
50. Langwell, W. H. "How Does Air Pollution Affect Books and Paper?" Address before the Library Circle Meeting, May 12, 1958. *Royal Institution of Great Britain. Proceedings* 37, pt. 2 (1958): 210–14.
51. Hudson, F. L., and Milner, W. D. "The Use of Radioactive Sulfur to Study the Pick-Up of Sulfur Dioxide by Paper." *Paper Technology* 2 (1961): 155–61.
52. Langwell, W. H. "Sulfur Dioxide Pollution of the Atmosphere." *Society of Archivists* 1 (October 1959): 291–93.
53. Luner, Philip. "Paper Permanence." *TAPPI* 52 (May 1969): 796–805.
54. Wilson, W. K., and Hebert, R. L. "Evaluation of the Stability of Record Papers." *TAPPI* 52 (August 1969): 1523–29.
55. Wilson, William K. "Selection, Use, and Storage of Records for the International Geophysical Year." Report 5321. National Bureau of Standards, June 12, 1957.
56. W. J. Barrow Research Laboratory. *Deterioration of Book Stock, Causes and Remedies: Two Studies on the Permanence of Book Paper.* Virginia State Library Publications, no. 10. Conducted by W. J. Barrow and edited by Randolph W. Church. Richmond: Virginia State Library, 1959.
57. Church, Randolph W., ed. *The Manufacture and Testing of Durable Book Papers.* Virginia State Library Publications, no. 13. Based on the investigations of W. J. Barrow. Richmond: Virginia State Library, 1960.
58. *Permanent Durable Book Paper: Summary of a Conference held in Washington, D. C., September 16, 1960.* Virginia State Library Publications, no. 16. Richmond: Virginia State Library, 1960.
59. W. J. Barrow Research Laboratory. *Permanence/Durability of the Book. I. A Two Year Research Program.* Richmond: Virginia State Library, 1963.
60. W. J. Barrow Research Laboratory. *Permanence/Durability of the Book. II. Test Data of Naturally Aged Paper.* Richmond: Virginia State Library, 1964.
61. W. J. Barrow Research Laboratory. *Permanence/Durability of the Book. III. Spray Deacidification.* Richmond: Virginia State Library, 1964.
62. W. J. Barrow Research Laboratory. *Permanence/Durability of the Book. IV. Polyvinyl Acetate (PVA) Adhesives for Use in Library Bookbindings.* Richmond: Virginia State Library, 1965.
63. W. J. Barrow Research Laboratory. *Permanence/Durability of the Book. V. Strength and Other Characteristics of Book Papers 1800–1899.* Richmond: Virginia State Library, 1967.
64. Lewis, Harry F. "The Deterioration of Book Paper in Library Use." *American Archivist* 22 (July 1959): 309–22.
65. Hudson, F. L. "Acidity of 17th and 18th Century Books in Two Libraries." *Paper Technology* 8 (June 1967): 189–90.
66. Hudson, F. L.; Grant, R. L.; and Hock-

ey, J. A. "The Pick-Up of Sulfur Dioxide by Paper." *Journal of Applied Chemistry* 14 (October 1964): 444–47.

67. Barrow W. J. "Migration of Impurities in Paper." *Archivum* 3 (1953): 105–8.
68. Smith, Richard D. "Paper Deacidification: A Preliminary Report." *Library Quarterly* 36 (October 1966): 273–92.
69. Smith, Richard D. "Guidelines for Preservation." *Special Libraries* 59 (May–June 1968): 346–52.
70. Rogers, J. S., and Beebe, C. W. "Leather Bookbindings, How to Preserve Them." Booklet No. 398. Washington, D. C.: U.S. Department of Agriculture, May, 1956.
71. Hebert, R. L.; Tryon, Max; and Wilson, W. K. "Differential Thermal Analysis of Some Papers and Carbohydrate Materials." *TAPPI* 52 (June 1969): 1183.
72. Minogue, Adelaide E. *The Repair and Preservation of Records.* Washington, D.C.: Government Printing Office, 1943.
73. Werner, Anthony E. A. "The Preservation of Archives." *Society of Archivists* 1 (October 1959): 282–88.
74. Launer, Herbert F., and Wilson, William K. "Photochemical Stability of Papers." *Journal of Research of the National Bureau of Standards* 30 (January 1943): 55–74.
75. Shaw, Merle B., and O'Leary, Martin J. "Study of the Effect of Fiber Components on the Stability of Book Papers." *Journal of Research of the National Bureau of Standards* 17 (December 1936): 859–69.
76. Browning, B. L., and Wink, W. A. "Studies on the Permanence and Durability of Paper. I. The Prediction of Paper Permanence." *TAPPI* 51 (April 1968): 156–63.
77. Wink, W. A. "The Effect of Relative Humidity and Temperature on Paper Properties." *TAPPI* 44 (June 1961): 171A–180A.
78. Mason, Ellsworth. "A Guide to the Librarian's Responsibility in Achieving Quality in Lighting and Ventilation." *Library Journal* 92 (January 1967): 201–6.
79. Storm, Colton. "Care, Maintenance, and Restoration." In *Rare Book Collections: Some Theoretical and Practical Suggestions for Use by Librarians and Students,* edited by H. Richard Archer. ACRL Monograph, no. 27. Chicago: American Library Association, 1965.
80. Noblecourt, A. *Protection of Cultural Property in the Event of Armed Conflict.* Paris: UNESCO, 1956.
81. Raistrick, A. S. "The Effect of Heat and Moisture in Leather." *Journal of the Society of Leather Trades' Chemists* 44 (April 1960): 167–68.
82. Stolow, Nathan. "The Action of Environment on Museum Objects. Pt. II. Light." *Curator* 9 (December 1966): 298–306.
83. Metcalf, Keyes D. *Planning Academic and Research Library Buildings.* New York: McGraw-Hill Book Co., 1965.
84. Feller, Robert L. "Control of Deteriorating Effects of Light Upon Museum Objects." *Museum* 17 (1964): 57–98.
85. Brommelle, N. W. "Museum Lighting. Pt. 3. Aspects of the Effects of Light on Deterioration." *Museums Journal* 62 (1962): 337–46.
86. Judd, Deane B. "Radiation Hazard of Museum Light Sources." Report 2254. Washington, D.C.: National Bureau of Standards, February, 1953.
87. Harrison, Laurence S. "Report on the Deteriorating Effects of Modern Light Sources." New York: Metropolitan Museum of Art, 1954.
88. White, Lucien W. "Library Lighting Standards." *Wilson Library Bulletin* 33 (December 1958): 297–301.
89. Thomson, Garry. "Visible and Ultraviolet Radiation." *Museums Journal* 57 (May 1957): 27–32.
90. Launer, Herbert F., and Wilson, William K. "The Photochemistry of Cellulose: Effects of Water Vapor and Oxygen in the Far and Near Ultraviolet Regions." *Journal of the American Chemical Society* 71 (1949): 958.
91. Feller, Robert L. "The Deteriorating Effect of Light on Museum Objects: Principles of Photochemistry, the Effect on Varnishes and Paint Vehicles and on Paper." *Museum News* 43 (June 1964), Technical supp. 3: i–viii.
92. Belaia, I. K. "Effect of Shortwave Ultraviolet Radiation from Bactericidal Lamps on Paper." *Bumazhnaya Promyshlennost* 32 (September 1957): 9–10.
93. Poole, Frazer G., ed. *The Library Environment, Aspects of Interior Planning: Proceedings of the Library Equipment Institute, St. Louis, Mo., June 26–27, 1964.*

Chicago: American Library Association, 1965.

94. Feller, Robert L. "Control of Deteriorating Effects of Light on Museum Objects: Heating Effects of Illumination of Incandescent Lamps." *Museum News* 46 (May 1968), Technical supp.: 39–47.

95. Harrison, Laurence S. "Evaluation of Spectral Radiation Hazards in Window-Lighted Galleries." Paper presented at the I.I.C. Conference, Rome, 1961.

96. Rohm & Haas Co. "Plexiglas Ultraviolet Filtering Formulations." Bulletin no. 612. Philadelphia: Rohm & Haas Co., November 1963.

97. Barrow, William K. "Black Writing Ink of the Colonial Period." *American Archivist* 11 (1948): 291–307.

98. Race, Edward. "The Degradation of Cotton during Atmospheric Exposure, Particularly in Industrial Regions." *Journal of the Society of Dyers and Colourists* 65 (1949): 56–63.

99. Egerton, G. S. "The Action of Light on Dyed and Undyed Cloth." *American Dyestuff Reporter* 36 (October 6, 1947): 561.

100. Wilson, William K., and Mandel, John. "Determination of Carboxyl in Cellulose: Comparison of Various Methods." *TAPPI* 44 (February 1961): 131–37.

101. Wilson, William K. "Determination of Aldehyde in Cellulose: A Review of Methods." *TAPPI* 38 (May 1955): 274–79.

102. "Preservation of the Declaration of Independence and the Constitution of the United States: A Report by the National Bureau of Standards to the Library of Congress." Circular 505. Washington, D.C.: National Bureau of Standards, July 2, 1951.

103. Merritt, Frederick S. *Building Construction Handbook*. New York: McGraw-Hill Book Co., 1958.

104. American Society of Heating, Refrigerating and Air-Conditioning Engineers. *ASHRAE Guide and Data Book, Applications for 1966–1967*. New York: ASHRAE, 1967.

105. Garver, Thomas H. "Control of Atmospheric Pollutants and Maintenance of Stable Climatic Conditions within Museum Buildings." In *Museum Climatology,* edited by G. Thomson. London: International Institute of Conservation, 1967.

106. Howorth, F. Hugh. "An Approach to Air Conditioning." In *Museum Climatology*, edited by G. Thomson. London: International Institute of Conservation, 1967.

107. Amdur, Elias J. "Humidity Control: Isolated Area Plan." *Museum News* 43 (December 1964), Technical supp. no. 6, pt. 2: 58–60.

108. Buck, Richard D. "A Specification for Museum Airconditioning." *Museum News* 43 (December 1964), Technical supp. no. 6, pt. 1: 53–57.

109. "New National Gallery of Art in Washington has 21-Zone Air Conditioning System." *Heating and Ventilating Magazine* 38 (April 1941): 39–41.

110. Stolow, Nathan. "The Action of Environment on Museum Objects. I. Humidity, Temperature, Atmospheric Pollution." *Curator* 9 (September 1966): 175–85.

111. Grad, Ian, and Greenberg, Alfred. "Air Conditioning for Books and People." *Architectural Record* 121 (June 1957): 231–34.

112. Pollak, H. "Dehumidification for the Preservation of Documents." *Mechanical World* 141 (August 1961): 268–70.

113. Pollak, H. "Dehumidification for the Preservation of Documents." *Mechanical World* 141 (September 1961): 302–304.

114. Warner, Burns, Tean, Lunde, Architects. *National Agricultural Library, Beltsville, Maryland, Specifications, Mechanical-Electrical.* Secs. 51 through 67. General Services Administration, Public Buildings Service, Washington, D.C.

115. Bell, Morton. "The Cost of Clean Air." *Air Conditioning, Heating and Ventilation* 65 (July 1968): 41–46.

116. Whitby, Kenneth T.; Lundgren, Dale A.; McFarland, Andrew R.; and Jordan, Richard C. "Evaluation of Air Cleaners for Occupied Spaces." *Journal of the Air Pollution Control Association* 11 (November 1961): 503–15.

PRESERVATION, DETERIORATION, RESTORATION OF PHOTOGRAPHIC IMAGES

GEORGE T. EATON

Librarians and library management are concerned with the preservation and restoration of all kinds of documents and records produced on a wide variety of materials. Photographic records represent an increasingly important segment of library acquisitions, especially in view of audiovisual needs, microfilm records, and the collection of valuable photographic prints.

In order to understand the deterioration, preservation, and restoration of photographic records, it is necessary to know the potential sources of trouble that may arise from the manufacture of the raw materials, the preparation of the photographic records, and the handling and storage of these records. Much has been published on most aspects of these problems; therefore, the significant factors are summarized here.

Originally the word "photography" meant "to write with light," but today it can be defined as follows: "to produce an image in a sensitive layer by some kind of radiation." There are many image-forming systems, but this discussion will be concerned only with those sensitive materials based upon the silver halide salts: silver chloride, silver bromide and silver iodide. These materials consist primarily of a support —glass, film, or paper—coated with the silver halide emulsion.

Library acquisitions can include motion picture films, sheet film and roll film negatives, microfilm records in a variety of formats, photographic prints on film or paper, and, possibly, color films and prints. Although a wide variety of photographic materials can be involved, the same care must be taken with each in the production of records required for archival purposes. Color films are not approved by USA Standard [1] for archival use, since dyes are known to fade over a period of years. However, modern color films, if processed and stored as recommended, will retain their original colors for many years.

The permanence of photographic records is dependent upon (1) the stability of the support, (2) the control and completeness of the processing operations, and (3) the storage environment. The stability of the unused photographic material is primarily the manufacturer's problem with respect, first, to the emulsion time of exposure and, second, to the support for its lifetime. Although the manufacturer can and does recommend processing and storage procedures, these are, respectively, the responsibility of the photographic processing laboratory and the ultimate owner of the record.

SUPPORTS FOR PHOTOGRAPHIC MATERIALS

GLASS

Glass plates are used in a considerable number of technical applications where dimensional stability is very significant. Carefully selected glass is used, free of irregularities in light transmission. There is no stability problem with glass except breakage.

FILM BASE

The evolution of film base from the early cellulose nitrate through the acetate "safety" film to the newer polyester bases has been well documented, particularly in relation to motion picture film [2, 3].

Cellulose nitrate film base is chemically unstable and a serious fire hazard but has not been employed in film manufacture since 1951. However, there are still thirty-five-millimeter motion picture films on nitrate base in some film storage vaults. Such films should be identified and segregated from all other materials and steps taken to duplicate the records [2]. *These films are not acceptable for any archival record use.*

"Acetate film" refers to any film having a base composed of cellulose diacetate, cellulose triacetate, or the mixed esters—cellulose acetate propionate or cellulose acetate butyrate. In any case, the support used for the production of archival records should conform to the USA Standards for safety film [4] and permanent record film [1]. Accelerated-aging laboratory tests [5, 6] and fifty years of experience have demonstrated the high degree of chemical stability of acetate films.

Polyester films were introduced about 1955 [7]. Although not yet included in the USA Standard for permanent record film [1], they do meet the USA Standard for safety film [4]. Accelerated-aging tests and experience to date show the polyester films equal to, or better than, cellulose triacetate film in permanence [3].

The commercial polyester films are of particular interest in special applications requiring high dimensional stability and film strength, as well as greater resistance to extremes of temperature.

PHOTOGRAPHIC PAPER SUPPORT

The problem of durability and permanence of paper is well known to librarians, archivists, and others. At least a few hundred manuscripts have been published on the subject which indicate the concern of the paper manufacturer and the consumer. The problem has been at least equally significant in the photographic industry.

The photographic paper base must be as durable and permanent as possible. It cannot chemically affect the silver halide emulsion coated upon it, and it must be resistant, physically and chemically, to the chemical processing required to produce the silver image. The photographic record obtained must then keep indefinitely if stored under optimum conditions. Obviously, it became necessary to investigate the manufacture of paper within the photographic industry to satisfy its very special requirements.

It was observed that there was a direct relationship between the yellowing of paper and the "keeping" or life of the silver halide emulsion coated on the paper. Therefore, the relative permanence of two papers could be determined by their effect on the photographic emulsion.

Because of the variability in the best white rags available, it was apparent that a uniform raw material must be found. Wood pulp was a potential source. Impurities were removed in such a manner that the cellulose purity was essentially equal to that of new-grown cotton.

The purity of this high-grade wood pulp must be retained in the finished paper, and, therefore, an extensive investigation of sizing materials was conducted to find a replacement for rosin, which was not sufficiently effective in wood-pulp paper. A combination of the purified wood pulp and a new sizing material produced paper at least equal in all respects to rag pulp-rosin paper. Additionally, a photographic emulsion coated on the new wood-pulp paper had keeping properties equal to the same emulsion coated on glass [8].

During the same period the National Bureau of Standards, studying the permanence of papers, employed an accelerated-aging test in which the paper was subjected to increased temperatures under controlled humidity and measured for changes in chemical and physical properties. The new purified wood-pulp papers showed a high order of permanence under these and other test conditions [9, 10, 11].

The durability and permanence of photographic paper continue to be problems in the photographic industry, and every effort is made to improve both the chemical and the physical properties.

PROCESSING OF PHOTOGRAPHIC MATERIALS

Those concerned with the storage of archival photographic records, unfortunately, do not usually know whether the exposed photographic material was properly processed unless they had direct responsibility for the work. In any case, knowledge of the important factors in processing relative to permanence can be helpful in procuring archival records, particularly when such records are being made currently.

Processing involves development, fixation, washing, and drying of exposed film or paper. Simply, development is the conversion of exposed silver halide to the metallic silver image; fixation is the conversion of the unexposed silver halide to soluble complex silver-hypo compounds; washing is the removal by water of the soluble silver-hypo complexes; and drying is removal of the bulk of water in the material. The chemistry and often the mechanical equipment are complex, and the recommended procedures and controls should be followed. With proper control of the process, stable images are produced, but improper control leads to instability or fading.

Inadequate fixation or washing can produce fading. If some of the silver-hypo complexes are left in the film or paper, they can decompose to produce an overall yellow brown stain of silver sulfide in the nonimage areas, particularly noticeable in photographic paper prints. When some of the fixing agent, hypo, is left in the film or paper because of poor washing, it can attack the silver image in a manner similar to "tarnishing" of silverware by sulfur-containing gases.

For permanent records it is necessary to obtain complete fixation and washing, that is, removal of essentially all residual silver and hypo salts. Because the damage from improper fixation and washing may not be evident for years, the Bureau of Standards and the USA Standards Institute [12, 1] have established specifications for maximum allowable residual silver and hypo and for tests to determine the success or control of the processing operations.

In many photographic applications today shortened processes are used in the interest of rapid access to the image and information. These processes must be passed by in favor of more time-consuming operations. However, there are certain factors that can be significant in providing more efficient and economical processing in the production of archival records.

The washing system, regardless of its design, must satisfy two conditions: (1) an adequate rate of renewal or change of water at the emulsion surface and (2) a sufficient rate of flow of water to accomplish the renewal rate. A complete change of the volume of water every five minutes will satisfy these requirements. Unless an efficient washing system is employed, other changes in processing conditions will have little effect.

Residual hypo and silver-hypo complexes are either strongly or weakly held according to the condition of the gelatin in the emulsion layer [13]. The gelatin is usually acidic in nature, and, when maintained in this condition, strongly retains hypo and silver-hypo salts, but any change in the process that makes the gelatin less acidic permits more rapid removal. The degree of acidity or alkalinity of the processing solutions affects the acidity of the gelatin.

The degree of acidity or alkalinity is expressed on a pH scale from 0 to 14 in which the neutral point is 7.0. Values below this indicate greater acidity as the number becomes lower, and values about 7.0 indicate increasing alkalinity. Gelatin in photographic emulsions is usually at pH = 4.9.

THE pH EFFECT

The initial pH value of a fixing bath is related to its composition, which is determined by such practical characteristics as rate of fixation, useful life, hardening properties, and sludging properties. Three acid fixing baths, such as Kodak F-5, F-10, and F-6, have initial pH values of 4.3, 4.6, and 4.9, respectively. Washing will remove hypo from film at a greater rate the higher the pH of the fixer (fig. 1).

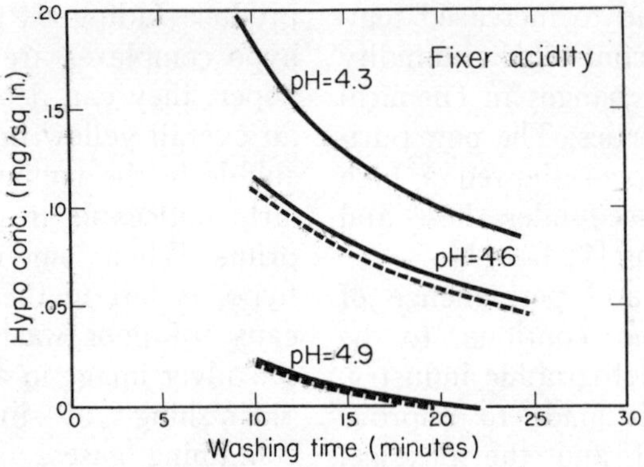

FIG. 1.—Effect of fixer pH on hypo removal. Solid curves show increased rate of removal as fixed pH increased. Dotted lines show effect of raising pH 4.3to 4.6 and pH 4.6 to 4.9.

In most large-volume, continuous processing systems this effect is not very significant because the gelatin pH of 4.9 has not been increased. The pH of the acid hardening fixers cannot be increased above 4.9 because the hardening properties must be maintained. However, in some small-volume, manual operations, hardening fixing baths at pH 5.0 have been employed.

The pH effect is much more pronounced when the pH of the wash water is raised above 5.0. Experimentally a 0.03 percent ammonia rinse increased the pH of the gelatin to values of 9.0 and 10.0, and the hypo was removed very rapidly (fig. 2). In a practical situation film is rinsed in running water immediately following fixation and prior to immersion in the ammonia bath to avoid sludging by reaction between the hardening agent, alum, and ammonia (fig. 3). This technique has been used in the processing of microfilm with definite advantages in saving time and water and permitting a simplified machine design.

The pH effect is observed and used only with film products; it is insignificant in the processing of photographic papers.

THE COMPOSITION OF THE FIXING BATH

Sodium thiosulfate (hypo) is the most commonly used fixing agent, but ammonium thiosulfate, used in rapid liquid fixers, reduces fixing time by about 50 percent when the two salts are used in equivalent concentrations. Films, but not photographic papers, are washed more rapidly following the use of ammonium thiosulfate fixers (fig. 4). The residual hypo content is reduced to zero in 50–65 percent of the time required for eliminating sodium thiosulfate.

It is important not to overuse fixing baths because the concentration of silver in the fixer gradually increases as more and more unexposed silver halides are dissolved. The silver-hypo salts formed become more complex and also more difficult to remove by washing. When the pH of the fixer is maintained constant during use, the amount of silver complexes (not metallic Ag) retained by the film increases with use (fig. 5). Little or no silver is retained if the pH of the fixer is not controlled by the use of a stop bath, but this effect

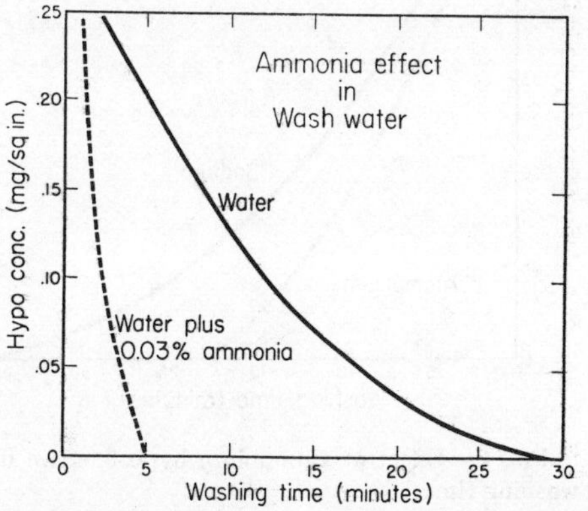

FIG. 2.—Effect of ammonia in wash water. Residual hypo in film completely removed in one-sixth the time.

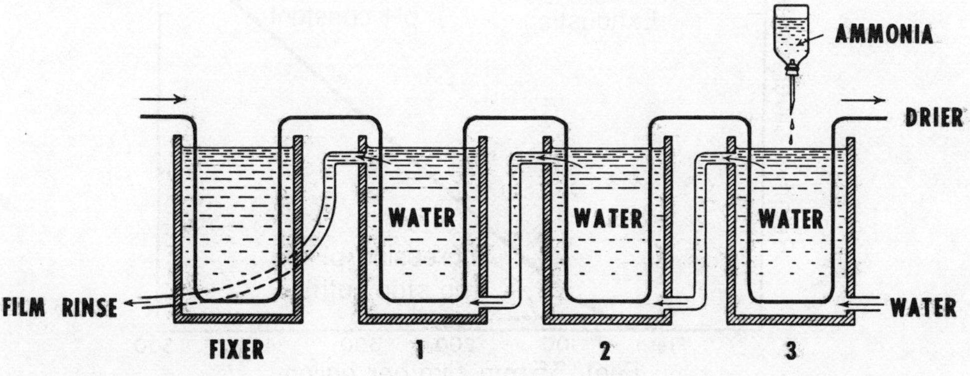

FIG. 3.—Practical arrangement for use of ammonia. Water flows counter to film and is used to rinse film after development.

cannot be used often in practice. Figure 5 shows data for thirty-five-millimeter film; the same retention of silver occurs in processing photographic prints.

Related to fixing bath exhaustion and retained silver complexes in both film and paper processing is the use of double fixation [14]. The larger percentage of unexposed silver in the emulsion is dissolved in the first bath, and fixation is then completed in an essentially fresh second bath having a very low concentration of silver. Under these conditions the amount of silver retained by the processed film or paper is very small and usually within specified amounts when the first fixing bath does not exceed the permissible concentration of silver [12] (fig. 6).

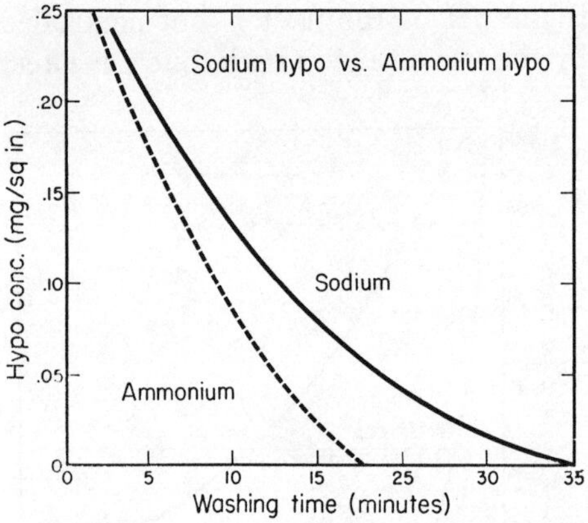

FIG. 4.—Effect of ammonium hypo fixer on film washing time.

TEMPERATURE OF THE WASH WATER

This is a factor of considerable practical importance. It is recommended that water tempered to 65–70° F is especially helpful when it is necessary to reduce washing time to a minimum and to conserve water supply. The effectiveness of temperature in washing both films and papers is indicated in figures 7 and 8. Generally, shorter washing times are required to reduce the residual hypo content to a low level if the temperature of the water is increased to 75° F. Complete washing is possible with films, but it is not easy to reach zero in prints because the paper fibers and reflection coatings (baryta) strongly hold hypo, as indicated in figure 8. Other treatments are required to remove the last traces of hypo from prints.

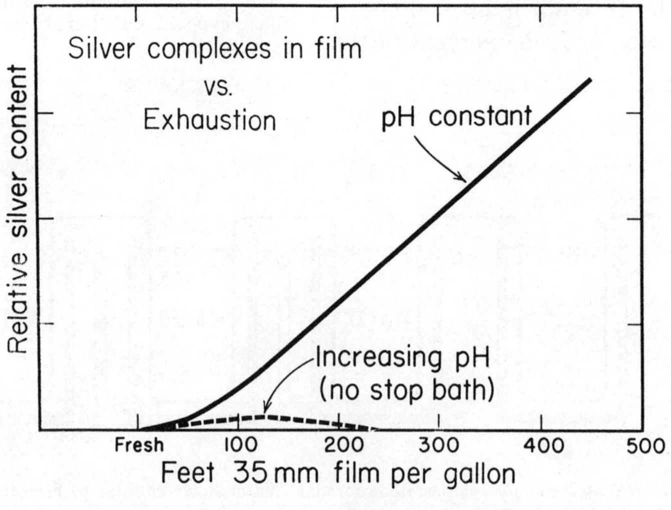

FIG. 5.—Fixing bath exhaustion vs. silver retention by film

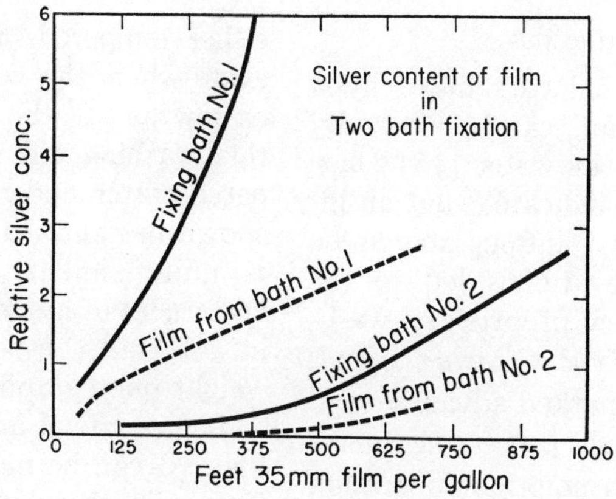

FIG. 6.—Silver retention by film in two-bath fixation. Solid lines: silver concentration in fixing baths with use; dotted lines: silver concentration in processed film.

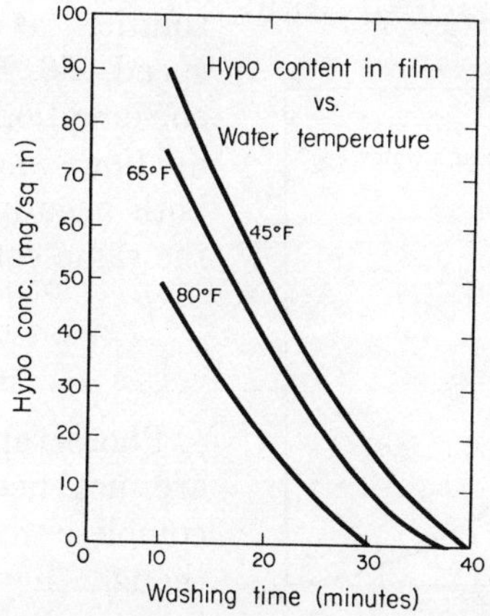

FIG. 7.—Effect of water temperature in film washing

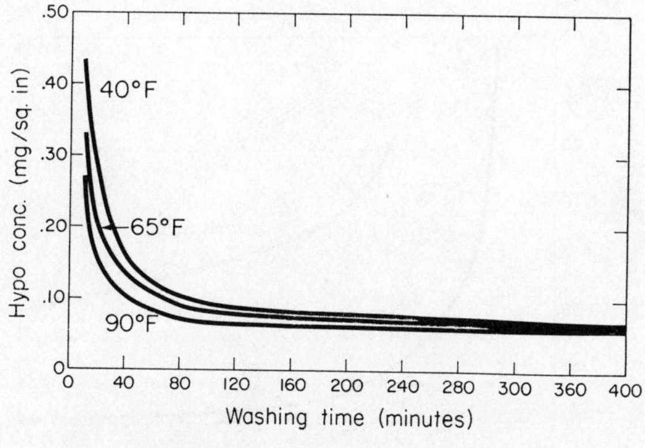

FIG. 8.—Effect of water temperature in paper washing

WASHING AIDS

The time required to remove hypo from films and prints can be markedly reduced by using sea water [15] (figs. 9, 10). This work indicated that an investigation of salt solutions should be made [16]. These studies led to the marketing of a new proprietary washing aid, *Kodak Hypo Clearing Agent*, which has shown marked advantages in both film and paper processing in regard to water consumption, operating time, and hypo elimination with respect to USA Standard specifications for permanent records. This washing aid is equally effective when used with either tempered or untempered water, even when the water temperature is as low as 40° F. The effectiveness of this washing aid compared with tempered water and ammoniated water is shown in figure 11 for films. The effect is quite similar for prints, but the last traces of hypo may not be removed in all cases, especially with double-weight photographic papers.

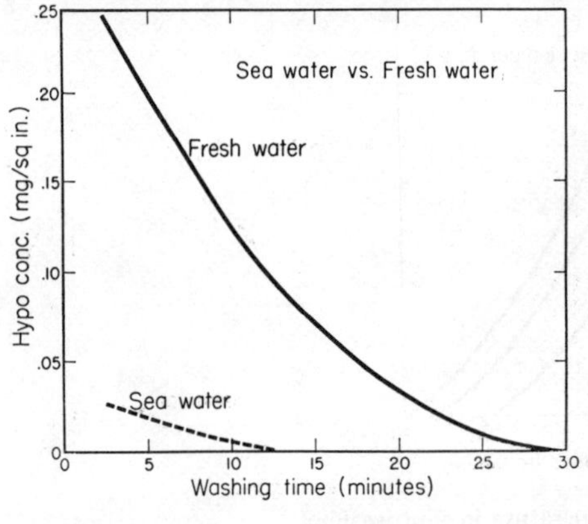

FIG. 9.—Hypo elimination from film in sea water and fresh water.

The practical arrangement shown in figure 3 can be modified to use Kodak Hypo Clearing Agent, as show in figure 12. A comparison of these two practical systems in the processing of microfilm shows the advantages of the salt solution as follows: greater machine speed, 50 percent reduction in water consumption, increased volume of production, and capability of processing both negative and positive films under the same conditions (table 1).

POSTPROCESSING STEPS FOR ARCHIVAL RECORDS

Photographic film and print images are not necessarily permanent after complete fixation and washing. Even though they contain very little or no hypo and silver salts [12], the images are susceptible to environmental conditions such as hydrogen sulfide, sulfur

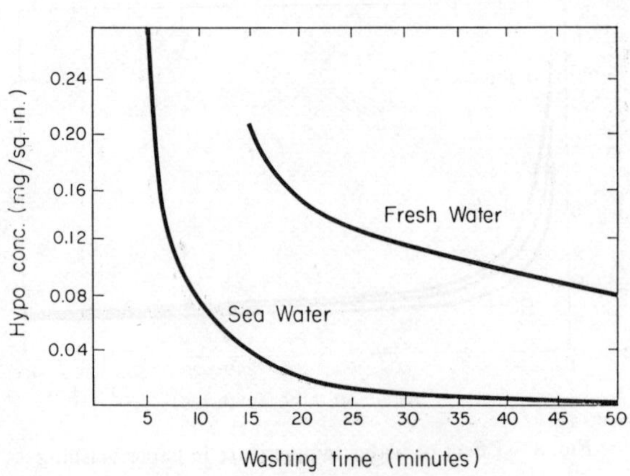

FIG. 10.—Hypo elimination from prints in sea water and fresh water

dioxide, hydrogen peroxide, certain organic vapors, high humidity, and temperature.

FILM RECORDS

Motion picture films and microfilms have probably received the greatest attention in processing and subsequent handling. Other films for archival record purposes should receive the same attention. All records should satisfy the USA Standard specifications for permanent records [12].

There are two quite significant aspects of film record preparation that should be mentioned: (1) the use of storage envelopes for sheet film negatives and (2) the prevention of "aging blemishes" on microfilm records.

Storage envelopes designed with a center seam should be avoided because the pastes or adhesives used are usually hygroscopic and retain moisture, which eventually promotes fading in an area of the negative corresponding to the seam. The material used in the manufacture of the envelopes must be free of sulfur. Specifications are stated in

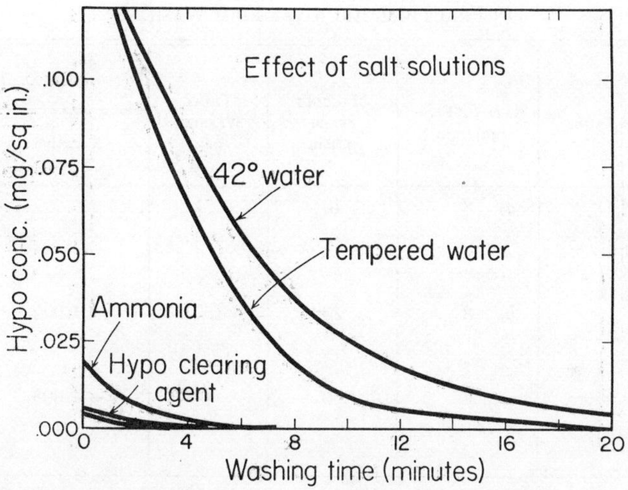

FIG. 11.—Relative effectiveness of Kodak Hypo Clearing Agent. Treatment in the washing aid provides relatively rapid hypo removal regardless of wash water temperature.

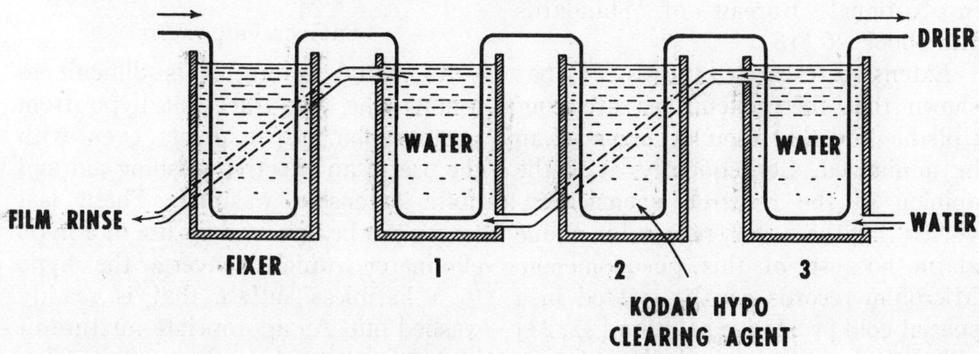

FIG. 12.—Practical arrangement for use of Kodak Hypo Clearing Agent. Water flows counter to film from tank 3 into tank 1 and then is used to rinse film between development and fixation. Tank 2 contains stagnant washing aid solution.

USA Standard for negative storage envelopes [17].

Aging blemishes or microspots were observed in stored rolls of microfilm as tiny circular spots on fogged opaque leader, the fogged edges of the first few feet and, in a few cases, the image areas. Inspection of thousands of rolls showed very few cases where the image area had been affected significantly in respect to image deterioration or impairment. A more detailed description of the blemishes and of the techniques used in inspecting microfilm is given in National Bureau of Standards Handbook 96 [18].

Extensive research [19, 20, 21] has shown that these blemishes are controllable and that their occurrence can be minimized. Consequently, it is the opinion of the research agencies involved that there is no reason for undue alarm because of this pheonomenon. Microfilm records can be treated in a special gold protective solution [22, 23] either during the original film processing or as a postprocessing treatment. This treatment is available from the Business Systems Marketing Division of the Eastman Kodak Company and provides the highest degree of protection.

The addition of 0.2 gram per liter of potassium iodide to the fixer in microfilm processing has proved very beneficial. Several files were inspected before and after the use of iodide, this being the only change in processing and storage. Few, if any, blemishes were observed after four years of storage. Table 2 shows the effectiveness of the iodide treatment.

TABLE 1

RELATIVE EFFECTIVENESS OF AMMONIA AND KODAK HYPO CLEARING AGENT IN PRACTICAL ARCHIVAL FILM WASHING

WASHING IN THREE TANKS	RATE OF FLOW (gal/min)	MACHINE SPEED (ft/min)	TOTAL WASHING (min)	RESIDUAL HYPO (mg/sq in)	
				Negative Films	Positive Films
Water (1 tank) + Tempered water and ammonia (1 tank) + Water (1 tank)	*a*) 8	40	$7\frac{1}{2}$	....	<0.005
	b) 8	20	15	<0.005	....
Water (1 tank) + KHCA (1 tank) + Water (1 tank)	4	50	4	<0.005	<0.005

PHOTOGRAPHIC PRINTS

As stated before, it is difficult to remove the last traces of hypo from photographic paper prints even with the use of an effective washing aid and quite extensive washing. These last traces can be removed by use of a hypo eliminator, which converts the hypo to a harmless sulfate that is readily washed out. An appropriate mixture of hydrogen peroxide and ammonia (Kodak Hypo Eliminator HE-1) is recommended [24]. This same paper suggests further means of protection against atmospheric conditions.

After treatment with the hypo eliminator and washing, the print images can be further protected by treatment in a dilute gold solution. This effectively coats the silver grains of the image with a layer of gold, which is much more resistant than the silver.

The washed and dried prints can then be mounted. The mounting board employed, at least for archival records, should be free from sulfur compounds and other constituents that might affect the print. Unfortunately, no standard specifications have been written for photographic mounting board.

The prints should be dry-mounted by using a dry-mounting tissue, which also provides a barrier between the print and the mounting board. Pastes, adhesives, and cements are generally hygroscopic or contain sulfur compounds and can cause "fading" in local areas.

Mounted prints can be overcoated with a suitable lacquer sprayed on to cover the print and the face of the mounting board, care being taken to coat the edges of the print.

ARCHIVAL STORAGE OF PHOTOGRAPHIC RECORDS

Basic storage concepts are equally applicable to commercial as well as archival records, but more care is required for the latter. In planning storage facilities one should consider temperature, humidity, air conditioning, air purification, water protection, and fire protection [25, 26].

HUMIDITY

Storage in moist air and above 50 percent relative humidity should be avoided. Relative humidities above 60 percent encourage fungus growth, while very low humidities can cause film brittleness, curl, and static charge. Properly controlled air conditioning of the storage area is recommended for longtime preservation of archival records. Generally, the relative humidity and temperature should be controlled to 40–50 RH and 70° F, respectively.

AIR PURIFICATION

Contaminants can come from illuminating gas, coal gas, and certain chemical manufacturing plants, especially in industrial and urban areas. Typical

TABLE 2

EFFECT OF IODIDE ON AGING BLEMISHES

Collection Designation	Processing Dates	Iodide in Fixer	No. of Films Examined	No. Having Spot Defect
A.	1/63–5/64	No	31	31
A.	6/64–1/66	Yes	19	0*
B.	8/63	No	5	5
B.	9/64	Yes	5	0*
C.	2/18/63–6/8/64	No	33	33
C.	6/29/64–1/24/66	Yes	25	0
D.	4/63–6/64	No	11	8
D.	7/64–8/65	Yes	8	0*

NOTE.—The latest 1964 date given indicates when iodide was added to fixer. All other conditions in processing and storage were the same before and after addition of iodide, i.e., same in each collection, but conditions varied between collections.

* A single spot (not a spotted roll) was found in one of the rolls.

contaminants are paint fumes, hydrogen sulfide, sulfur dioxide and similar gases. When these cannot be avoided in the storage area, air conditioning designed to remove contaminating gases must be installed [27].

WATER PROTECTION

Storage facilities should be located above basement level, and steps should be taken to make sure that all records are protected from water damage such as leaks, fire-sprinkler discharge, and flooding [25].

FIRE PROTECTION

According to the number of records to be stored, cabinets, safes, and storage vaults should be considered to provide the highest degree of protection. Such storage facilities should satisfy the Fire Underwriters regulations and requirements of the National Fire Protection Association [28] for a valuable-record room.

PACKAGING FOR ARCHIVAL STORAGE

Most photographic records are stored in some kind of container which is carefully selected with respect to its composition and possible effect on the photographic image. Reels of valuable films like microfilms and motion picture films are usually stored in metal cans designed for the purpose. The cans may or may not be sealed, depending on the storage facilities and the film usage. A good-quality, rubber-base pressure-sensitive tape is used for sealing the cans. Roll film negatives can be stored in a similar manner. Sheet films and paper prints should be stored in separate envelopes meeting the specification of USA Standard for negative storage envelopes [18].

Often sheet film negatives and positives as well as photographic prints are stacked with plastic interleaving sheets. These sheets contain plasticizers, some of which can affect the photographic image. There are no USA Standard specifications at present, but recommendations are available from photographic manufacturers. Aluminum foil and polyethylene appear to be practical.

Interleaved stacks of negatives and prints are usually stored in a container. Cardboard boxes are suspect unless the cardboard is known to be free of sulfur compounds. Metal cabinets designed specially for the purpose will likely provide the highest degree of protection [28]. Completely fixed and washed unexposed photographic paper has been used as a satisfactory interleaver.

The use of rubber bands around rolls of films should be avoided because the rubber can contain residual sulfur used in vulcanization. Adhesive tapes, tape splices, bleached papers, and printing inks may have the same undesirable effect [25].

RESTORATION OF DETERIORATED PHOTOGRAPHIC RECORDS

Restoration techniques are required primarily with sheet film records and photographic prints that have been affected by poor storage conditions, that is, high relative humidity, temperature, and often external contaminants. Reels of processed films, especially in the case of valuable or archival records, are usually duplicated and stored in a safe place. The special case of microscopic blemishes was discussed earlier.

With all valuable records it is advisable to attempt duplication by photography before testing or treating the record chemically. Film negatives can often be contact-printed onto a second film to restore near-original contrast and quality. Film negatives and paper prints, especially if faded or stained, can often be photographed on a copy camera with appropriate filters. In fact, this may be the only satisfactory technique when the stain results from incomplete fixation or from the accidental spillage of solutions [29].

Before any chemical restoration treatment is attempted on either films or paper prints, it is necessary to determine what the stain is and how it was probably produced [30]. The most common "stain" encountered is the result of fading, which can result from residual hypo or from silver-hypo complexes in the processed record. When the image has been attacked by hypo and has turned brown to yellowish brown, it can be restored by a bleach and redevelopment process. The whole image, silver and brownish silver sulfide, is converted to a silver salt, like silver bromide, and then treated in a developer to produce a whole black silver image. This technique is not applicable when there is a uniform stain resulting from the decomposition of silver-hypo complexes to form silver sulfide. The result would be a grayish stain of silver.

One other change that occurs in time is the formation of silver mirrors. These are quite readily removed by immersion in an ammonium hypo reducer [31].

The factors involved in the deterioration, preservation and restoration of photographic records have been reviewed. The significance of these relative to the value of the records can be appreciated, and, therefore, the necessary steps can be taken to assure correctly processed images and appropriate preparation for storage of the records.

REFERENCES

1. USA Standard Specifications for Photographic Films for Permanent Records PH 1.28—1957. Obtainable from USA Standards Institute, Inc., 10 East 40th Street, New York, New York 10016.
2. Calhoun, John M. "The Preservation of Motion-Picture Film." *American Archivist* 30 (July 1967):517–25.
3. Adelstein, P. Z., and McCrea, J. L. "Permanence of Processed ESTAR Polyester Base Photographic Films." *Photographic Science and Engineering* 9 (September-October 1965):305–13.
4. USA Standard Specifications for Safety Photographic Film, PH 1.25—1965. Obtainable from the USA Standards Institute, Inc., 10 East 40th Street, New York, New York 10016.
5. Hill, J. R., and Weber, C. G. "Stability of Motion-Picture Films as Determined by Accelerated Aging." *Journal of the Society of Motion Picture Engineers* 27 (December 1936):677–90.
6. Fordyce, C. R. "Improved Safety Motion-Picture Film Support." *Journal of the Society of Motion Picture Engineers* 51 (October 1948):331–50.
7. White, Deane R.; Gass, Charles J.; Meschter, Emery; and Holm, Wilton R. "Polyester Photographic Film Base." *Journal of the Society of Motion Picture Engineers* 64 (December 1955):674–78.
8. Lane, Gerould T. *Permanence of Paper.* Rochester, N.Y.: Eastman Kodak Co., 1935.
9. Rasch, R. H., and Scribner, B. W. "Comparison of Natural Aging of Paper with Accelerated Aging by Heating." *Journal of Research of the National Bureau of Standards* 11 (December 1933):727–32.
10. Rasch, R. H.; Shaw, M. B.; and Bicking, G. W. "Highly Purified Wood Fibers as Paper-Making Material." *Journal of Research of the National Bureau of Standards* 7 (November 1931):765–82.
11. Scribner, B. W. "Comparison of Accelerated Aging of Record Papers with Normal Aging for 8 Years." *Journal of Research of the National Bureau of Standards* 23 (September 1939):405–13.

12. American Standard Methods for Predicting the Permanency of the Silver Images of Processed Films, Plates and Papers. Z 38.8.17 (1948). Available from USA Standards Institute, Inc., 10 East 40th Street, New York, New York 10016.
13. Crabtree, J. I.; Eaton, G. T.; and Meuhler, L. E. "The Removal of Hypo and Silver Salts from Photographic Materials as Affected by the Composition of the Processing Solutions." *Journal of the Society of Motion Picture Engineers* 41 (1943):9–68.
14. Crabtree, J. O.; Henn, R. W.; and Edgerton, R. F. "Two-Bath Fixation of Prints." *Photographic Society of America Journal,* sec. B, 19B (February 1953):10–16.
15. Eaton, G. T., and Crabtree, J. I. "Washing Photographic Films and Prints in Sea Water." *Journal of the Society of Motion Picture Engineers* 40 (June 1943):380–91.
16. Henn, R. W.; King, Nancy H.; and Crabtree, J. I. "The Effect of Salt Baths on Hypo and Silver Elimination." *Photographic Engineering* 7 (1956):153–64.
17. USA Standard Requirement for Photographic Filing Enclosures for Storing Processed Photographic Films, Plates, and Papers PH 4.20—1958. Obtainable from USA Standards Institute, Inc., 10 East 40th Street, New York, New York 10016.
18. McCamy, C. S. *Inspection of Processed Photographic Record Films for Aging Blemishes.* National Bureau of Standards Handbook 96. Washington, D.C.: National Bureau of Standards, 1964.
19. Wiest, D. G., and Henn, R. W. "Microscopic Spots: A Progress Report." *National Micro-News* 70 (June 1964):249–57.
20. Henn, R. W., and Wiest, D. G. "Microscopic Spots in Processed Microfilm: Their Nature and Prevention." *Photographic Science and Engineering* 7 (September-October 1963):253–61.
21. Henn, R. W.; Wiest, D. G.; and Mack, Bernadette D. "Microscopic Spots in Processed Microfilm: The Effect of Iodide." *Photographic Science and Engineering* 9 (May-June 1965): 167–73.
22. Henn, R. W., and Mack, Bernadette D. "A Gold Protective Treatment for Microfilm." *Photographic Science and Engineering* 9 (November-December 1965):378–84.
23. Henn, R. W., and Wiest, D. G. "Properties of Gold-Treated Microfilm Images." *Photographic Science and Engineering* 10 (January-February 1966):15–22.
24. Crabtree, J. I.; Eaton, G. T.; and Muehler, L. E. "The Elimination of Hypo from Photographic Images." *Journal of the Society of Motion Picture Engineers* 35 (May 1940):484–506.
25. *Storage and Preservation of Microfilms.* Kodak Data Book no. P-108. Rochester, N.Y.: Eastman Kodak Co., 1965.
26. *Storage and Preservation of Motion-Picture Film.* Kodak Data Book no. H-8. Rochester, N.Y.: Eastman Kodak Co., 1957.
27. Saurwein, G. K. "Air Conditioning for Protection." *Heating, Piping and Air Conditioning* 13 (May 1941):311–13.
28. Protection of Records, Standard no. 232—1963, National Fire Protection Association, 60 Batterymarch Street, Boston, Massachusetts 02110.
29. *Copying.* Kodak Data Book no. M-1. Rochester, N.Y.: Eastman Kodak Co., 1968.
30. *Stains on Negatives and Prints.* Kodak Data Book no. J-18. Rochester, N.Y.: Eastman Kodak Co., 1950.
31. Henn, R. W.; Crabtree, J. I.; and Russell, H. D. "An Ammonium Hypo Reducer." *Photographic Society of American Journal* 17B (November 1951):110–13.

ALKALINE PRINTING PAPERS: PROMISE AND PERFORMANCE

JOSEPH J. THOMAS

INTRODUCTION

The printed word remains the backbone of the record of man in all of his activities whether they be in the social, industrial, political, scientific, economic, or artistic worlds. "Hard copy" of the written word still involves paper in spite of the many technological processes of recording that utilize photographic, magnetic, electronic and/or other new techniques. Invariably we come back to the "image on paper" as the real workhorse in our daily work of living and doing. Hence it is pertinent that we today talk about paper as one of mankind's primary raw materials. That such recording should have permanence seems obvious, but only now are we really doing something actively about its longevity.

Paper in the educational field, as the vehicle for the transmission of information, is but one of its many uses, because we have learned to apply paper to all facets of life. Today we have many different kinds of paper to do many different kinds of jobs. World War II was a major stimulus to our research and development in the paper industry to make paper perform jobs that hitherto had not been dreamed of. Paper was applied extensively in the war effort, in packaging, in industrial usages, and in many other jobs as other raw materials became scarce or nonexistent. Today paper has come of age and is the tenth largest industry in the United States.

This discussion, however, will be primarily concerned with "printing paper" and, therefore, we must define the properties of such paper in terms of its use for printing and publishing. Certainly we should not apply to printing paper the criteria and specifications that we would apply to industrial papers. In other words, the end use should truly be reflected in the properties and specifications that we delineate. In the case of book manufacture, such paper is to receive accurately the image from the printing plate; it must handle well through the presses and the bindery; and finally it must perform in the hands of the reader. Thus, manifold uses should be covered in the so-called specifications. Economically, it would be wasteful to build more into the paper than is needed for its optimum performance; on the other hand, adequate properties to embrace optimum manufacturing and usage must be covered. Paper's composition, its method of manufacture, conversion to use, storage, and utilization should all be weighed in consideration of specifications. For example, newsprint with its temporary, transient use certainly differs in requirements from the permanent, archival uses of the historian. Likewise, the properties required in papers for machine-shop manuals, army maps or navy charts differ from those needed for insurance rate-books or chemical handbooks whose usage will be rendered obsolete with time as technological progress out-dates the information contained therein. Papers for electrophotographic printing or for magnetic recording must have a different definition from paper to be printed by gravure and used as a label on a bottle or tin can.

Therefore, my remarks on paper will be confined to the end uses of printing, publishing, binding, and finally as a book in your hands in the library, where it should remain available and usable to posterity 100 or 200 years from now.

HISTORICAL

Examination of the literature shows that there has been a great deal of interest in the permanizing of man's records by studying the substrate paper. There seems to have been much talk but little action until W. J. Barrow really lit a fire on the subject in the 1950s and 1960s. Two papers with comprehensive bibliographies on paper durability are U.S. Government Printing Office Technical Bulletin no. 22, published in 1940 and entitled "Permanence and Durability of Paper, an Annotated Bibliography from 1885 A.D. to 1939 A.D." and "Paper Performance" by Philip Luner in *TAPPI* magazine (52, no. 5 [May 1969]: 801). For those who wish a comprehensive study on the subject I would recommend these two references for good historical and technical background.

Back in the good old days when life moved a little more leisurely and there were fewer economic and competitive pressures, rag papers made in a slow careful way seemed to be the answer to the longevity problem; but this was not wholly true, especially if sizing was obtained by the use of alum with rosin. However, as economic pressures demanded more and more production at lower costs the change to wood fibers met the ever-increasing demand for paper. Mass production became the "paper way of life" and we lost something. Alum became the papermaker's panacea, for it not only set rosin to give sizing a temporary resistance to water, but it also made the wet fibrous slurry on the Fourdrinier wire more free to drain water and thus increased production. Despite these advantages, however, the use of alum resulted in acid paper.

ORIGIN OF ALKALINE PAPERS

I would like to be able to say that we in our company had the perspicacity to see the evil of alum and to predict our alkaline future, but, as in many discoveries, the real stimulation was pressure to utilize a by-product that came from our soda process in isolating fibers from trees. Lime mud resulted from our recovery of soda-cooking liquors, when we treated the ash from the burning of our pulp-cooking liquor with slaked lime (fig. 1). This regenerated our soda chemicals to be used in cooking more wood, but the resulting useless precipitate was calcium carbonate, which we could only pile up behind the mill. Its nice white color made it look tempting, and we hoped to find a use for this by-product since the bleached purified cellulosic fibers coming from that pulp mill made such excellent book paper. We had already established to our own satisfaction that cellulose fibers regardless of their source, whether it be rags or trees, if purified, were of a durable and permanent character and that we could make good and lasting paper from properly purified wood fibers.

Credit for much of this thinking goes to the father of paper chemistry, Edwin Sutermeister, who had come to us as a new graduate from the Massachusetts Institute of Technology in 1899. It was he who, in 1901, made the experiments with lime mud and set aside a series of papers that he examined periodically to see the effect of this by-product on the paper versus the usual paper making techniques extant. Specifically, he set aside six "super" plain papers that had been manufactured between 1896 and 1901; five were clay filled and one had lime mud as filler. The fiber furnish varied from all rag, to mixtures of rag and sulphite wood pulp, to all wood fibers (mixtures of bleached sulphite and soda pulps). The sixth sample which had the lime mud was 75 percent sulphite and 25 percent soda wood fibers; it had a pH of 8.9, while the other five samples had pH values varying from 3.6 to 4.3. When Edwin Sutermeister examined the samples in 1929

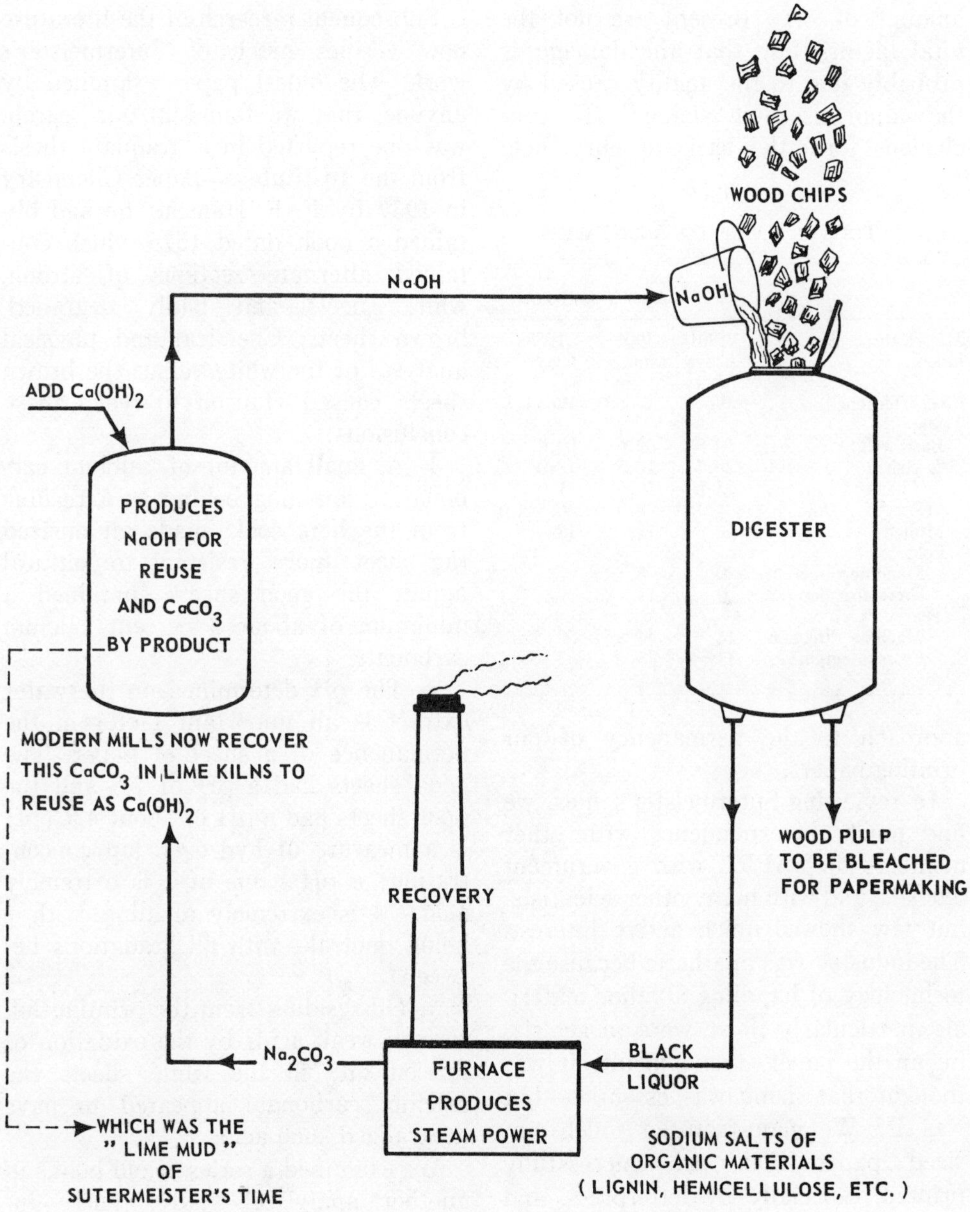

FIG. 1

and retested them, his report said "all of the acid samples were badly discolored and were absolutely without strength while the lime mud sample was much whiter and seemed as strong as ever." He concluded that "from the present samples it appears that the nature of the fiber content and the amount of clay present are not the vital factors but that the damage is probably due to the acidity caused by the alum used in sizing." His conclusions form the basis of our whole approach to the permanency of our printing papers.

TABLE 1

1958 TESTS ON NATURALLY AGED PAPERS

	Acid	Alkaline	Neutral
Mfg. Date	1901	1901	1958
Filler	Clay	Lime mud	Clay
Fibers (bleached)	Wood	Wood	Wood
Tests:			
Basis weight	60.8	62.6	60.0
% Ash	29.7	16.5	18.0
% Filler	33.8	29.5	21.0
pH	4.3	8.9	6.5–7.0
Mullen	6	18	18
Fold:			
Machine direction	0	8	7
Cross direction	0	14	7
Tear:			
Machine direction	14	44	50
Cross direction	13	45	55

In reviewing Sutermeister's files, we find much correspondence with other members of TAPPI, with government officials, and with many other scientists, but few showed much active interest. The industry was apathetic because the technology of handling alkaline materials, particularly if we were to get sizing in the paper, was difficult; it was thought that sizing was essential—but was it? We manufactured much unsized paper that was successfully printed, especially by letterpress, and made into books. The government's attitude was one of conservatism. "Sutie's" frustration showed through readily in this correspondence, but he and we kept plugging. In time we overcame many of the technological obstacles, including the sizing problem.

OLD BOOKS AND PAPERS

Subsequent research of the literature now verifies much of Sutermeister's work. The oldest paper examined by anyone, that we found in our search, was one reported in a graduate thesis from the Institute of Paper Chemistry in 1937 by F. F. Hanson; he had obtained a book dated 1576 which contained alternate sections of strong, white sheets and badly degraded, brown sheets. Chemical and physical analyses of the white versus the brown sheets caused Hanson to reach these conclusions:

1. A small amount of calcium carbonate, remaining behind as a residue from the lime cook, made an unsized rag sheet more resistant to natural aging; the good sheets contained a minimum of about 2 percent calcium carbonate.

2. The pH determined on the water extract is an important factor in the permanence of a sheet of paper. The good sheets had a pH of 7.5 and the poor sheets had a pH of about 4.9 (pH is a measure of hydrogen ion concentration; a pH value of 1 is extremely acid, 14 is extremely alkaline, with 7 being neutral—with all gradations between).

3. Oil residues from the printing ink formed weak acids by the oxidation of linseed oil; in the white sheets the calcium carbonate appeared to have neutralized such acids.

We examined a series of old books in another analytical study. These involved a book made in 1859 of all rag paper; it was unsized; it had a pH of 7.5; after 103 years it was in excellent condition and still had a fold test value of over 50. This book contrasted with one made in 1891 of all wood fibers, having a pH of 4.4 and a fold of only 1. The third book was made in 1912 of wood fibers and had a pH of 4.8 and a fold of 7. The oldest book could be easily handled, while the other two had to be handled somewhat "like eggs" if they were to be studied by users in the library.

Table 1 summarizes work we did in 1958 on Sutermeister's acid and alkaline papers of 1901 vs. a publisher's grade being satisfactorily made and used at that time. Unfortunately, we cannot find the analytical data on these samples at the time they were made. These data were either lost from the files or the tests themselves were made by methods not comparable to those being used today. But it is obvious that the neutral or alkaline pH was the major cause for retention of strength.

Those papers are available for examination. The acid one has to be enclosed in a plastic envelope because it is so brittle it would fall apart in one's fingers if handled. The alkaline paper made in 1901 feels as though it were made yesterday.

DURABILITY VERSUS PERMANENCE

In preparing this article I spent much time in our company files for background information as well as for evidence and proof of our major thesis that a neutral or preferably alkaline sheet of paper connotes permanence. I found much of Sutermeister's writing more poignant than anything I could say; hence I shall quote from his report of 1941.

In the strict sense of the word, as defined in a dictionary, there is no such thing as a "permanent" paper. This is recognized by the Technical Association of the Pulp and Paper Industry which defines permanence as the degree to which paper resists chemical action which may result from impurities in the paper itself or agents from the surrounding atmosphere. Durability, on the other hand, is defined as the degree to which a paper retains its original qualities under continual usage. The word "usage" should be particularly noted as being very different from storage; usage implies the mechanical handling of the paper.

According to these definitions a paper may be highly permanent but not at all durable because, for example, of structural weakness in the original sheet. On the other hand, it may be relatively durable but not permanent although it is difficult to see how any serious chemical degradation can take place without at the same time lowering the durability of the paper. The problem of durability is largely one for the paper maker as it depends chiefly on the type of fibrous material used and the treatment given it in the manufacturing operations. The permanence of paper also depends on the paper maker but almost equally on storage conditions which are beyond his control. Permanence has received more attention than durability and as far back as 1824 much concern was felt in regard to the condition of books and records. . . . The washing of the bleached fiber prior to its use in the beater is of some importance in regard to permanence. If the soluble chlorides from the bleach residues are not washed out they may react with the alum used in sizing and form hydrochloric acid which is particularly harmful to paper and even worse than sulphuric acid. Of the other materials going into paper, rosin and alum are generally admitted to be harmful if used in too large quantities as is generally the case with alum. This is the chief reason for the acid condition of rosin sized papers and even the acidity thus caused is very injurious. Conversely, the presence of an alkaline filler such as calcium carbonate tends to keep the paper in an alkaline condition and prevent its deterioration. The sharp contrast between the acid and alkaline conditions was shown by a package of samples which had been kept in a rather warm place for about 34 years; the acid papers were dark in color and very brittle while those with an alkaline filler were apparently as good as when first made. . . . It is fully realized that the conditions under which a book or document is stored have a tremendous influence on its longevity.

The factors which must be taken into consideration are light, heat, air, moisture, dust, gases etc.

It is very important that we understand the difference between durability and permanence because the latter is the retention of significant use properties while the other is retention of original quality under continual use. For example, a business machine tabulation card under continual use certainly must be durable and resist handling abuse; a book on the library shelf is consulted only occasionally and is handled far more gently. While it does not have to have the same initial strength, it should retain its ability to be consulted and endure over a prolonged period of time. If you recall my original statements about fitting the manufacture of paper to the end use, you will begin to appreciate that book papers can be produced from pure fibers and nondeteriorating chemicals which enable it to be uniformly printed, collated, and bound into a permanent book. The strength needed is that required to go efficiently through the various processes of the print shop and the bindery and then to be capable of final usage (reading and/or consulting of it). It would be economically unsound to use expensive, strong pulps simply to get durability; in addition such fibers do not print well, have no mellowness, or aesthetic appeal. The papermaker balances his so-called furnish to meet the end use best, and in the case of book papers there need be no compromise on permanence. The recipe used should be pure pulps with other chemicals added only to the extent that they enable the printing paper to perform its job. If sizing is required, it should be done from an alkaline medium; by sizing we mean sufficient resistance to water to be lithographically printed and/or written upon with water inks if this is indicated. For many years this question of sizing was the excuse for using rosin and alum, but in the 1950s Hercules Powder Company came out with an alkaline sizing material known as "Aquapel"; there are now other competitive products on the market. Warren was one of the first to take advantage of this new alkaline sizing material and we developed proprietary methods for incorporating it into our paper along with the filler, calcium carbonate, which gave permanence through its buffering ability to keep the paper neutral or slightly alkaline. We have made thousands of tons of book papers by these techniques over the past twelve to fifteen years; this paper has been sucessfully processed through our customer plants and onto library shelves. Furthermore, our proprietary techniques for alkaline sizing and filling are through licensing being used in many overseas paper mills.

Calcium carbonate is an inert, white, bright pigment; it simply is dormant in the paper and available if any acid is encountered, such as in uncontrolled storage conditions. In other words, calcium carbonate is a slightly alkaline, inert buffer which stands guard against acidic conditions. We believe that all book papers should contain a residual of some calcium carbonate regardless of what other fillers may be present, be they clay or TiO_2. The permanence of calcium carbonate itself is attested to by the fact that marble is the purest natural form of calcium carbonate and, as you well know, marble has been used for centuries in the artistic sculptural world for statuary.

Other means of obtaining neutral or alkaline conditions can be utilized in the manufacture of paper, even if they are less ideal than the use of our inert filler calcium carbonate. For example, many good and permanent papers are made by combinations of basic bodystock paper plus surface size and/or plus coatings. We have seen in our own work where alkaline coatings such as those containing satin white placed upon a slightly acidic bodystock gave a composite pH on the neutral or alkaline side. For example, we made such a composite coated sheet in 1931 and have followed its natural aging characteristics over the years—as shown in figure 2. Its extracted pH is 7.9. Note that we have tried to draw a smooth curve through the average values for Mullen (burst), M.I.T. 1 kg. folding endurance and Elmendorf tear strength (cross and with grain data combined). The test numbers show some variance, probably due to operator, instrument, and/or sampling techniques over such a forty-year span, but it is clear that this coated paper has leveled off in its strength properties with time; it still is in good condition and usable. Parenthetically it should be mentioned that the heavy weight of this type of coating, which was usually applied at that time, put a burden on fold—but it still was sufficient for making into a book.

Admittedly, these sandwiches or composites are not ideal, but they are certainly better than a totally acidic paper. The question is just how far down these superimposed layers penetrate to neutralize any acidity in the base, and when they do, what the effects of the residual neutralized salts are. Obviously, a uniform alkaline or neutral paper throughout its cross-section is better than a sandwich of different layers, but if the composite is neutral or alkaline, the odds are good that permanence also will be good.

TESTING METHODS

Methods of testing have been controversial in this permanence field for years, and the battle still rages. Sutermeister's work does show, however, that the alkaline theory has stood the test of time of natural aging; witness the 1901 samples already cited. But we cannot wait for fifty or 100 years to do the testing, so we must rely upon accelerated aging tests such as TAPPI, P453 which is a seventy-two-hour aging at 105° C, then measuring folding endurance; results are expressed as the percentage of the fold retained after the exposure. Barrow recommends a similar test. But does resistance to simple dry heat indicate permanence or just resistance to heat degradation? For this reason, Gray of Eastman Kodak in a paper published in *TAPPI* (February 1969) feels that moisture should be added to the test. Likewise, Luner in the reference cited earlier recommends a test in which the exposure would be from 80°–100° C but in an atmosphere of 3–8 percent moisture, which he feels would better correspond to the chemical reactions occurring at room temperature with time; he recommends the folding test as the best criterion after such exposure. Qualitative spot testing that the Barrow laboratory recommends currently does give quick indications of potential permanence by the measure of pH, groundwood content, and the presence of alum and rosin. Of all these tests, pH determination is the most significant one; we concur in Barrow's recommendation of 6.5 or above as a good criterion of longevity. The initial physical strength tests, however, we feel do not necessarily have to be fixed but should be correlated with the end use of the paper.

The ultimate accelerated test for longevity will be one that not only

NATURAL AGING OF AN ALKALINE COATING ON AN ACID BODYSTOCK

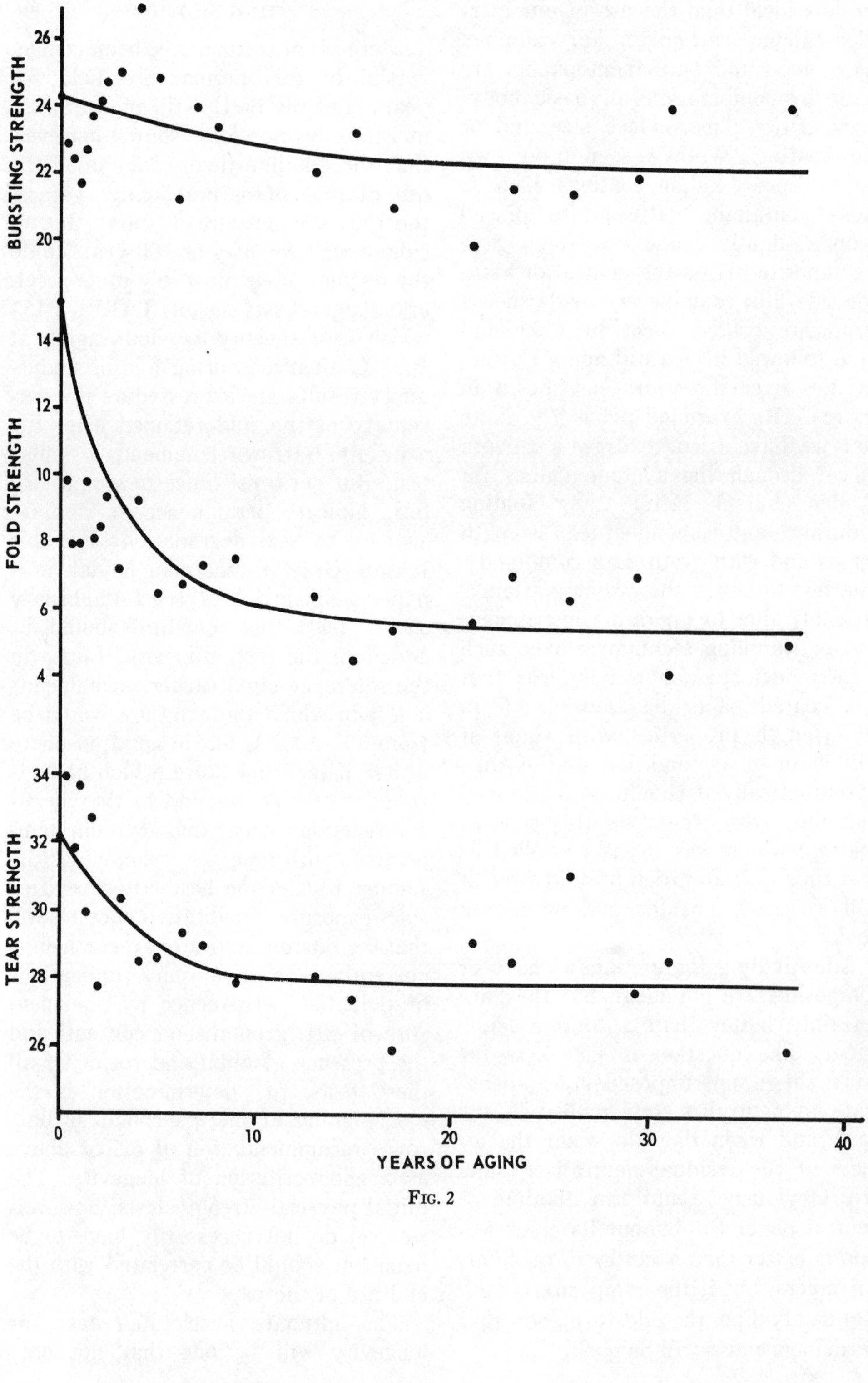

FIG. 2

takes into account the initial recipe but also the conditions that the paper will encounter in its processing, usage, and storage.

CONVERTING AND STORAGE

There are many chemical influences to which a book paper is subjected in its life history. Printing processes in themselves may add chemicals, such as residues from the fountain solutions and/or inks. Generally speaking, the tests from our print shop research indicate that these influences are minor—that if calcium carbonate is used it generally will cope with any acidic additive. We have definitely shown a correlation between alkaline pH and good ink drying, especially in the normal relative humidity ranges of the print shop of 40–60 percent. Also, the binding chemicals, the adhesives used there, can have an effect especially if these are acidic; but here again our panacea, calcium carbonate, may well handle this too. Atmospheric exposure, such as to the burning of fossil fuels which may give rise to sulfur dioxide (SO_2) and carbon dioxide (CO_2) must be taken into account; air conditioning and air filtering should help. Here again, residual calcium carbonate will act as a buffer. Certainly we should avoid light and extremes of temperature and humidity, as well as guarding against the attacks of insects and vermin.

FORECASTING THE FUTURE

What about the future? As long as purified cellulosic wood fibers can be obtained economically and under good conservation practices they will probably form the lowest cost substrate for the printed medium, whether the basic paper itself be filled, surface-sized, coated, or converted in some other way. This presumes that materials added to paper do not cause chemical deterioration. The best insurance against this, of course, is the neutral buffer, calcium carbonate. Our crystal ball does have a picture of plastics some day filling some role, although their permanence too will have to be established by adequate test techniques. Some plastic papers for printing are being made today, especially in Japan, but they are currently so expensive that we need not consider them for general printing uses. Just when the petrochemical or plastic industry can produce a product as low in cost and effective in use as nature's cellulose remains to be weighed as technological progress is made with time. Certainly for the present and foreseeable future, the work done by Sutermeister and well substantiated and proclaimed by Barrow still holds. The best insurance for permanence of the printed word is on paper made on the neutral or preferably alkaline side. Present technology is such that book papers can be so made whether they be sized or not, whether they be coated or not. The costs may be slightly higher today, but, as more and more mills shift to alkaline paper manufacturing, this disadvantage should disappear. Librarians can have confidence in this approach to making paper—and their future worries about permanence will be minimized.

DISCUSSION

GREER ALLEN

Joseph J. Thomas has recounted the way in which the S. D. Warren Paper Company shifted its book paper production to papers of higher alkalinity—thus insuring, according to current research, papers of greater permanence. This is a remarkable history of Yankee opportunism and good luck. The company managed to arrange its methods some years back to solve problems that were to reach critical magnitude half a century later.

This was Mr. Thomas's assignment, to discuss the making of permanent book papers. His technical presentation of the subject is impressive as befits his eminent qualifications. I am in no position to criticize it, because I am a printer rather than a paper chemist. My assignment is to comment on the printer's reaction to the emphasis on permanence and durability in papers as compared to other qualities that are necessary to produce good printing. Elsewhere in these papers, Leonard Shatzkin discusses these qualities from the standpoint of a publisher. I shall take you into the shop where such standard but diversified items as paper, ink, type, presses, folding machines, binding thread, and glue have to be arranged and managed in order to produce a good book.

It is important for the printer to have a voice in the great permanence and durability debate. Usually whenever people assemble to discuss processes and solutions to the problems of bringing modern commercial publishing papers to a state of longevity that they have not heretofore enjoyed, the exchange of views is restricted to three principal parties: the papermaker, the publisher, and the librarian. Surely, I would not want to omit one of these. Each spends a great deal of time performing some critical service connected with the life of the paper in question. But it is only natural that when they get together each seeks to grind a particular axe. It is only fair, since the printer is equally involved, for him to have a turn at the grindstone.

The papermaker recounts how he has been introducing chemicals and manufacturing systems which precipitate and neutralize impurities, conjuring up (as he goes along) visions akin to those soapsuds commericals on television, where we are treated to a view of smiling, eager little enzymes gobbling up a veritable panoply of offending ingredients.

Then there is the publisher, oppressed on the one hand by the stringent demands of purchasing committees to make his books withstand abuses from an ever more licensed and uncontained body of young people; chided on the other by the librarian who seems never so smug and delighted as when he is pointing to browned edges and frayed bindings; and finally he is constrained by an awareness of his own reputation—that marketable yet elusive asset, the view taken of him by his buying public, his agents (the bookstores), and (quite vital) his authors.

The third man in the discussion is the custodian of books, the librarian himself. He is never quite sure whether he is serving learning by making his volumes convenient to the readers or running a sort of "geriatric nursing home" for decrepit books; and all the while he thrashes about trying to find a culprit on whom to pin the ills of his deteriorating charges.

The view of the commercial printer-and-binder in relation to paper permanence is rarely called for, hardly ever articulated; it is generally misunderstood and more often than anything, it is inaccurately presumed. Consequently I am writing, not as a service-oriented printer in a great research and teaching institution (where responsibility beyond one's immediate purview is part of the job), but I aim to set forth the views of "the average commercial printer" touching permanence in paper.

I imagine that there is a general eagerness to hear what he thinks about; because it is for him and not for me, that Mr. Thomas and his brothers in industry churn their Fourdrinier machines so endlessly; and it is to him, and not to me, that Mr. Shatzkin (and his publishing colleagues) turn to have their many new titles and reprints fabricated each year. And finally, Mr. Soderland must admit that his library shelves are filled to the brim, not with a harvest from my presses but from his.

The concern of the average commercial printer for paper permanence is remarkable. Is the reader ready to discover it? I seriously wonder if he can take it. The truth is that the average commercial printer could not care less. He "does not give a damn" (if I may quote one informant in my recent survey). Despite responsible-sounding sales talks and other public utterances which he feels obliged to make, just catch such a printer over a martini after a day filled with machine costs, tax adjustments, wage settlements, and work spoilage. Then he will own that permanence in paper is just not very high on his list of pressing distractions.

I stress his position because it is important to know it. As we comb over the finer points of technology, we had better remember this small (but critical) slice of reality and drop in a pinch now and then to leaven our debates.

When I claimed earlier that the commercial printer's position is inaccurately presumed, I meant that too often we realize in a benumbed sort of way that the printer is not very bothered about paper permanence; yet underlying all this is a stifled sense of outrage because, "God knows, he most certainly ought to be!" Therein lies the problem.

The printer operates in a highly competitive market with a rather mean profit margin. Unless the world can make it worth his while (in dollars and cents) to exercise a preference for permanent papers (or at least to feel equivocal about printing on them), then we will get nowhere in overcoming his indifference. This is not surprising. Others involved in the debate have economic interests, too.

Concern for permanence has, of course, been profitable (yea, vital!) for librarians. Who would be a custodian for long if he were expected to spend his time among shelves of crumbled, pulverized fragments which had once been books? The published, as another party, feels the dollar pinch when, for example, he loses a large state adoption because his sample book did not hold up as it careened through that ingenious bibliographic amusement park: the text-book testing laboratory. And Mr. Thomas can recount (if not measure precisely) the tangible benefits reaped by at least one papermaker who early grew concerned about self-destruction in paper, took manufacturing steps to end it, and was not at all bashful about letting his customers (the publishers) know just what he had done.

But commercial printers (except for a handful of highly specialized book manufacturers and binders) are at best unconcerned and more typically quite ignorant of these matters. Printers familiar with permanence view it as a quality on which a few particular clients insist and one which often compounds the already complex problem of getting the ink down on the paper as quickly as possible—all the while meeting prearranged quality standards.

To get the printer who is involved in paper selection interested in permanence we will have to show him, on the one hand, that specifying permanent papers is an important service to his clients and, on the other, that it will cost him no more than it is worth in dollars and cents—either in cash or in terms of production time. In doing this, the paper manufacturer will have to see to it that "paper made to last" carries the same built-in defenses against the common printing and binding ills that all well-constructed printing papers now carry.

Let me share with you some of my experiences with permanized papers and describe a few of the critical qualities which concern the printer. For example, a few years ago, at a time when we were becoming eager to avoid self-destructive papers and were proceeding with some degree of success in selecting publishing sheets with a preference for less acidity, we encountered a client who insisted that his job be run on a paper with the highest pH factor we could find. The job in question was an offset book with small halftones. It carried photos of equipment in subtle gradations to distinguish essential details. We tested a number of sheets and found a shockingly positive correlation between acidity and clear reproduction; the more alkaline sheets available at the time just would not hold the best images. When faced with the decision between publishing on a more permanent sheet and obtaining the best photoreproduction, (I told him we would not "stand behind the reproduction on just any old sheet") this very responsible client knuckled under and selected the acid content sheet. The job was completed, and I have not heard if the books are still intact.

Two factors concerned us as printers in this particular case: brightness and ink holdout. Brighter, whiter papers permit halftone dot photoreproductions to show the maximum contrast between black and white and consequent definition of detail. Ink holdout is the ability of the paper to trap the ink chemicals on the paper surface, to dry right there, and in doing so to permit the ink to show off its varnished shine and its blackness. Thus it does not sink deep into the paper leaving the image lifeless and washed out. Here, very poignantly, is the conflict between responsibility and reputation. If we had run the job on the alkaline sheet, all the world would have seen "what miserable printers we are."

Take another case. It may indicate why printers shy from involvement in what appear to be experiments. It illustrates what I meant earlier when I said that permanence and durability must be built into papers without altering the printing and handling characteristics which the printer has grown to expect if he is to become anything but livid when confronted with the sheets. This is the tale of a client who did not knuckle under and of a university printer who unwittingly walked smack into a technological mine field.

When we contemplate printing on acetate, or vegetable parchment, or some vinyl-coated substance, we of course, make tests and careful inquiries to select the proper inks, drying agents, and sprays to be sure the sheets will dry promptly without offsetting (that is, allowing the wet image to print on the underside of the sheet above it, in the delivery pile). But when we prepare to print on a so-called text or antique finish book paper, we (and other job printers like us) have found from general experience that the behavior of all these sheets falls within normal parameters; or, in other words, the pressman knows what to expect when he puts the job on the press. He might have to dope up his ink, add driers, extenders (thinners), adjust the lithographic water-ink balance, or repack his impression cylinder to obtain the most suitable pressure; but he usually feels he is working within limits that he knows.

However, on the particular job I am about to describe, the client called for a specific brand name of paper. The sheet was one constructed primarily as a permanent and durable paper—which indeed it was and is! But its printing qualities (as printers have come to know them) appear to have been secondary considerations in its manufacture. For one thing, it was rather more transparent than sheets of similar substance. Its opacity was low. To overcome this, we increased the weight of the paper selected from seventy pounds per standard ream to eighty, knowing full well that it might double the sheetwork (the folding and sewing). But it seemed worth the effort and the cost.

When we put it on the offset press and applied the usual amount of ink, we found that it did not behave in the expected way. Our pressman experimented with it; after much delay, he found that we could run the sheets without offsetting, but with the result that the image was weaker than we would have wished it to be. On later investigation we found that an obscure additive would have inhibited the offsetting adequately.

We folded the sheets without mishap and sewed them successfully. The job was to be a paperback with glued-on covers. We put it on our covering machine only to find that the paper repelled our natural adhesives. We lifted the job and rushed it to another binder whose polyvinyl actetate emulsion succeeded admirably in gluing the covers to the books and meeting the deadline.

This account will show the sorts of traps a printer may stumble into unless such papers come to him with better information and warnings. The second time around, of course, it was easy. Admittedly, this was a rather abrupt introduction to printing on permanent papers—ideal from the standpoint of paper endurance, but it tried the endurance of the printer who was as ill prepared as most commercial printers tend to be under similar conditions, because most of the permanized publication papers to which the printer must be introduced possess printing and binding properties indistinguishable from their acidic siblings.

Now we have covered brightness, opacity, receptivity to adhesives, ink-holdout, and drying qualities. What are some of the other paper characteristics which mean so much to us printers? Several fall under the heading of runability: "How will the sheet run or feed through systems in which the sheet is passed from the skid at the feed end of the press by an elaborate system of vacuum cups, little metal gripping fingers, positioning guides, tape conveying belts and rolls to a pile of printed sheets at the delivery end of the press?" Dimensional stability and flatness are two vital concerns in running a job. The sheets simply cannot vary in size on a high-speed, carefully calibrated modern press. They will crumble and bunch up. Nor can they be anything but flat. The vacuum feed-system will not pick up sheets from a wobbly, wavy skid of paper. Here moisture stability is important, the critical property in a paper which must remain flat under normal conditions.

Moisture stability figures prominently in the next general area, printability: the ease with which ink can be transferred onto the paper and stay there the way we want it to. Again, moisture content affects paper's receptivity to ink. Here, too, we should consider the smoothness of the surface. In letterpress printing, of course, it must be sufficiently smooth; for offset lithography it cannot be porous. Nor can the sheets afford to pick (lose surface fibres) or to carry paper dust on their surfaces or edges, which will end as unsightly spots on the printed pages.

Another general heading includes binding and handling qualities. Is the bulk or caliper uniform? Covers are preprinted, boxes made, and machines set for certain prearranged thicknesses of books. They cannot vary from standard without bringing on disaster. The sheets, too, must be strong enough to withstand the ordeal of folding and sewing, or simply getting through roll-fed, high-speed, web-press systems.

Then there are the aesthetic properties of color and what (for want of a better phrase) is termed in the trade "a bookish feel." Although these tend to appear arbitrary, if a bit traditional, they are nonetheless real to the printer.

So we see that a number of hidden concerns and factors must be known and attended to as printers are enlisted into the general march toward permanence and durability. Certainly the printers' ignorance and indifference can block progress just as their intelligent participation can speed things up. To enlist that intelligent participation, proponents of greater permanence and durability in printing papers need also to understand and take into account the qualities that a printer seeks in papers.

PUBLISHING ON PERMANENT PAPERS

LEONARD SHATZKIN

Untimely deterioration has put book paper squarely in the center of the stage under a very bright spotlight. This is certainly not the way we would have chosen for paper to attract the interest and attention of the users of books. Quite aside from the question of how long the paper will function satisfactorily, the objective is to have the paper in the book noticed as little as possible. The more the reader notices the paper, the more he is distracted from the words and pictures which the paper is intended to hold before him. Yet, for all its planned unobtrusiveness, paper characteristics are important in the highly complicated functions of the manufacturing process and in the final book itself. So specific are these functions that book paper is considered a special product to be manufactured only by paper mills which have the particular equipment, talent, and experience to provide paper specifically for books.

Book paper (which, incidentally, accounts for about one-third of the cost of the finished physical book) resembles other paper, including tissues, writing papers, paper plates, and other familiar papers, in being essentially a matting of cellulose fibers. The cellulose fibers for all modern papers are obtained from wood, either by simply grinding it, as for newsprint, or by separating it into individual fibers by one of several complicated processes of chemical extraction. The cellulose fibers are quite small. If you put a powerful magnifying glass to a Kleenex tissue, you will be able to make out the larger fibers, but not the smaller ones.

After the fibers are extracted, by whatever method, they have to be bleached. Actually, bleaching alone is not sufficicent to bring the cellulose to the desired color, or lack of color. Dyes are added to bring the resulting paper to the specified whiteness, or off-whiteness, depending upon the publisher's preference for color and the nature of the book for which the paper is intended. For a "reading" book, with no illustrations, a cream white or pinkish white paper would be preferred as being less fatiguing and less likely to strain the eyes. For a book with many illustrations, a neutral white or blue white paper would enhance the beauty and clarity of the illustrations at some small sacrifice of the ease of reading the text.

Control of color in book papers, even after a particular color is chosen, must be very precise, more so than for printing papers in general. Very slight variations in shade, virtually impossible to detect with the untrained naked eye, can cause unpleasant streaks along the edge of the final book if some pages are printed on one shade of paper and some on the other. Since even in one lot of paper delivered for printing a book, succeeding sheets may have been manufactured several days apart, color control is no simple problem. Moreover, publishers like to be able to use paper left over from a previous pressrun with additional paper delivered weeks or months later.

The cellulose fibers are formed into paper by being suspended in water—

only about 1 percent of the mixture is fiber and 99 percent is water—and passed over a moving screen of very fine mesh. The screen permits the water and only the very finest of the fibers to pass through, leaving the bulk of the fibers on the wire as a thin matting from which the remaining water is then pressed and dried to leave the continuous sheet of paper.

Here, too, the special requirements of book publishers create special problems. First, there are the fibers themselves. They differ not only by the way in which they are processed from the wood log but also by the species of tree. One way in which fibers differ is simply by their length. The longer fibers from coniferous woods make a stronger paper but one which is less opaque and with a surface much less suitable for printing. The shorter fibers from deciduous woods improve opacity by scattering more light. They also add some bulk to the paper for equivalent weight and, together with the filler pigments, provide a better printing surface and make a limper sheet, one which will lie flat when the book is open and will be softer and more pleasant to the touch. Depending upon the nature of the book and the printing process being used, the publisher will want a particular balance of long and short fibers.

Second, there is the mechanical pretreatment. The fibers are passed through refining devices which abrade their surfaces and fray their ends, thus providing better opportunity for the fibers to "hook on" to each other and "swell" so that they adhere better to each other, making a stronger paper. But the more the fiber is beaten, the less opaque the paper and the tinnier it is, excellent for letterheads but very unpleasant in a book.

Third is the way in which the fiber is fed onto the wire. All paper to be printed must have a high degree of uniformity. A halftone picture coarse enough to be printed on an uncoated paper would still have over 12,000 individual dots per square inch of paper surface. If the paper accepts ink from these dots differently, it is clear the resulting picture will suffer and will differ from one impression to the next. Therefore, paper produced for printing, whether advertising pieces, magazines, or books, must not have soft spots and hard spots and must be uniformly resilient.

But books require an additional uniformity which is not easy to achieve: uniformity of thickness. The binding process requires that all the books in any one binding run be of uniform thickness to go through the machines. The case, the stamping dies, and the dust jacket are made, in advance, to fit a predicted thickness of the pages of the book. The pages in the front, or the middle, or the back of the book may be printed on paper made at different times. Indeed, since the book is printed in segments rather than all at once, we may be sure that any one book combines paper from widely separated parts of the paper alloted to that book. This means that the thickness of paper must be very closely controlled from run to run and also controlled across the width of the papermaker's wire for each run. When we consider that the width of the paper being made can be 80,000 times the thickness, the difficulty of controlling the uniformity of that thickness at extremely high speeds becomes apparent.

Fourth is the way in which the paper is matted on the wire. Since the wire is traveling at high speed, it tends to place the fibers so that most of them lie parallel to the direction of motion, particularly if the fibers are long. This results in a paper grain, with some important effects on both printing and binding. As paper takes on moisture, as it inevitably does in printing by the offset process, it tends to swell across the grain, which makes it difficult to print several colors successively in precise relation to each other. This and other characteristics of paper with a pronounced grain direction make it undesirable for use in books.

A fifth problem in making paper for books is the tendency for the lower surface, the wire side, to differ in appearance, texture, and ink receptivity from the upper surface, the felt side. For many purposes, even printing purposes, considerable difference between the two sides of the paper can be tolerated, but not in books. Even minor two-sidedness, as this tendency is called, would be too obvious in the repeated comparison offered as one turns the pages of a book, so the papermaker goes to great efforts to make the paper surfaces as nearly alike as possible.

As I have pointed out, paper is primarily a matting of fine cellulose fibers extracted from wood. But, of course, it is a great deal more complicated than that. Paradoxically, cellulose is not very ink-receptive, so filler materials are added to the pulp to increase opacity and also to make the finished sheet friendlier to ink. Also, to keep ink from spreading and to slow the absorption of water, the paper must be made moisture-resistant by adding other materials. This process is called sizing. Starch, glue, and other materials have been used. The widespread use of rosin and alum for sizing, which renders the finished paper acidic, has been identified as a principal cause for paper deterioration. But even if we avoid rosin and alum because it has disastrous side effects, we cannot avoid sizing. For example, unsized paper such as used in towels, facial tissue, and blotting paper would not make desirable book paper. The need for sizing varies with the printing process. Paper for letterpress printing requires very lilttle; gravure paper needs more. Unfortunately, paper for offset printing, which has in recent years become the most widely used process in book production, and is becoming more so, requires a great deal of sizing.

Offset printing makes a further demand on paper, one which is of minor consequence in letterpress and was of no concern when the papers that W. J. Barrow studied were manufactured. That is the stronger adherence of the fibers themselves to each other. The offset process requires a tacky ink, and generally the tackier the ink, the better the print. Also, the rubber surface which transfers the ink to the paper exerts a very strong pull on the fibers of the paper, as is clearly evident when one watches an offset press in operation and sees the paper literally pulled away from the rubber printing cylinder. Any material picked off the paper, whether it is fiber or some additive, works itself back into the ink and quickly degrades the print quality, making it necessary to stop and clean the press frequently. The better the adherence of the fibers and the filler material, the less difficulty the paper creates on the offset press.

The growing use of large rotary presses, particularly offset presses, printing directly on rolls of paper and delivering folded signatures, has presented a whole new set of demands upon the paper. The paper is pulled through these presses under great tension. Slight defects in the paper are enough to cause it to tear under such tension with traumatic effect upon the cost of printing that book. Even if, without tearing, the paper only stretches under tension, the changes in dimension (just like a change in dimension due to moisture absorption) may ruin print quality if more than one color is being laid down.

These presses, becoming increasingly more important in book manufacturing print at such high speeds that drying of ink, which must take place before the paper is folded, cannot be left to normal evaporation or oxidation. The presses are fitted with large ovens maintained at several hundred degrees, through which the paper is passed. Minute pockets of moisture in the paper may explode under this heat, causing blisters. This is an extreme, though not uncommon, danger. An everyday problem is to have the paper pass through the oven without embrittlement or other similar deterioration.

Opacity is another demand which books place on paper to a greater degree than other paper uses. Years ago when books were simply evenly spaced lines of type, it was possible to mask some of the translucency of the paper by printing the lines of each page so that they corresponded exactly to the lines of the reverse page. With the increased use of illustration and mathematical formulas, and a generally freer use of white space in book design, we have to make greater demands upon the opacity of the paper to avoid the unpleasant intrusion of other pages on the page being read. This is increasingly a problem as we try to reduce the weight and thickness of books by using lighter and thinner papers. Opacity in paper is improved by the addition of filler such as clay, calcium carbonate, titanium dioxide, or other white pigments, all of which have in common that, while their role in keeping the printing from showing through to the other side is essential, they add nothing to the strength of the paper but in fact detract from it by interfering with fiber-to-fiber bonding.

The growing demand for improved print quality and the greater use of illustrations in books have led to a marked increase in the use of coated papers in books. These papers were virtually unknown during the period from which Barrow collected his aged samples. Coating is a fine powdery material held together by binders and applied like a paint to the paper to give a smoother, more ink-receptive surface and one that reflects more light. The effect of these coatings, which tend to be alkaline or neutral, upon the life expectancy of an acidic supporting fiber mat has not yet been definitely established. They have, however, definitely brought a new set of conditions into the printing and binding of books with corresponding new demands upon the papermaker's skill.

In one important respect the demands from the book publisher tend to create more difficulty than those from other users of coated papers. In advertising, and to a lesser degree in magazine publishing, the shininess of coated paper is an advantage. It makes pictures more brilliant and attracts a casual viewer's attention. Shiny coated paper is much easier to make than nonshiny coated paper. But shininess makes reading difficult and may cause eyestrain, though the reader may not be aware that the reflections from the paper are the cause of his difficulty. We insist on as little shininess as possible in coated book papers, but we insist on retaining the same smoothness of surface achieved with shiny papers.

This gives some idea, perhaps, of

how paper functions in the manufacture of the book and its final appearance and use. I do not suggest that these considerations, and I have by no means enumerated all of them, make the permanence or, more exactly, the long life of paper unimportant. Not at all! In a sense, the life expectancy of paper is quite apart and in no way contradictory to the ways in which paper takes ink and goes through presses or binding machines, or how it looks and feels in the finished book. But it should be clear that all of these characteristics, including life expectancy, are relative. A paper does not take ink either perfectly or not at all; it does not change dimension either under all press conditions or under none; it does not either crumble immediately or last forever. Therefore we try to achieve a balance of the desirable characteristics of paper without assigning an absolute limit to any one.

We are now conscious that life expectancy has not been given the attention it deserves and that a new balance of paper characteristics is required. If some of the experts in the field are cautious about how far to go in arriving at the new balance, such caution is understandable, even by those of us who are determined to take the essential steps toward adjustment without delay.

Making paper last longer can be accomplished in two general ways. The first of these is to make it stronger to begin with. In current terminology, this is making the paper more durable. The second way is to make it retain its strength over a longer period. This is called making the paper more permanent—which is a great idea but an unfortunate distortion of the word "permanent." Making the paper stronger may be accomplished by using more long fibers, or prolonged beating, or the addition of strong binders, any of which may detract from the other characteristics we consider so desirable. Moreover, there is some question about where to stop in adding strength as long as the ultimate has not been reached.

Fortunately, today's papers, because of the demands of today's book manufacturing methods, are considerably stronger than the papers used 100 years ago or even fifty and twenty-five years ago. These papers, if the rate of deterioration can be slowed, may very possibly be sufficiently strong to exceed librarians' standards for longevity. That is why there is some reluctance to endanger the balance of paper characteristics by introducing an overriding and somewhat arbitrary standard for fold strength or tear strength.

On the other hand, the shifting of paper from the acid to the alkaline side or making it neutral, which is the principal method proposed by Barrow and others to slow its deterioration, seems to be easier and more fruitful. Nothing in the way a book is manufactured or the finished book is used makes acidity of the paper an advantage. And although the shift from acidity is not easily made, and involves considerable change in the papermaking process for some mills, it seems not to require a change in the balance of the other paper chracteristics I have described which are so important to the functioning of paper in the book.

As I have already suggested, the principal cause of acidity in paper, though perhaps not the only one, is the use of rosin and alum sizing in the papermaking process to make the paper less receptive to moisture. The shift away from acid requires that some nonacid or nonacid-producing material be used to accomplish the same purpose accomplished by rosin and alum. Glue, which is not appropriate today, was used before the introduction of rosin and alum. There are other materials, unfortunately proprietary, which are being used successfully by some paper manufacturers and which avoid residual acidity in the finished paper.

Faced with the fact of speedy deterioration of paper widely used in books and the heavy weight of evidence that this deterioration is being accelerated by residual acidity in the paper itself, what should the publisher do? He has obligations in at least two directions. On the one hand, the author is his client, relying on the publisher's business expertise as well as upon his ethical and moral sense. The publisher accepts the obligation to bring the author's ideas to the widest possible reading audience in a form appropriate to those ideas. That implies a great deal about the design of the book itself, the advertising and promotional campaign, the activity of the publisher's salesmen, and everything that goes into producing and marketing the book. Clearly, as part of his obligation to the author, the publisher must suit the physical specification to the content and purpose of the book. Some books, or some editions of other books, are clearly intended to be read and discarded, and they may be made by processes and with materials of a life expectancy secondary to the lower retail prices which their economies make possible.

But when the author has written for future readers as well as present ones, where the book is intended to survive some immediate role of mass-distributed tract or casual entertainer, it must, within the sensible limits of good business, be made of materials and by printing and binding methods that will not thwart the author's intent. These are things which the author need not specify to his publisher or even know about. They are inherent in the author-publisher relationship.

The publisher has an obligation to the purchaser of the book as well. The book buyer understands fully that the paperback in the newsstand rack is not meant to last, and he is not shocked or disappointed when it does not. On the contrary, building unnecessary durability into such a book, at the expense of increasing its retail price, would be a disservice to the buyer. But the buyer expects the book which by its content, format, and price clearly labels itself a candidate for his permanent collection, to have the qualities, within the practical limits of available technology, suitable to such a collection. He does not look for a guarantee on the copyright page. The nature of the book is its own unwritten warranty from the publisher.

Publishers have assumed these obligations to author and book buyer seriously and generally have performed well. Now we are face-to-face with the fact that, notwithstanding good intentions, we have not delivered the quality we thought we were delivering. The assumptions we were making about paper quality simply do not correspond to the facts.

The principal credit for the increased concern clearly evident among publishers over the quality of paper used in books belongs to the Council on Library Resources and to Mr. W. J. Barrow, whose research on durability and permanence was financed by the council. This is due as much to the timing of this research and the energy and clarity with which the results have been presented to the concerned parties as it is to the specific results themselves.

It seems that much of Barrow's work was anticipated by Sutermeister and by others. It is even probably true that Barrow's conclusions tend to be somewhat oversimplified. But if the effect of residual acid in paper was understood in some circles in the paper industry before Barrow, this understanding had certainly not penetrated to its publisher-customers. And perhaps the simplicity of Barrow's message—acid papers decay rapidly, alkaline or neutral papers decay slowly—provided the sharpness that enabled it to penetrate places where useful action could be taken.

It is probably true that the conditions under which books are used and stored markedly affects the rate of paper decay. Polluted air may be killing off books even more effectively than it is killing off the readers of books. We know from aging tests that both atmospheric moisture and temperature affect paper life, and not even in a consistent, predictable way. It may be necessary for libraries to protect their collections by controlling the atmospheres in which they are housed. But in spite of this, Barrow's admonition is still valid—acid papers decay rapidly; alkaline or neutral papers decay slowly.

It is the nature of the publishing business that the specialization which has taken place over the years has shifted more of the responsibility for the manufacture of books and the materials that go into them from the publishers themselves to the suppliers to the publishing industry. The publisher is well aware of the qualities that are visually discernible—the sharpness of the ink impression, the evenness of the round, the accuracy of the folding. He is much less aware of the qualities which can be determined only by chemical or physical tests—the rub resistance of the cloth, the strength of the threads, the plasticity of the glue, and the longevity of the paper.

It is the rare publisher who has on his staff a chemist or engineer, except in an editorial capacity, and even rarer is the one who has a program for routinely testing the materials which go into the books, or the books themselves. Insofar as he must specify materials or the methods of manufacture, the publisher depends upon his suppliers to describe the alternatives, explain the practical effect of their differences, and specify the cost of each alternative so that the publisher can pick what suits his own general purposes and the requirements of each particular book.

Until the reports from libraries of the widespread deterioration of books on their shelves, and the disclosure by Barrow of the effect of the acidic residues of prevailing papermaking methods, the publisher believed he had a simple and straightforward choice among paper alternatives. In the pre-Barrow world, paper was divided into two broad classifications. The first of these was the papers which consisted largely of groundwood, or contained any appreciable groundwood. These papers were considered to be short-lived, in direct proportion to the percentage of groundwood. It was easy to demonstrate that they would turn brown and brittle if left in the open sun on the publisher's own windowsill, and it was understood that the same thing happened, though at a much slower rate, even in the absence of direct ultraviolet light. Such paper, when used in books at all, was used in books of passing interest which were not expected ever to enter permanent collections of either individuals or libraries.

The other broad classification was papers made exclusively of cellulose fibers chemically abstracted from wood. These were free of any contamination from groundwood, and were therefore called "free sheets." According to our pre-Barrow understanding, these free sheets, being pure cellulose, to which were added only what we believed to be relatively stable agents designed to retard moisture penetration, improve opacity, and provide a more ink-receptive surface, would, if properly cared for, last as long as papyrus or the handmade rag papers of the early days of printing.

We now know that this was an unfortunate oversimplification. Removing the lignins and other impurities which seem so destructive in groundwood is not sufficient to guarantee long life to the resulting paper. As a matter of fact, when we conducted aging tests according to Barrow's procedure, we discovered to our horror that one free sheet we were using showed an estimated life-span of less than twenty-five years compared with more than 100 years for some of our groundwood papers, which, in turn, is substantially shorter than the more than 300 years we expect from neutral free sheets.

Of all those involved in the movement of the idea from the author's mind to the library's shelf, the publisher is in the best position to do something about the revelation that residual acid destroys paper surely and quickly. After, all, he buys or specifies the paper used in his books. Since it is being produced commercially, and the ways to produce it are well known, he need only specify neutral or alkaline paper and he will have neutral or alkaline paper. As a matter of fact, this is exactly what a number of publishers have done. In time, no doubt others will take the same step. Hesitation, aside from the normal lag in reacting to any new development, is rationalized in varying degrees on four grounds.

1. *Permanence is not the only quality to be considered, and one must establish that other important paper qualities are not sacrificed to achieve small improvements in permanence.* True. It is certainly true that in order to be manufactured at all, the book, and particularly the paper, goes through extremely demanding operations during which it is pulled, twisted, sheared, folded, yanked, perforated, scorched, dampened, pinched, sewed, and put through every conceivable torture test, often at incredibly high speeds.

In addition to surviving the physical trials of printing and binding, the paper must have the properties essential to the book itself. As already noted, it must be opaque and completely uniform in thickness and have a surface which accepts and holds ink nicely and is pleasant to the sight and to the touch, and for some applications (not popular with librarians) accepts fountain pen ink. It must have all these physical and cosmetic properties, even if it is very thin and light in weight, because bulky books are hard to read, cost too much to ship, and occupy too much valuable shelf space.

One cannot ignore the fact that survival is not the sole purpose of the book and that the physical demands of the manufacturing process are difficult to deny. However, except in minor matters, there does not seem reason for real concern. For example, though it appears to be very difficult to produce tinted papers, particularly strong tints, by acid-free manufacturing methods, such papers are rarely used and can hardly be considered essential in any book. All of our experience with alkaline papers indicates that the other qualities we look for in paper have not suffered. Actually, we believe that ink drying has improved and that press conditions in offset lithographic printing are less critical than with acid papers.

2. *Acidity is not the only factor determining the useful life of the paper.* True. Barrow himself pointed out that paper must begin with a substantial resistance to tear and fold in order to last longer, whatever its rate of decay in strength. But Barrow's work also shows that acidity exercises much more leverage than can any conceivable improvement in starting strength. According to Barrow, paper with a pH of 7.0 lasts twenty times longer than paper with a pH of 4.8. In other words, one would have to make a paper twenty times as strong at pH 4.8 to achieve the equivalent longevity of paper at pH 7.0. Quite aside from the fact that strengthening the paper so drastically would be costly, if not impossible, the paper manufacturers assure us that such strength could only be achieved at the expense of other important paper characteristics, notably opacity, ink receptivity, ease of binding, and the feel of the finished book. Therefore, the attack on acidity is the best way to obtain balanced paper characteristics plus long life. Even if putting all the blame on acidity is oversimplification, if other additives or pollutants in the water may have serious aging effects, this does not argue for delaying a shift from acid papers but rather that the research should not stop there.

3. *Neutral paper is more costly.* True. There are three factors tending to increase cost. The chemicals are more expensive; the papermaking machines cannot run so fast; the limited number of producers inhibits competition. The last of these will become less important as publishers specify neutral papers and mills are encouraged to enter the field. The first two may cause somewhat higher costs for neutral papers for a long period. But the choice between acid and neutral papers represents today's version of yesterday's choice between groundwood and "free sheets." Inevitably the choice must go the same way—in favor of quality even if costs do rise slightly.

4. *A wholesale shift to neutral paper would disrupt the paper industry.* True. An orderly transition requires time. Mill managements must sort out the alternative manufacturing methods available to them. They may have to make changes in equipment or acquire the right to use patented processes. New process control methods have to be learned and installed.

It is by no means an easy change for the paper manufacturer to make. Not only must each publisher respect his papermaker's difficulties for the practical reasons that he must solve them if the paper is to be available, but, morally and ethically, he is obligated to allow time for the change in the light of those difficulties, regardless of how suddenly he, the publisher, has discovered the need for change. However, it is hard to believe that the present pace of conversion to neutral papers cannot be greatly accelerated. Those of us who have shifted virtually all of our hard cover production to neutral paper do not seem to be using enough paper to strain the capacity to produce it. And a number of mills seem to be in transition toward acid-free production methods, so additional capacity will soon be available. Whatever the actual capacity may be, publishers, as the customers, should be asking the paper industry to do a little more than it can, rather than a little less.

The revelations of Barrow and the new and proper concern of librarians about the strength and longevity of paper do not change the publisher's obligations to author or book buyer—they simply redefine them. We now know that for many years the publisher has unwittingly compromised his standards of quality. There is no question of attempting to justify or to perpetuate an error made out of ignorance. Present knowledge dictates the use of acid-free papers for all books which openly, or by implication, are intended to have long life.

DISCUSSION

FORREST F. CARHART, JR.

Mr. Shatzkin has listed many of the practical factors that pertain to the manufacture of book papers and their utilization by publishers. To most of us who are not directly involved in publishing activities, this is informative and provides a useful background but is hardly a basis for intensive argument. My approach, then, will be to repeat for emphasis some of Shatzkin's principal statements, to point out areas of modest disagreement, to tell some of the experiences gained in the Library Technology Program's studies on papers and card stocks, and finally, to offer some suggestions for future action.

Shatzkin has very succinctly stated the difficulties that publishers face when they plan the production of a book. Each element that goes into the building of a sheet of paper used by the printer has an immediate effect on the publisher's finished product. To most of us who are librarians, many of these factors have not previously come to our attention. For most of us, one piece of paper seems to be like any other. Obviously, this is not the case. It is commonly said that papermaking is still an art, not a science. But the precision of measurement and demands discussed by Shatzkin and others indicate that papermaking is becoming less of an art and is coming closer to being a science.

We should dispose of a semantic problem before we proceed further. Shatzkin states that the use of the word "permanent" in relation to paper is an unfortunate distortion of the usual use of the word. Perhaps our immediate goal is paper with greater longevity, permanence being the ideal which we are hoping to attain.

It is well known that residual acid in paper is a principal cause for paper deterioration. It has also been well established that paper is likely to have a greater longevity and durability, if, among other things, it possesses a high degree of initial strength.

There are, of course, other factors which affect the deterioration of book papers. The handling that the book receives from the library staff and the borrowing public has a bit to do with its life expectancy. Still other factors are the conditions under which the book is stored before it reaches the library, the transportation conditions, the storage environment in the library, etc. Many of these are conditions over which librarians have little or no control. Thus, it is important to them that book papers be of the highest practical quality when they are procured by the publisher.

Sizing has a great deal to do with the printability of the sheets and is very important to the printer and the publisher. Shatzkin has indicated that most of the residual acid in papers comes from the sizing which is applied to the paper either internally or externally during the manufacturing process.

A highly alkaline condition in paper is possibly just as injurious as a highly acidic condition. It has been shown by many that papers in the neutral pH range have a better chance of long life than do those which are acidic or alkaline.

That this is not new information is shown by the number of paper manufacturers who are aware of the qualities of better book papers and the number of publishers who are using such papers. Indeed, Shatzkin's firm quietly announced some time past that it would print all of its future books on papers which would apparently have a longer life.

Not only are initially strong papers needed to guard against later physical abuses, but they are necessary in order that we can all take advantage of the economics of the use of new high-speed web offset presses. But we have heard that such presses involve the use of a high-temperature drying cycle. Such an exposure to high heat argues for initial strength as well as all of the other qualities which make for longevity and durability.

Much progress is being made toward the end result we all desire—books possessing the characteristics of greater durability and longevity. The need has been recognized by publishers as well as librarians, and now publishers are working with paper manufacturers to bring a better product to the printer—a mutually happy circumstance.

I wish that Shatzkin had emphasized the need for strength as much as he did the need for acid-free papers. Obviously, we should build strength into papers in such a way that other desirable factors are not compromised. He mentions that one of the ways in which strength can be attained is through the use of long-fiber woods in the papermaking process. Long-fiber woods (i.e., coniferous) are most typically used by southern paper mills, while short-fiber woods (i.e., deciduous) are more typically used by northern paper mills. The mill from which paper is procured and its location may have much to do with the nature of the sheet. It is possible to produce a strong sheet with good printing qualities from long-fiber woods. There are practical limits to the strength obtained by using short fibers, strong binders, and prolonged beating. Shatzkin says "There is some question about where to stop in adding strength as long as the ultimate has not been reached." I do not believe we are ready—any of us—to say that there are limits we wish to establish relative to the durability of our papers or their longevity. Neither are we ready to say we have reached the ultimate in printability qualities.

Shatzkin suggests that there are at least four rationalizations which can be cited as delaying the general adoption of long-life papers for book publication. The first is that permanence is not the only quality that must be considered. I disagree that some other important qualities cannot be overlooked to achieve small improvements in longevity. But we can note with great pleasure that efforts to produce better papers are not inimical to the production of papers suitable to the satisfaction of publishers. Neither the physical demands of the manufacturing process nor the survival factor can be ignored. But publishers are becoming alert to the dual needs, and this is progress—not enough, but progress.

The third rationalization states that "neutral paper is more costly." This I find hard to accept as a flat statement. I can accept the fourth rationalization, "a wholesale shift to neutral paper would disrupt the paper industry," but I cannot accept what is to be inferred from this statement. If there were to be a sudden wholesale switch to the use of so-called permanent and durable papers for book publishing, one segment of the paper industry would indeed be disrupted. But the normal development of demand will bring about an appropriate supply. It is almost impossible that all publishers will decide simultaneously to use long-life papers. Thus, the changeover will inevitably be natural and gradual.

The Library Technology Program (LTP) of the American Library Association mailed two small questionnaires in the spring of 1968. This was done as a bit of staff work for the American Book Publishers Council–Resources and Technical Services Division (American Library Association) Joint Committee. One questionnaire went to publishers to identify the relative quantity of publishing being done on permanent and/or durable papers. The second questionnaire was addressed to paper manufacturers. It sought information on the mill capacity for the manufacture of long-life papers compared with recent mill production. We found that there is much unused mill capacity available. We also discovered that in some instances there is a price differential between permanent and durable book papers and book papers of comparable quality lacking long-life characteristics. Usually, however, such price differentials were minor.

The cost of changing a paper machine from acid to low alkaline or neutral production has been made without inordinate expenditures. Possibly it has been difficult for some mills to adjust to new production methods, but many mills, I am told, have found it to be a reasonably simple process. Perhaps I would be guilty of an overstatement if I said it was simply a matter of cleaning up a machine so that traces of acid were no longer detectable. Overstatement or not—this has been a common experience.

Before we talk of the future, it may be interesting to note a few other observations from LTP's work which, like Barrow's, was financed by the Council on Library Resources. A few years ago, LTP gave one of its book printers eight papers on which we wanted some experiments conducted. Basically, we wanted to know whether permanent and durable papers were more difficult for the printer to use than ordinary book papers. All of the papers (five were permanent and durable) were found to be superior among those papers with which the printers usually worked. And this applied to offset as well as letterpress printing. Of course, we could see some differences in printing results because some of the papers were designed for offset and some for letterpress work. But basically—all eight were very workable papers. The tired old objections of some printers were unmasked as simple objections to change.

Another example of the fear of change arose during the work and discussions which have led to the adoption of USA Standard Z85.1, a performance standard relating to permanent and durable catalog cards. We found that the paper converters and some paper mills were afraid to change the basis on which they historically had specified their card stocks. Rather than a recipe for combining materials, the new standard calls for a minimum performance of the finished product whatever its ingredients. It was even feared that the neutral pH requirement and a minimum level of folding endurance (one measure of strength) would be difficult (if not impossible) to attain. By the time the standard was adopted by the U.S.A. Standards Institute in 1969, no questions were being asked regarding the pH requirement, and at least one manufacturer was regularly exceeding the minimum folding endurance level by more than 100 percent. The experience of the last few years shows it is likely that an upward revision of performance levels can now be discussed with profit. An earnest desire to provide a better product plus a willingness to experiment on the part of knowledgeable people brought about this new U.S.A. Standard.

And these were the ingredients of Barrow's efforts. After working with the restoration of old papers, he concluded independently that there should be a way to make paper from wood which would have the long-lasting characteristics of the best rag papers and that the wood pulp papers so made could be commercially competitive with the best rag papers. Printability was not his goal.

His first attack was to study the causes of paper deterioration and seek remedies for paper failures. The papers he studied first were manufactured between 1900 and 1949. Typically, these were uncoated papers, but not exclusively so. Those with coatings generally showed alkaline characteristics on the surface but had acidic cores. Barrow's own observations, stimulated by his intuition and later confirmed by his readings and laboratory investigations, brought him to the conclusions that initial strength and neutral pH values are important to the durability and longevity of paper.

One of Barrow's signal contributions was to tell all of us loudly, clearly, and concisely that we must seek acid-free and stronger papers. Barrow's concern has finally penetrated our consciousness and possibly is one of the reasons for this conference. We have recognized a problem, want to learn more about it, and seek solutions for the future.

In the course of many years and particularly in recent meetings of the ABPC-RTSD (ALA) Joint Committee, librarians have urged publishers to print more books on permanent and durable paper. Now the publishers have, among other things, asked the library representatives on the committee to identify those materials which should be printed on long-lasting papers and those which can be printed on cheaper short-lived papers. After all these years, we have no definitive answer.

A thought expressed by Gordon Williams of the Center for Research Libraries is that from now on we should print everything on long-life paper. The economic factors which have precluded the use of permanent and durable papers in past years now seem to be disappearing, and Williams' suggestion is not flippant, but highly appropriate under the circumstances. Many times we are unable to distinguish, in the early days of its existence, ephemera from material of permanent importance. Thus, if books were printed on permanent and durable papers, we would have them available for a longer period of time than if printed on groundwood pulp. Not all paperbacks from the newsstand rack are subject to immediate discard, for two reasons: first, some of these are the only available reprints which can be used to replenish library stocks; and second, some items of lasting importance published in paperback versions are never published in the so-called hardbound editions.

As librarians, we cannot presume to devise a recipe for better book papers, but we must take the responsibility for telling publishers and paper manufacturers what is expected of the books they manufacture for us. Perhaps it is sufficient to say that we want books which will last as long as the knowledge in them will be useful to mankind. This is a goal which may be very difficult to attain. It may be one that is impossible to attain, but unless we set our eyes on a goal someplace along a continuum, we will make little or no progress in that direction.

Barrow's work has indicated not only that residual acid is a factor which tends to make paper deteriorate but also that the constant flexing of papers in books is another factor. These seem so self-evident now that there is little question about these two factors being causes of deterioration. Thus it would seem that we might additionally suggest to publishers and papermakers that we need both as much strength as it is feasible to build into new paper and at the same time paper that is neutral in a balance between acidity and alkalinity.

How can we communicate to publishers (and they in turn to paper manufacturers) the qualities which are desired and necessary? Normally a specification or standard is the format used. In recent years, some contention has been noted because of embryonic activities toward the development of performance standards for book papers. These efforts have been called "arbitrary" and even worse names. But the enunciation by Barrow in 1960 of a proposed standard did bring attention to our paper problems, as Shatzkin has stated, and has stimulated discussion and interest. Whether Barrow's proposal was arbitrary is, I think, an academic question. The result has been salutary.

Only when a standard is needed but does not exist do we become painfully aware of its importance to us. The determination of a minimum standard for the performance of book papers will certainly not inhibit innovation and lead to undesirable uniformity, as has been claimed. Rather the setting of clear norms for desirable characteristics eliminates the need to establish such values repetitively. Standards are the language for the dialogue between buyer and seller by specifying either a recipe for the material or the behavior of the material. Among other things, standards result in a greater confidence of the consumer in the material, a better understanding of how to use the material, better quality control, lower inventories by elimination of unnecessary grades, better performance at lower prices through the reduced need for negotiations, more efficient inspection and testing, and, finally, lower prices to consumers through a rational basis for competitive bidding.

The goal of the development of a performance standard for book papers is, in my estimation, a long-range goal. In the meantime, we must all insist that publishers require their paper manufacturers to supply increasingly improved book papers. Constant experimentation with various combinations will show us the appropriate balances of factors governing paper manufacture which will provide improved papers. Testing, probing, and experimentation must not stop. We must continue to do more.

Whether or not long-lasting papers are more costly (and they do not seem to be significantly more so), the law of demand and supply will bring the price still lower. Competition caused by desire to serve is marvelous for this purpose. Obviously, manufacturers have been afraid to go into the field of neutral papers in wholesale quantities because they have not seen the market for the papers. They have not found the market because publishers have not pushed for such papers, since librarians have not pushed the publishers. The transition in the paper mills will take a little time but only as much as we will allow. Economics will not hinder progress as much as lack of desire.

As custodians of the books, librarians have one responsibility they cannot side-step. They must do all in their power to provide a proper environment for the books manufactured by the publishers. To ignore this responsibility would be a gross dereliction of duty.

Fortunately, there are several publishers, as represented by Shatzkin, who have realized that the long life of a paper for books is an important thing for scholarship and, although economic considerations should have some attention, they should not have paramount bearing on the decision to use long-life papers in the printing of books. At the present time, it is not entirely feasible to print all kinds of materials on the long-life papers presently available; but it is possible to print a great variety of materials on long-life papers, as has been proven by a great many publishers. The fact that we will soon be able to print more and more of our materials on long-life papers is due in great part to the knowledge, efforts, and sincere desire on the part of publishers to present a product that is needed by scholarship. The publisher must continue to weigh the relative balance of the various factors that make up a good paper for the particular book he is printing. As long as he is looking for better papers and calls upon his papermakers to provide him with papers that will have a longer life in libraries, we will move forward toward the goal that we want to achieve—that is, books that will stay in our libraries as long as they are needed.

To repeat and summarize, these are some future steps which must be taken: (1) librarians must identify those items which are to be published on long-lasting paper; (2) they must remind publishers of the need for long-life papers in their books; (3) publishers must insist that paper makers provide long-life papers; (4) librarians must provide proper environments for storing the books; (5) librarians, publishers, and papermakers must develop some commonly understood measures of book behavior or performance standards; (6) finally—librarians must urge publishers to insist that the paper industry do a little bit more than it can rather than a little bit less.

BINDING PRACTICE AS RELATED TO THE PRESERVATION OF BOOKS

HAROLD W. TRIBOLET

It has been reported that the work assignments in the western European monasteries before the age of printing were very simple. If a monk could read and write, or possibly just write, he was developed as a calligrapher. Those who did not have writing skills were sent to the garden or were taught bookbinding. This story was probably related by a waggish calligrapher. Nevertheless, the work of the early binder is truly remarkable. He conceived sound constructional techniques, some of which have survived for 1,000 years. Unmistakable evidence of his fundamentals and ingenuity remains in much of our binding technology of today, particularly in books with rigid covers. As in the past, we continue to secure and hinge the leaves at one edge, a process which enables one to read from one page of text to another in a convenient, rapid manner. Many books have a concave fore edge together with a rounded backbone, again a reflection of early construction. The fiber boards on the sides of a modern binding, inspired by the wooden panels used in the past, give protective support to the less rigid leaves of the book. Finally, although the covering material on the exterior of most of the present-day machine-made books is unlike the leathers used several hundred years ago, its prime purpose remains to protect the underlying construction.

Shortly after the invention of the printing press, book production grew rapidly in Europe. The binders, unlike the newly trained compositors and pressmen, were not required to master a new craft, for they simply continued the time-consuming traditional techniques developed earlier for the binding of manuscript leaves. As the demand for printed books increased, it is apparent that the quality of binding suffered because inexperienced help with questionable talent was recruited to supplement the output of the skilled binders.

Shortcuts followed, and by the eighteenth century one can see evidence of these in the construction and materials used for binding. The evolution of the mass-produced binding to its present-day form reflects the continuing struggle of the binder to keep pace with the printing press and the demands of the publishers. Perhaps the most significant breakthrough came with the creation of the case binding, estimated to have occurred about 1825–30, shortly after the introduction of cloth for a covering material. Case binding illustrated the prefabrication concept. It involved a group of sewn signatures, glued, rounded, and backed, to be put in a cover or case made of two boards and a covering material produced as a separate unit—both held together with an adhesive. Although this binding was designed to be produced by hand, it was actually the prototype for the machine-made binding introduced shortly before the turn of this century. It was a departure from the costly hand binding of the past; now books could be made available to the millions who wanted them at reasonable prices; the binder in collaboration with the engineer had learned to accept the tools and conditions of an industrial society. But the basic fashion of binding was not changed. Many evolutionary variants in binding styles have developed during the past several centuries; yet, as Klinefelter reminds us: "If Christopher Columbus were to return to earth today, one of the things in daily use that he would easily recognize would be a book" [1, p. v].

The structural success of a book is dependent upon the satisfactory function of the construction and all of the material involved. An elegant or simple binding on a book made of paper with a very limited life, or with leaves that do not open easily because the paper is rigid or badly sewn, is an inexcusable waste of skill and money. When a new book is being conceived, the binder should be involved in the planning stage, since he is responsible for an important component of the construction. The kind of paper, its thickness, the direction of grain, signature size, dimension of the gutter margin, type of sewing, edge treatment, style of binding, covering material, and related details should not be the undivided responsibility of the designer. If rebinding or restoration is necessary, it is imperative that the binder or conservator fully understand the purpose of his craft in providing a workable extension to the life of the book.

In planning a new book, the selection of paper should be made after consultation with a person who knows binding. The paper in existing books that require rebinding or restoration, however, presents another problem; here the mistakes of the past are frequently seen and must be resolved. The binder must carefully decide whether the leaves require washing, deacidification, sizing, total physical support with a supplemental material, repair of the folds of the signatures—decisions that he should make after discussing the problems with the owner of the book or the librarian, who are best qualified to judge the importance of an item and the manner in which it is to be used. Although paper is the most important element of the physical book and the binding is a protective shell, often the binding outlasts the paper, a condition too frequently seen in many books produced during the past century.

Middleton, in his thorough book on binding techniques, describes the stabbing of papyrus leaves with thread through one of the margins as the most primitive form of consolidation [2]. Today some mechanized sewing is not unlike this early process, and these kinds of curious similarities can be seen in many other variants of the sewing operation.

Another example of the effect of the past is the raised thong or cord sewing, probably developed in the tenth century, in which the thread is inside the signatures, parallel to the folds and anchored to the thongs or cords positioned outside the signatures at the backbone. This sewing has stood the test of time and is still used today by many hand binders who are determined to create durable bindings. Furthermore, the basic concept undoubtedly inspired the inventors of the Smyth sewing machine and similar ones developed during the latter half of the last century, which automatically introduce thread to the signatures as in the raised-cord sewing, then knot them together, but without the protruding cords on the backbone. This type of mechanical sewing, used on millions of books being manufactured today, provides strength and flexibility. On heavy books subject to frequent handling, cotton tapes are usually included at the backbone, through which the sewing is passed. The tapes, longer than the thickness of the book, are anchored to the inside of the case as part of the endsheet.

This sewing is employed in some European countries for rebinding circulating books, after the folds of the signatures are repaired, because of the flexibility advantages. Library binders in our country have not adopted the process, claiming that the preparatory work on the signatures is too expensive.

Prior to the invention of the sewing machine, the pressures of production brought about compromises in sewing that enabled the binder to produce books rapidly, though hand labor was still employed. He found that hand sewing a book on a few hemp cords recessed in the backbone was faster than sewing on the traditional five raised cords. Frequently the covering material on publishers' bindings sewn in this way was paper or cloth, used as a substitute for the more expensive leather.

Some of the present-day hand binders involved in leather binding also favor recessed cord sewing, combined with a hollow backbone. This backbone is a tubelike, partially laminated paper lining, to which are sometimes attached artificial raised bands made of strips of cardboard or leather. The hollow backbone makes it possible to open a book to the farthest point of the gutter margin, and it also provides a relatively inflexible area for gold tooling.

The advantage of easier opening in the recessed-cord, hollow-backbone construction, as in a book with abnormally stiff leaves, is offset by significant defects. Saw cuts across the folds of the signatures are necessary to accommodate the sewing cords, a form of mutilation that weakens the paper in a critical area. When the book is opened, a severe arch forms at the backbone, opposed to its normal shape, thus causing a strain on the sewing cords. Then, as the binding ages, the leather wears away in the joint area, followed by the disintegration of the paper folds of the hollow backbone. Finally, the entire backbone comes loose from the binding, thus creating the need for an immediate major restoration operation.

The edition or publishers' binding will withstand normal usage in the private library, but it suffers when given heavy use in a circulating library. Frequently the leaves become detached, the case loosens from the body, and the covering material breaks down. Prolonging the life of the book is the logical objective in most instances. However, the manner in which this is done requires intelligent judgment. If the book is a rarity it should be set aside for special treatment in the hands of a skilled binder, who would have the competence to restore or rebind it. An intermediate category should be recognized for those books too significant for the so-called library binding, yet not qualified for the special treatment. The third category should include books that justify simple rebinding.

Within each of the three categories mentioned, there are many routes to follow in deciding precisely what should be done with a particular book. Sorting a collection of books in need of attention requires the knowledgeable judgment of the librarian, or book owner, who understands the advantages of consulting a qualified binder or conservator.

Simple rebinding could mean the utilization of the existing sewing, new endpapers of durable, permanent, acid-free paper, the relining of the backbone, and a strong case binding of cloth or a suitable material. If resewing is necessary, overcasting or oversewing is generally used, done by machine or by hand. Here the folds of the signatures are cut away, and thread is introduced through the gutter margins of the leaves, consuming the last one-quarter inch of each leaf. Unless the paper is thin as well as flexible, a binding sewn in this way opens poorly, and one must exert force on the pages during the reading process. It is, however, a strong sewing technique.

Side sewing (not to be confused with that used on pamphlets and slightly related to overcasting), used on many new, mass-produced school and reference case-bound books destined for heavy use, is undoubtably the most distinctive innovation in commerical binding. Holes are drilled at high speeds through the gutter margins of the leaves at a ninety-degree angle, and thread is drawn through the entire book in one operation. Again reflecting the traditional form, side-sewn books are frequently rounded and backed. Although the sewing goes through a portion of the gutter margin, books manufactured with this construction in mind are designed with a larger-than-normal binding or gutter margin, so they can be comfortably read.

Considering simple rebinding, Grove [3] points out that some binderies use the adhesive binding techinque (also called "perfect," "threadless," "unsewn," or "flex") rather than overcasting, particularly if a book with unusually narrow gutter margins is being rebound. The folds of the signatures are trimmed off, and the single leaves are then held together with an adhesive, applied to the binding edge so that a small amount of it holds each leaf to the adjoining one. In some instances the binding edge is serrated to increase the surface, and hemp cords are placed in saw cuts across the backbone. Additional strength is gained with linings of cloth, paper, or a combination of the two materials. Adhesive bindings can be rounded, backed, and put into covers as a case binding, or treated as the familiar paperback. Flexibility and durability at the backbone can be expected if the paper is pliant and, of course, if the correct adhesive is properly applied. The process has its place, and many new and old books have been successfully bound in this way, but it should not be used on valuable and rare books.

Adhesive binding is not new. Over 100 years ago gutta-percha and other rubberlike substances were used on a large number of new books. Some of these were rather elegant publications. By now, most of these books have probably broken apart as the bonding material crystallized. The process was, however, a beginning; its survival is due chiefly to the improved adhesives made available during the past fifty years.

Shortly after the turn of the century, the eminent hand bookbinder, Cockerell, focused attention on the rebinding of books in the intermediate category. He described them as "books of permanent interest, but of no special value, that require to be well and strongly bound, but for which the best and most careful work would be too expensive" [4, p. 94]. Such work must be done by hand, and the materials, which are a minor part of the total cost, should be stout as well as free of injurious ingredients that would shorten the book's life. Books of this kind should be bound to open easily, which excludes overcasting in most instances.

Sewing with linen thread over cotton or linen tapes, combined with split boards on heavy books, is a desirable preliminary treatment. Strong cloth or the most durable leather, or a combination of the two as on a quarter binding, should be considered for the covering material. Unfortunately, too frequently books in this category are subjected to casual treatment at the lowest possible price, resulting in irreversible damage.

The rare, valuable book in need of rebinding or restoration in a collection should be given to a professional who not only has the skills to bind well but who fully understands the characteristics of *all* materials involved—those he is asked to work on as well as the ones he will add. He is professionally obligated to recognize the great wealth of knowledge gathered over the centuries of good bookbinding and to accept new techniques and materials only after they are carefully tested and proven. Constructional innovations have appeared in extra bound books, some of which are excellent, but the traditional laced-in raised-cord, sewn-headband, tight-backbone binding, with a covering of leather free of excessive acid, is generally accepted as best. In some instances, replica or period bindings are produced when none or very little of the original binding exists and it is desirable to recreate the early appearance. Here, too, the materials should be carefully selected, the historic construction observed, and skilled craftsmanship maintained.

Although the uncut deckle edges one sees on some books is usually viewed with appreciation, this irregular surface of white paper is the conservator's burden. The edge is not under compression, so dirt and other atmospheric pollutants easily creep into the leaves and cause discoloration. The trimmed edge, burnished, stained, marbled, sprinkled, or gilded, provides a relatively solid surface from which dirt can be readily removed, and some of these treatments protect the paper from the penetration of contaminants.

The wooden panels used on the sides of early manuscripts and printed books served their purpose extremely well. Their weight and rigidity, together with the fore-edge clasps frequently used, kept the books under favorable compression. As books became smaller and were produced in greater numbers, a more manageable and cheaper substitute was found in fiber board, which is now used everywhere in most bindings. Today, there are interesting variants of the use of individual boards front and back. Some cases consist of a single board which continues over the backbone from the sides; another is made of an extruded plastic sheeting which is stiff enough not to require boards; but all give the traditional protection to the leaves of the book.

Although, in earliest bindings, the boards did not always extend beyond the leaves, evidence of the intentional square or projecting board was seen by the middle of the fifteenth century, according to Middleton [2]. This custom has undoubtably survived because the extra dimension of the board provides a degree of protection to the edges of the book. In modern construction, by hand or machine, we should minimize the size of the square, for it creates a problem that affects the life and appearance of the binding. A book placed vertically on a shelf will sag in a clockwise direction, that is, the leaves at the fore edge will drop the distance of the square until they rest on the shelving, exerting a strain on the joints and the backbone. As a result, the backbones of most books become slightly more convex at the bottom than at the top, and the joints of casebindings usually loosen.

In the earliest bindings, leather, either tawed with alum and salt or tanned with vegetable products such as wood and bark, was applied to the book to protect the backbone construction and to serve as a supplemental hinge over the laced-in cords or thongs. The binders sought a flexible material that could be made durable, and it is obvious their choice was excellent, for much of the leather has lasted for centuries. During the last century, tanners made an effort to expedite the process and at the same time gain an unnatural evenness of color by the application of acids that have proved to be injurious and have resulted in an inferior product. The decline of quality tannage is particularly evident in many bindings produced during the latter half of the nineteenth century.

In 1900, the Council of the [Royal] Society of Arts of England established a Committee on Leather for Bookbinding to investigate the problem and make recommendations for improved tannage as well as binding techniques. Although this was a commendable beginning, it was apparent that further scientific work had to be done. As a result, in 1932, the Printing Industry Research Association and the British Leather Manufacturers' Research Association, with the strong support of R. Faraday Innes, the distinguished English leather chemist, continued the investigation. Briefly, the group determined that protective organic salts found in early vegetable-tanned skins were being washed out in the modern processes, and that potassium lactate should be applied to newly tanned skins. The purpose of the potassium lactate is to prevent the sulphur dioxide absorbed from the urban atmosphere from causing early disintegration in vegetable-tanned leather. While other salts have been found to have good protective characteristics, most binders involved in treating bound books use potassium lactate. The peroxide test was also introduced for determining the durability of leather, and it was proposed that skins tanned in the approved way be stamped "Guaranteed to resist P.I.R.A. [Printing Industry Research Association] Test." This superior leather is available today.

Skins converted into leather by another process, known as chrome tannage, have had a very limited use in binding. Although it is more resistant than vegetable-tanned leather to fungal growth and deterioration from injurious atmospheric gases, leather created in this way is not easily fabricated. A combination of chrome and vegetable tannage, which is supposed to have the advantages of each, is now being applied to goatskins.

Vellum, also made of animal skins, has been a strong and enduring covering material for centuries, although it is sensitive to humidity and temperature variations, which results in warping. It is a hardy material that has a natural resistance to the atmospheric gases and only requires an occasional cleaning with an eraser or saddle soap. Books bound in vellum can be kept more or less compact with fore-edge clasps or ties, but they should also be shelved under moderate pressure.

Although various fabrics have been used as book-covering materials for centuries, the popular use of cloth for publishers' bindings developed during the early 1820s. This was a woven cotton material prepared with a gelatine size or starch to prevent the penetration of the glue used for bonding. The advantages of an inexpensive mass-produced covering material were obvious to the publishers and the binders, and cloth manufacturers soon responded with a variety of textures, finishes, and base fabrics in various weights. Today, we have plain starch-filled cloths that give excellent service, as well as a variety of impregnated and coated fabrics that can be easily washed and are usually resistant to vermin. As a conservation measure, it is important in rebinding or in planning a new binding to select a cloth (if that is the preferred material) with a suitable base fabric that is strong and will adequately support the book.

Currently, nonwoven covering material's are being used on bindings, but it is too early to judge their lasting properties. One is made of granulated leather and paper fibers bonded with latex. Another is composed of impregnated paper fibers. A product that deserves special attention consists of matted polyethylene fibers and is remarkably strong even in its thinnest form. Compositions of this kind are usually treated with a pyroxylin or the superior acrylic coating, are colored, and can be grained or textured in an unlimited variety of patterns. It is also possible to print or hot-stamp designs on the surface. I have described some of these modern materials science has made possible, for it appears they offer economic advantages and can be made strong. The materials are now on trial, and later we will know more about their permanence.

Only recently has the craft of binding restoration been recognized as one that requires the skills of the highly competent hand binder, coupled with ingenuity and a thorough knowledge of materials and constructional techniques. Everything possible should be done to retain what remains of the original, and added materials should be functional, chemically safe, strong, durable, and unobtrusive. I do not support the idea that added materials should be obviously unlike the original, for too frequently this theory becomes the crutch of the haphazard worker who cannot or will not trouble to produce a good restoration. The restorer is interested not in deception, for little can be done that would escape detection, but rather in a sensitive, pleasant result.

Should an important book that is disintegrating only be preserved, or should it be restored? Such an item could be wrapped in acid-free paper, or placed in a protective container, which would preserve it somewhat, but it would be little more than a museum piece with a very restricted life. A book, in my opinion, should be made usable, and restoration is the logical solution. If it is important to retain evidence of constructional details, photographs and other records can be made before the repairs are begun, then kept with the book. In addition, such a report should include information regarding the new materials used, the operations performed, the date, and the name of the restorer.

First-aid repairs by a well-meaning person unfamiliar with materials and techniques frequently result in serious problems that cause irreversible damage to a book. Not many years ago the useful polyvinyl acetate emulsion adhesive was advocated for the reattachment of loose boards on leather bindings. The adhesive was spread over the surface of the leather adjoining the joint area, so it included a portion of the backbone as well as the board. Upon drying, it appeared that the hinge had again been made functional and that a minor miracle had been performed—but this was a temporary and false impression. Ultimately the adhesive peeled away, taking the surface of the weak leather with it, thus making a sophisticated restoration impossible. A parallel illustration involves the familiar, handy, pressure-sensitive tape which has also been misused on valuable bindings.

Many book materials are attractive to vermin and insects, support mold spores and bacteria, degenerate in the presence of ultraviolet light, require favorable humidity and temperature controls, suffer in a polluted atmosphere, support combustion, and create major problems if they become wet—yet it is within the scope of human ingenuity to minimize or eliminate these weaknesses. The problems of book conservation are not new, and a multitude of solutions have been proposed and developed over the years, but we must learn to reject or accept them with caution. Too frequently the well-meaning scientist, publisher, manufacturer, supplier, binder, or conservator, or the urgency of the problem, causes to be brought forth a material or a process that has not been thoroughly tested under realistic circumstances. We are, however, in an exciting age of innovations and synthetics, and a healthy relationship exists between the scientist and the practitioner, all of which should bring us closer to our goal.

What can you do, as a conscientious librarian or book owner, to fulfill your responsibility as a custodian? Here are a few suggestions:

1. Should you find evidence of vermin or insects, enlist the help of an exterminator or entomologist to undertake a professional control program. Poison baits can be used, and you can find reference to many of them, but it is best to employ a specialist.

2. If you suspect or see evidence of the development of mold, initiate plans for an air-conditioning system, with positive control over humidity, temperature, and acidic urban pollution. If such a system is not immediately possible, excessive humidity, in some instances, can be reduced with mechanical or chemical dehumidifiers. Early sterilization should be considered for important books. Of course, one should not wait for mold to develop to use controlled air, for all materials in the book will live longer in a favorable environment.

3. The problem of ultraviolet light can be diminished by painting over clear glass windows, by installing drapes or blinds over natural light openings, and by using plastic filters on light fixtures or fluorescent tubes with built-in filtration properties.

4. Understand binding, restoration, and preservation techniques, not as a practitioner, but as an informed person who can request intelligent help from the specialist.

5. Become familiar with approved book-cleaning and leather-treatment methods. The booklet *Cleaning and Preserving Bindings and Related Materials*, by Horton [5], is highly recommended.[1] This is the first of a series of manuals on the conservation of library materials, made possible by a grant from the Council on Library Resources, Inc. Other manuals yet to be produced will be equally useful.

[1] A selected bibliography of materials on book preservation appears below.

Over the years we have progressed in many areas; books are being produced more efficiently, conservation techniques are becoming more sophisticated, but we are also becoming increasingly aware of our ignorance. Many questions require the undivided attention of the scientist and the binder/conservator. Finally, we must increase training facilities for the hand craftsman who will continue to establish the quality standards important to those involved in the mass-production of books.

REFERENCES

1. Klinefelter, L. M. *Bookbinding Made Easy.* Milwaukee, Wis.: Bruce Publishing Co., 1960.
2. Middleton, B. C. *A History of English Craft Bookbinding Technique.* New York: Hafner Publishing Co., 1963.
3. Grove, L. E. "Adhesive Bookbinding: A Practice Reviewed." *Library Resources and Technical Services* 6 (Spring 1962):143–60.
4. Cockerell, D. *A Note on Bookbinding.* London: W. H. Smith & Son, 1904.
5. Horton, C. *Cleaning and Preserving Bindings and Related Materials.* Chicago: American Library Association, Library Technology Program, 1967.

BIBLIOGRAPHY

Adams, R. G. "Librarians as Enemies of Books." *Library Quarterly* 7 (1937):317–31.

Archer, H. R. *Rare Book Collections.* Chicago: American Library Association, 1965.

Banks, P. N. "Some Problems in Book Conservation." *Library Resources and Technical Services* 12 (Summer 1968):330–38.

Bookbinding Leather Committee. *The Causes and Prevention of the Decay of Bookbinding Leather.* London: Printing Industry Research Association and British Leather Manufacturers' Research Association, 1936.

Cockerell, D. *Some Notes on Bookbinding.* London: Oxford University Press, 1929.

Cockerell, D. *A Note on Bookbinding.* London: W. H. Smith & Son, 1904.

Cockerell, S. M. *The Repairing of Books.* London: Sheppard Press, 1958.

Cunha, G. D. M. *Conservation of Library Materials: A Manual and Bibliography on the Care, Repair and Restoration of Library Materials.* Metuchen, N.J.: Scarecrow Press, 1967.

Dutton, M. K. *Historical Sketch of Bookbinding as an Art.* Norwood, Mass.: Holliston Mills, Inc., 1926.

Gardner, A. "The Ethics of Book Repairs." *Library,* 5th ser. 9 (September 1954):194–98.

Greathouse, G. A., and Wessel, C. J. *Deterioration of Materials.* New York: Reinhold Publishing Corp., 1954.

Grove, L. E. "Adhesive Bookbinding: A Practice Reviewed." *Library Resources and Technical Services* 6 (Spring 1962):143–60.

Harrison, T. "Fragments of Bookbinding Technique." From articles in *Paper and Print,* n.d.

Haselden, R. B. *Scientific Aids for the Study of Manuscripts.* London: Bibliographical Society, 1935.

Horton, C. *Cleaning and Preserving Bindings and Related Materials.* Chicago: American Library Association, Library Technology Program, 1967.

Iiams, T. M., and Beckwith, T. D. "Notes on the Causes and Prevention of Foxing in Books." *Library Quarterly* 5 (1935):407–18.

Innes, R. F. "The Preservation of Vegetable-Tanned Leather against Deterioration." In *Progress in Leather Science: 1920–1945.* London: British Leather Manufacturers' Research Association, 1948.

Innes, R. F. "The Preservation of Bookbinding Leathers." *Library Association Record* 52 (December 1950): 458–61.

Klinefelter, L. M. *Bookbinding Made Easy.* Milwaukee, Wis.: Bruce Publishing Co., 1960.

Langwell, W. H. *The Conservation of Books and Documents.* London: I. Pitman, 1957.

Lehmann-Haupt, H.; French, H. D.; and Rogers, J. W. *Bookbinding in America.* New York: R. R. Bowker Co., 1967.

Lydenberg, H. M.; Archer, J.; and Alden, J.

The Care and Repair of Books. New York: R. R. Bowker Co., 1960.
Middleton, B. C. *A History of English Craft Bookbinding Technique*. New York: Hafner Publishing Co., 1963.
Plenderleith, H. J. *The Conservation of Antiquities and Works of Art*. London: Oxford University Press, 1956.
Plenderleith, H. J. *The Preservation of Leather Bookbindings*. London: Trustees of the British Museum, 1947.
Pollard, G. "Changes in the Style of Bookbinding: 1550–1830." *Library* 11 (June 1956):71–94.
Prideaux, S. R. *Bookbinders and Their Craft*. New York: Charles Scribner's Sons, 1903.
Smith, R. D. "Guidelines for Preservation." *Special Libraries* 59 (May–June 1968): 346–52.
Smith, R. D. "The Preservation of Leather Bookbindings from Sulfuric Acid Deterioration." Masters paper, Graduate School of Librarianship, University of Denver, 1964.
Weiss, H. B., and Carruthers, R. H. *Insect Enemies of Books*. New York: New York Public Library, 1937.
Wheatley, H. B. *Bookbinding*. London: W. Trounce, 1880.

DISCUSSION

KENNETH W. SODERLAND

Harold Tribolet has presented a very lucid description of binding practices and the many paths to follow—each with its particular effect on the preservation of books. How do these variants affect the practicing librarian who has to make these choices day by day? First, even if the librarian knows a sufficient amount about binding (although this is too often not the case, unfortunately), still the type of library, its content, its use, its purpose, greatly influence his choices. My experience has been in research libraries, and I will limit my remarks to the situations encountered in libraries of that type, including larger public libraries.

Tribolet has suggested that books to be rebound fall into three broad categories: rare books, those which are "too significant for the so-called library binding," and those where simple rebinding is justified. One can hardly disagree with this, but it may be difficult to identify material in the intermediate category. This category may contain on the one extreme a few titles thought to be semi-rare, or which may qualify as rare books fifty years from now. On the other extreme, this category could include almost any noncurrent imprint that is the library's only copy. This consideration of copies is important because multiple copies in heavier than average use present a preservation problem different from the one normally meant when we speak of preservation. The danger in this case is wear and tear from use; the strongest binding (i.e., oversewing) may be the best from all standpoints. When the use has subsided, extra copies will probably be discarded. Since the recommended and approved practice for this intermediate category is handwork, doing as little damage to the original book as possible, it raises the great economic question. Can libraries with millions of books, or even hundreds of thousands, afford to give this better, hand treatment to a very large percentage of its collections? While most people will agree that this intermediate category is necesary, the biggest question in the mind of the librarian is how large to make it.

Unless a library has a very ample binding budget which can cover the costs of hand binding at about four times the rate of machine sewing, it is probably paying more attention to another factor, the condition of the paper. Mr. Williams discussed earlier the state of deterioration of library collections. The paper in a great many books has become brittle and no longer has the strength to stand machine sewing. Excluding from discussion those volumes which are normally not considered rebindable, one seems to have two choices—either repair and hand sew or use adhesive binding.

Adhesive or "perfect" binding, as Tribolet points out, is not new, but it really came into its own seven or eight years ago when new glues were found which remain more flexible and new machinery was developed for better and more efficicent handling. When the binders began promoting adhesive bindings, they advertised them as the answer to binding those paperbacks which lack adequate sewing margins. They looked so good and initial tests were so promising that some librarians began binding a great many other paperbound volumes this way, since the binding is so economical and since many new accessions in research libraries are not expected to get heavy use. Smaller-than-average volumes, which do not have glossy paper, lend themselves particularly well to adhesive binding.

Also adhesive binding for those books in which the paper has become brittle has seemed to be a great boon, for it has allowed libraries to keep in circulating condition many volumes which otherwise would have had to be replaced by reproductions. Adhesive bindings also offer a wide selection of cases; one has a choice of gold-stamped cloth casebindings, plastic-covered cases, etc.

The quality of materials going into bindings deserves further comment. The quality and permanence of the paper going into books is finally receiving serious attention, but more attention should be given to binding materials. Binders seem to be alert to using materials with sufficient initial strength, but who worries about the permanence of these materials? Are the endpapers acid-free and permanent? Is the binding cloth so acidic that it is causing deterioration? Is that why it gives way so soon at the hinges? Does the pyroxylin-impregnated cloth, so popular with library binders now, deteriorate faster than the starch-filled cloths? Are the presently used glues causing deterioration of the paper? Answers to these and many more related questions are needed. In the absence of scientific answers, some librarians have been asking for a wider use of mylar-covered cases, since mylar is reported to be an inert material.

Field tests of new materials and new processes should prove satisfactory before one uses them to a great extent, but someone has to do the testing. Mylar was so widely accepted on the paperback bindings that proceeding with mylar cases over sewn bindings seemed worth the risk. The University of Chicago library has been using them for about four years now on a limited quantity of new materials with apparently very satisfactory results. The fact that a mylar binding is cheaper than cloth binding is an added inducement.

Some should be testing the permanence of binding materials. At any rate, more librarians should begin to show some concern over these problems, so that the binders will take greater note of what they are doing for libraries.

NEW APPROACHES TO PRESERVATION[1]

RICHARD DANIEL SMITH

I. INTRODUCTION

The preservation of library materials is a major concern of librarians. Increasing numbers of books are so badly deteriorated they cannot be circulated. Persons in many fields are experimenting with and searching for ways to improve preservation practices. The objectives of this discussion are to review existing technology and report upon new approaches that librarians may apply to preserving and restoring library paper materials.

In the future, highly stable printing papers and book components will be more widely used in the manufacture of books. Present-day library collections, however, are largely composed of books printed on unstable paper. A substantial percentage of these books were not manufactured for permanent use, and libraries will continue to acquire significant works printed on impermanent paper. The novel preservation treatments presented in this report are applicable for most books already in libraries and for books to be printed on unstable papers of the foreseeable future.

The preservation of books and records is not a new problem. Over 3,000 years ago, an Egyptian scribe reported that papyrus scrolls in his charge had to be dried and unrolled to determine whether the rain had washed off the ink writing [1, p. 18, line 12–p. 19, line 2; 2]. Within a century or two after the invention of paper in China, the Chinese were treating paper to prevent attack by insects and book worms. By A.D. 500, they felt they knew enough to preserve paper for several hundred years [3, pp. 152–53].

In 1594 Shakespeare wrote: "So should my papers, yellowed with their age, / Be scorn'd like old men of less truth than tongue" [4, p. 290]. In the early 1700s, European scholars complained that irresponsible and profiteering papermakers were selling dirty thin paper [5, p. 2]. The scholars believed the government should force papermakers to produce good paper, just like the paper produced in Shakespeare's time.

We also show a tendency to view the

[1] This investigation was made possible by encouragement, guidance, and support from the Chicago Testing Laboratory, Chicago, Ill.; the Council on Library Resources, Inc., Washington, D.C.; the Institute of Paper Chemistry, Appleton, Wis.; and the Department of Chemistry, the Oriental Institute, the Toxicity Laboratory, and the Graduate Library School of the University of Chicago, Chicago, Ill. The Allied Chemical Corp., Chicago, Ill.; E. I. duPont de Nemours & Co., Chicago, Ill.; Harshaw Chemical Co., Hinsdale, Ill.; Hercules Incorporated, Chicago, Ill.; M & T Chemicals, Inc., Rahway, N.J.; Morton Chemical Co., Chicago, Ill.; and Stauffer Chemical Co., New York, N.Y., kindly donated many of the chemicals used in the experimental work. A large number of individuals, both within and without the above organizations, made contributions to this research. Particularly significant assistance from five of them calls for recognition: Howard W. Winger, professor, the Graduate Library School, brought the problem to my attention; Don R. Swanson, dean, the Graduate Library School, supported my research; Bertie L. Browning, senior research associate, the Institute of Paper Chemistry, gave me an appreciation for the complex nature of paper and guided much of the research; Harold W. Tribolet, manager, Department of Extra Binding, R. R. Donnelley & Sons Co., Chicago, Ill., evaluated my ideas from the viewpoint of a practicing conservator; and Walter A. Wozniak, chief chemist, the Chicago Testing Laboratory, helped me with experimental and testing problems. The results presented represent a summary of the author's doctoral research.

past through rose-colored glasses. Today librarians have few problems with rain, insects, book worms, and dirty thin paper; but they complain about the impermanence of paper produced since the introduction of wood fiber sources during the 1860s. This emphasis on the period beginning with 1860 is not 100 percent accurate.

Fifty years ago, Chapman investigated the condition of paper in books of the Imperial Library in Calcutta, India [6–8]. He discovered that books published before 1860 were also deteriorating and that some of these books were in a far more critical condition than books published after 1860. He identified bleaching practices and new paper fiber sources as the probable causes of the unstable paper manufactured between 1800 and 1820, and recognized that a solution to the problem of deteriorating books would require the efforts of many specialists.

Chapman compared books from the Imperial Library with identical copies from other libraries located on the hot Indian plains, in the Himalayan foothills, part time on the plains and part time in the foothills, and in England. He found that books stored under cooler conditions, in England and in the Himalayan foothills, had longer useful lives. Likewise, moving the books from the plains to the foothills reduced the rate of deterioration. In 1920, Chapman was so agitated about book losses that he actually proposed moving the Imperial Library collection to the foothills, 500 miles from the reading rooms in Calcutta [7, p. 243]. By 1922, he modified his stand and wanted to air-condition the proposed new library building [8, pp. 452–53]. Air-conditioning using refrigerants for cooling did not really begin to develop until the early 1930s. Chapman's desire for air-conditoning was no less radical (farsighted?) than his desire to move the collection.

Chapman fully appreciated the effect of storage conditions on the life of books and, through chemical analyses, established that an association existed between acidity and paper deterioration. We now know that acidity in paper is the main cause of paper deterioration and that poor storage conditions accelerate the rate of paper deterioration. The reactions which cause books to deteriorate occur after the books are received by libraries. Theoretically, therefore, librarians have the ability to make decisions and take whatever action is necessary to stretch out the useful life of books. Some knowledge about the manner in which paper deteriorates may be helpful in planning and scheduling preservation work in libraries.

2. THE NATURE OF PAPER DETERIORATION

The manner in which paper deteriorates is highly significant. Permanence and durability are the two characteristics of paper involved. Permanence is the capacity of paper to retain its original characteristics, and durability reflects the ability of paper to stand up in use [9]. All book papers probably have more durability than would be required for use in research libraries if the use occurred when the papers were new and strong. Unfortunately, research library patrons do not use books only when the paper is new and strong. A book may be used infrequently in research libraries and over prolonged periods of time.

The disintegration of books has been predicted by generations of librarians, but the books still stand upon the shelves, embrittled perhaps, but intact. To explain this, we must understand that the real-life rate of deterioration is not a straight line. It is an exponential curve, descending sharply at first, and then leveling off to push total disintegration into the far distant future.

The straight and curved lines in figure 1 are two ways of visualizing the very same loss in folding endurance. Because time is not specified, figure 1 can be considered as a generalization for all types of paper. The left axis and the straight line represent the logarithmic relationship. This form is highly regarded by scientists because the line can be extended to make a prediction of future properties. The right axis and curved or exponential line give information more significant to librarians because the curve represents the actual number of folds before the paper breaks. Paper loses folding endurance very rapidly at first and then more and more slowly as time goes on. (It may be helpful when considering fig. 1 to remember that the logarithmic numbers 2.0, 1.0, 0.0, and —0.8 are equal to 100, 10, 1, and about 0.16.)

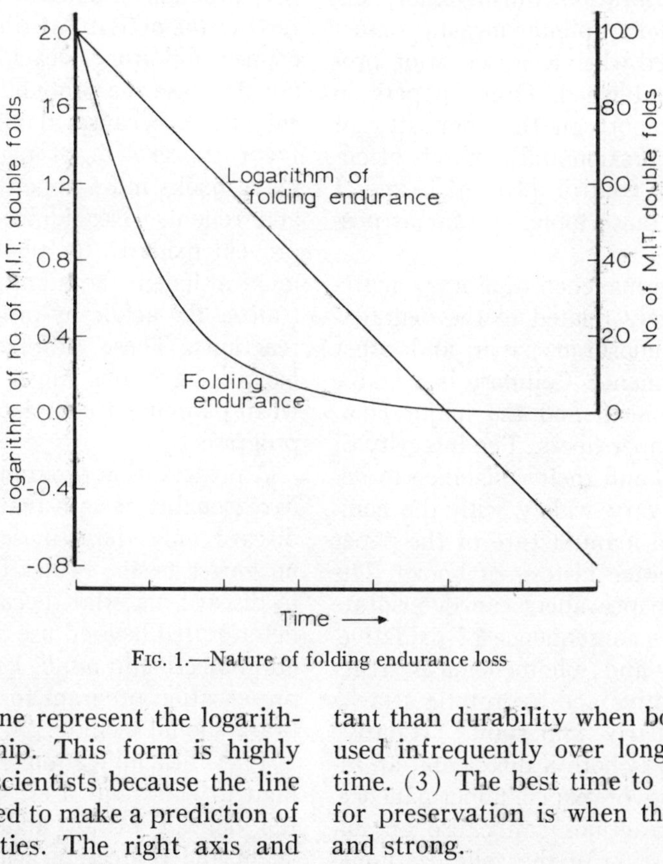

FIG. 1.—Nature of folding endurance loss

The exponential rate of paper deterioration suggests three things: (1) Books will remain intact on the shelves indefinitely after their leaves become so embrittled that the pages cannot be turned (papyrus scrolls are examples of this effect). (2) Permanence or a low rate of deterioration is far more important than durability when books will be used infrequently over long periods of time. (3) The best time to treat books for preservation is when they are new and strong.

3. A PROGRAM FOR PRESERVATION

Each library must consider its own responsibilities and means when planning a preservation program. No single plan can be recommended for all libraries. Popular libraries of ready reference tools and best sellers are chiefly interested in durability, not permanence. Research libraries are interested primarily in permanence, or maintaining their collections over an indefinite period of time. This discussion is directed toward the needs of the research library, but the suggestions can be modified to suit libraries with less permanent collections.

Books in research collections are likely to be exposed to all the causes of paper deterioration during their expected lifetime. Counter-measures must be considered when a preservation program is established. Other papers in this issue report on the chemistry of paper deterioration and methods of environmental control [10, 11], and I shall avoid these topics insofar as possible.

The impermanence of library materials is largely related to the degradation of cellulose in paper and other book components. Cellulose is a stable organic chemical and the major component of paper fibers. The integrity of paper fibers and their resistance to deterioration vary widely with the composition and manufacture of the paper and the storage history of books. The quality of paper fibers can deteriorate rapidly as a consequence of oxidative, hydrolytic, and photochemical reactions. Oxidative and hydrolytic attacks are particularly important. Oxidative degradation is both a direct and an indirect cause of paper impermanence. Oxidative reactions can cause an immediate scission of the cellulose molecule or prepare the way for other undesirable reactions. Oxidized cellulose is unstable and particularly liable to discoloration. However, the presence of oxygen is required for the production of oxidized cellulose, and its formation normally proceeds very much more slowly than that of hydrolyzed cellulose.

The preservation of library materials is contingent on minimizing the rate of hydrolytic acidic attack. The accepted preservation treatment for unstable book paper includes neutralization as well as the deposit of a benign, alkaline buffering agent in the treated paper. Such a treatment does not, however, strengthen weakened or embrittled paper, although an alkaline condition does restrict the activity of trace metals like copper and iron. Deacidification does not decrease the probability of biological attack because alkaline conditions favor the growth of many fungi and make books more appetizing to insects and rodents. Deacidification does not prevent oxidative or photochemical attack, although the alkaline buffer neutralizes the acidic by-products of these reactions. These problems and other hazards to books must be considered when planning a complete preservation program.

A preservation program should make it reasonably certain that a library can discard only those materials which it no longer needs, rather than be forced to discard materials because they have deteriorated beyond use. With this general objective in mind, I propose that a preservation program for a research library should include:

1. A deacidification treatment, benign to book and user, which includes the deposit of an alkaline buffering agent and protection against biological attack.

2. A strengthening and restoration treatment capable of improving the durability of heavily used materials and restoring the condition of borderline books so they can be rebound and circulated.

3. A method for protecting infrequently used books by storing them, preferably as individual units, in cheap, transparent, and disposable containers.

My specific preservation program, which I shall call the Chicago Process, will be discussed in four parts: (1) paper deacidification, (2) protection from living organisms, (3) paper strengthening, and (4) prolonged storage. Some emphasis will be given in this discussion to the work of earlier investigators whose work is scattered and frequently overlooked.

4. PAPER DEACIDIFICATION

4.1 INTRODUCTION

Acidic attack is the most significant cause of deterioration in library materials. The best publicized source of acidity is papermaker's alum, which is introduced principally during the manufacture of paper. Books are also destroyed by acidity which develops while the books are stored in libraries [12]. The sources of this acidity include air pollutants and the oxidation products of paper fibers and printing ink mediums.

For purposes of perspective in paper deacidification technology, I will first consider the use of organic deacidification agents, then inorganic deacidification agents, and finally nonaqueous deacidification.

Some methods of deacidification, as, for example, the sprinkling of alkaline inorganic powders like chalk on paper, are unlikely to be effective. Kathpalia [13, p. 251] reported unsatisfactory results with chalk powder (calcium carbonate). Another authority studied an acidic paper coated with an alkaline coating. The TAPPI water extract pH was alkaline as a result of the coating, but the paper was impermanent because its center remained acidic [14; 15, pp. 1524, 1527].

The ideal deacidification treatment would avoid the problem of wetting and drying books by using a gaseous process. Regrettably, gaseous treatments are not permanent because the deacidification agent escapes by volatilizing back out of the book, and the book reverts to its acidic condition. Other difficulties with gaseous processes include undesirable side reactions and the hazardous properties of available chemicals.

4.2 ORGANIC DEACIDIFICATION AGENTS

Organic alkalies, based on nitrogen, are effective deacidification agents. Amines or their derivatives have been widely applied to produce an alkaline condition and thereby stabilize paper or prevent metal corrosion or tarnishing. Low-molecular-weight amines are used as gases or vapors, and heavier amines are used as liquids or dissolved in suitable solvents.

The potential benefit of amines in deacidifying library materials, however, can be outweighed by the problems which amines may cause under library conditions. These problems originate in the side reactions and effects which amines undergo and cause. Most amines have physiological effects on human beings, and many amines present toxicity hazards at rather low levels of concentration. Organic alkalies, which contain nitrogen, discolor paper by reacting with the carbohydrates in paper to form brown, nitrogen-containing polymers. "Browning reactions" are a widespread phenomena in carbohydrate chemistry, and food and paper scientists have published much research [16–33]. (For purposes of completeness, the references cited [16–33] discuss the browning reactions of amines and carbohydrates as well as the more ordinary causes of color reversion in paper.)

Some applications of amines and their derivatives in stabilizing paper were enumerated in a previous *Library Quarterly* article [34, p. 281]. In addition, amines have been patented as vapor-phase corrosion inhibitors in antitarnishing wrapping papers [35] and used to stabilize dark-colored and black cellulosic plastic-molded products [36, p. 361; J. T. Bent, district sales manager, Plastics Division, Eastman Chemical Products, Inc., Rochester, N.Y., personal correspondence]. Amines are used to stabilize electrical papers against heat degradation [37, 38]. Gaines [39] and Volgenau [40] investigated the effect of gaseous, liquid, and solid amines on the thermal stability of cellulose. They found that the amines which were effective in stabilizing the strength properties of paper also caused the paper to discolor. Langwell [41, p. 27] asserted that the simplest organic alkali, ammonia, as an air pollutant, is a cause of paper discoloration.

A thorough discussion of amines is beyond the scope of this paper, but the Langwell vapor-phase deacidification (VPD) process [42–44] requires comment. The need for comment exists because the data on which Langwell [42, 43] asserts the safety of his VPD process under library conditions is incomplete. Moreover, some research applicable to the toxicology of the VPD process has not heretofore been discussed in library literature.

The Langwell VPD process is similar to the use of moth balls, where a solid material is placed close to the endangered goods and protection is conveyed via a vapor phase. The solid agent in the VPD process is cyclohexylamine carbonate (cyclohexanecarbamic acid cyclohexylammonium salt), manufactured by bubbling carbon dioxide through cyclohexylamine under appropriate conditions. The chemical reaction is shown by figure 2. Cyclohexylamine carbonate is acidic rather than alkaline, so it cannot be the deacidification agent. On vaporizing, therefore, it may reasonably be assumed that a major portion of the solid agent must revert to the alkaline chemical, cyclohexylamine. Consequently, this discussion will focus on cyclohexylamine, the deacidification agent in the VPD process.

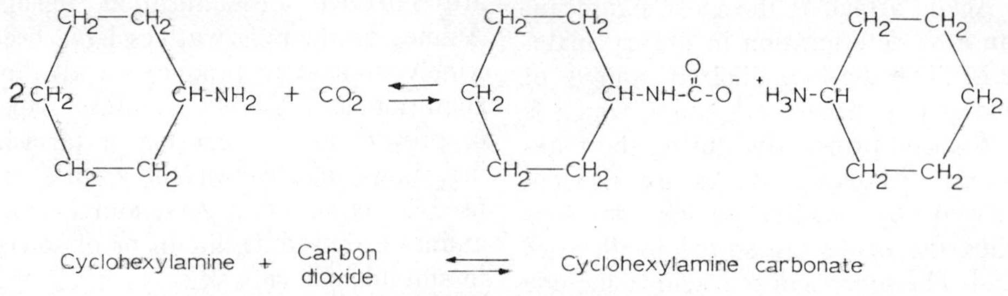

FIG. 2.—Formation of cyclohexylamine carbonate

Research on cyclohexylamine is currently stimulated because some people produce it as a metabolic product of the cyclamate family of artificial sweeteners. The U.S. Food and Drug Administration is concerned about the toxicity of cyclohexylamine and is developing information on the quantities of cyclamates safe for human consumption. In the process, they may establish safe ingestion levels for cyclohexylamine. The toxicology of cyclohexylamine has been reviewed [45], and small quantities have been found to be hazardous to health [46–48].

The Royal Air Force Laboratories in Porton, England, investigated the toxicity of cyclohexylamine carbonate in 1956 [49]. The report of this investigation has been identified as the Porton Report, and it has been cited as indicating that cyclohexylamine carbonate was safe for use in libraries [42, 43]. The Porton Report presented data obtained by short-term and relatively gross tests to justify the use of cyclohexylamine carbonate for the vapor-phase prevention of metal corrosion. Kenneth P. DuBois, professor of pharmacology and director of the Toxicity Laboratory, the University of Chicago, advised me that the Porton Report contained some evidence which suggests that an occasional and brief exposure to cyclohexylamine carbonate vapor would not be harmful. He stated further that the report contained no information to support the contention that humans could tolerate long-term exposure to cyclohexylamine carbonate vapor.

The Porton Report included data which can be interpreted as showing the necessity for further investigation before the VPD process is widely applied in libraries. It stated that the cyclohexylamine carbonate vapor concentration at 65° F (18° C) would approach five to six grams per cubic meter under saturated conditions and ranged from one to two grams when fresh air was introduced. The lowest vapor concentration reported was 1.1 grams per cubic meter, that is, about one part per thousand, when trays containing cyclohexylamine carbonate were placed, together with experimental animals, in a static ten-cubic-meter test chamber.

In the VPD process for deacidifying books, sheets of paper, impregnated with cyclohexylamine carbonate, are inserted at twenty-five-page intervals for books printed on heavily sized or coated papers and at fifty-page intervals for books printed on porous papers [43, 44]. One publication [43] recommends the impregnated paper not extend beyond the pages of the books being treated. Another publication [44] recommends the impregnated paper be sized larger so it will extend beyond the pages of the books undergoing treatment. The cyclohexylamine carbonate contained in or migrating to the periphery of the book or the protruding edge of the impregnated paper volatilizes into the surrounding air similarly to the volatilization of the cyclohexylamine carbonate placed on trays during the Porton experiments.

The Porton Report does not specify the rate of air change during the two-hour animal exposure experiments when the cyclohexylamine carbonate vapor concentration ranged between one and two grams per cubic meter of air. Consequently, this data cannot be applied directly to library book stacks but can be used to establish a possible concentration of cyclohexylamine carbonate vapor. Air in low-use areas like library book stacks that are air-conditioned is typically recirculated three to four times per hour and changed completely once per hour. In dynamic test chambers, the conventional practice is to change the air once per minute, so it is reasonable to assume that the unspecified rate of fresh air introduction in the Porton experiment changed the air at least once per hour. Hence, it is plausible that, if many of the books in an air-conditioned book stack were deacidified according to the VPD process, the book stack air would also contain about one gram of cyclohexylamine equivalent per cubic meter of air. Temperatures in American book stacks are customarily maintained about 75°–77° F instead of at 65° F as in the Porton experiments. This higher temperature would favor a higher concentration of cyclohexylamine carbonate vapor.

In 1961, after a variety of experiments including inhalation studies where exposures continued four hours per day over a five-month period, Lemonova [50] recommended that the maximum concentration of cyclohexylamine in air not be allowed to exceed 0.001 grams per cubic meter, that is, about one part per million. (For comparison, the longest exposure of the Porton investigation lasted thirty hours, six hours per day for five days.) Accordingly, this argument at least suggests the possibility that the Langwell VPD process (one part per thousand) might expose library personnel to 1,000 times the maximum amount of cyclohexylamine Lemonova concluded it was safe for Russian factory workers to breathe. It follows that, before cyclohexylamine carbonate can be used without hesitation by librarians, the safety of air-borne concentrations of cyclohexylamine carbonate which actually occur under practical book stack conditions must be determined by appropriate inhalation studies. In addition, it would be desirable to establish the dissociation rate of cyclohexylamine carbonate into cyclohexylamine, as this information does not appear to be available in the literature. Likewise, the rates at which cyclohexylamine carbonate vapor evolves from treated books should be investigated, both when the impregnated paper protrudes and when it does not protrude from the treated books. More precise information should be developed on the rate of browning and the degree to which discoloration would affect legibility and colored illustrations. Such a study might also consider the problem of how frequently the cyclohexylamine carbonate lost by volatilization should be replaced to maintain the condition of alkalinity.

If the safety of the VPD process is assured under normal conditions, librarians should consider that large-scale applications would require the presence of substantial quantities of cyclohexylamine carbonate and that these quantities could become hazardous in case of fire. Ten grams of cyclohexylamine carbonate are recommended when deacidifying two pounds of loose papers contained in a closed box [44]. More than 95 percent of the books in urban research libraries are in need of a deacidification treatment.[2] Hence, a 3,000,000 book library (given that the average book weighed two pounds) could contain about 30,000,000 grams or thirty-three tons of cyclohexylamine carbonate. Cyclohexylamine carbonate, like cyclohexylamine [47, p. 605], would undoubtedly be classed as having dangerous properties.

4.3 INORGANIC DEACIDIFICATION AGENTS

Calcium and magnesium carbonates are stabilizing agents. They are found in stable, old papers and probably were introduced accidentally during the process of preparing the fibers or intentionally to cheapen and whiten the paper and improve its printability. Early papermakers probably used limestone and dolomite stone rolls and containers for fiber maceration. Hard water, commonly used as the vehicle to work up

[2] The figure of 95 percent is based on data from a study I am currently conducting at the Newberry Library, Chicago, Ill.

paper fibers, contains appreciable quantities of calcium and magnesium compounds. Lime (calcium hydroxide) was thrown on old rags to hasten their disintegration, and any residue would have converted naturally to the carbonate. High-quality, finely pulverized limestone (calcium carbonate) is called whiting. It is and was widely used as a low-cost extender, filler, and whitener.

Actually, the providential use of mild, alkaline buffering agents to preserve cellulosic materials preceded papermaking. The Egyptians used natron, a natural and impure form of sodium bicarbonate (common baking soda), in mummification [51, pp. 317–47]. Plenderleith [52, p. 94] reported that certain mummy wrappings, which I believe contained natron, had an astonishingly fresh appearance. Sodium bicarbonate was tested as a deacidification agent by Barrow [53, p. 45] and, after accelerated aging tests, was reported to have detrimental effects on paper. Sodium bicarbonate begins to lose carbon dioxide at 50° C (122° F) [46]. By 100° C (212° F), the temperature of accelerated aging, it is converted into sodium carbonate, a strong alkali, that would be harmful to paper. The condition of mummy wrappings some thousands of years old is impressive testimony on the stability of cellulose in the presence of moderately alkaline compounds like sodium bicarbonate.

During the 1930s, many groups were seeking solutions to the problem of impermanent paper. The Brown Company, the Institute of Paper Chemistry, the Ontario Research Foundation, the S. D. Warren Company [54], and the U.S. Department of Agriculture, National Archives, and National Bureau of Standards worked on the problem [55, 56]. In these organizations and elsewhere [57–59], the contribution of moderate alkalinity to paper permanence was recognized. Then World War II diverted attention from the problem of deteriorating paper, and it became difficult for the library community [60] as well as industry to apply the developments of the 1930s.

Early aqueous deacidification methods involved the deposit of alkaline materials to solve an air-pollution laundry problem, and they are reported by the U.S. Bureau of Standards [61; 62, p. 189]. Present-day aqueous deacidification treatments are modifications of an invention made at the Ontario Research Foundation in Toronto by Otto Schierholtz [63], who received a U.S. patent entitled *Process for the Chemical Stabilization of Paper and Product* in 1936. Schierholtz immersed paper in or sprayed paper with aqueous solutions of barium, calcium, or strontium bicarbonates or hydroxides. His immersion times varied from five seconds to about two minutes. Then the wetted paper was dried to deposit the alkaline earth metal carbonate throughout the stabilized sheet of paper. Schierholtz recommended a carbon dioxide gas treatment to convert hydroxides to carbonates and, when necessary, a suspension of carbonates in the treatment solution to increase the neutralizing potential of the treatment. He reported that more concentrated bicarbonate solutions could be prepared by using carbon dioxide gas under pressure, and advised that the pH of a water extract from paper treated by his process should exceed a value of 6.5 and that a deposit of up to 2 percent by weight might be required for stabilizing groundwood papers like newsprint. He was aware that acidity causes instability in alum-rosin-sized papers and asserted that treatment according to his invention would make alum-rosin-sized papers more durable with age.

The deacidification treatments attributed to the late W. J. Barrow are so well known and appreciated that it is not necessary to discuss them in detail. Barrow [53, pp. 44–45; 64, p. 286] originally used a calcium bicarbonate immersion method. During the mid-1940s, he developed his two stage immersion process which consisted of twenty-minute immersions in a saturated solution of calcium hydroxide followed by a saturated solution of calcium bicarbonate. Instructions on how to prepare these solutions and deacidify paper have been published [13, 53, 65–67].

During the 1940s and 1950s, the Barrow immersion process was widely applied. In 1957, Gear [68, p. 296; personal correspondence] installed his one-stage (magnesium bicarbonate) thirty-minute immersion process in the U.S. National Archives Document Reproduction and Preservation Branch. In 1959, a saturated solution of calcium and magnesium bicarbonates was recommended for spray deacidification [65, p. 50]. The calcium bicarbonate was subsequently deleted [69, pp. 19–20], but magnesium bicarbonate apparently has not been recommended in an immersion process by the Barrow Research Laboratory [70, pp. 31–32]. The possibility of using deacidification agents other than calcium and magnesium salts was considered in 1965 [69, pp. 14–17], but the laboratory made no additional recommendations. Russian workers [71], however, have expanded the list of choices to include pH buffered solutions of borates and phosphates.

Until recently, all liquid deacidification treatments used water as a carrier for and solvent of one or another inorganic chemical deacidification agents. Water has advantages. Aqueous immersion treatments make it possible to stabilize paper from acidic attack to dissolve or carry away many of the harmful products of paper deterioration. The wetting of paper and its subsequent drying under pressure may strengthen it by improving fiber-to-fiber bonding. On the other hand, water has expensive liabilities. It can be difficult to wet sized paper, and all wet paper is relatively slow and/or expensive to dry. Paper takes up about twice its weight in water and, when wetted, expands considerably. Paper and books may be seriously damaged on wetting if they are constrained. Book and writing papers usually retain 10 percent or less of their dry strength while they are wet. Wet, weak paper is easy to damage in handling, and a high degree of craft skill is essential for deacidifying paper with aqueous treatments.

Aqueous deacidification solutions have a long history of effectiveness. Inorganic chemicals providentially stabilized certain mummy wrappings for thousands of years and some early papers for several hundreds of years. A variety of deacidifying treatments have been developed in the last forty years, and many of these treatments are in use for stabilizing rare and valuable library materials.

The problem of treating whole books and entire library collections, however, has not been solved by conventional aqueous deacidification treatments. The need for a nonaqueous deacidification treatment was succinctly stated by the American Group of the International Institute for Conservation of Historic and Artistic Works in October 1968. Their Committee for Paper Problems reported: "A non-aqueous means of deacidification that would not be harmful to paper, pigments, and the various media must be developed" [72, p. 30]. In the following section, I will review the literature pertaining to non-aqueous deacidification treatments and then describe a novel method for meeting the specifications of this committee.

4.4 NONAQUEOUS DEACIDIFICATION

Nonaqueous deacidification treatments involve the use of a nonaqueous solution composed of a deacidification agent and an organic solvent. The major advantage of using organic solvents is the possibility of treating whole books and therefore libraries. Organic solvents are available as liquids over a wide range of temperatures, and they can be blended together to obtain specific working properties. Far less heat energy is required to dry organic solvents from paper because suitable solvents have much lower specific heats of vaporization than water does.

On the other hand, certain organic solvents are poisonous or hazardous to health. Some organic solvents have flammable vapors that can burn with explosive speed. The dyestuffs in some inks and paper are more or less soluble in organic solvents. Fat and other skin components can be dissolved and dermatitis problems can arise from prolonged contact with many organic solvents. These hazards must be considered and safety measures incorporated when designing a nonaqueous deacidification treatment.

Barrow recognized the possibility for improvement and described two attempts at nonaqueous deacidification [69, p. 16]. The first attempt, using diglycolamine, failed because the treated paper did not remain alkaline on accelerated aging. The reacidification could have occurred because diglycolamine volatilized out of the paper or because the chemical reacted further with the cellulose to produce an acidic condition. The second attempt used a solution of magnesium acetate dissolved in water and mechanically mixed with trichlorethylene. The results presumably were erratic because magnesium acetate is not soluble in trichlorethylene, and because water and trichlorethylene, like water and oil, are immiscible liquids. Langwell [73, p. 493] reviewed nonaqueous systems, concluded they had advantages over aqueous treatments, but emphasized their lack of usefulness due to cost, flammability, and toxicity of the solvents. Baynes-Cope [74] has proposed the use of barium hydroxide, a toxic chemical, in methanol (wood or methyl alcohol). Regrettably, he found it necessary to limit this method to "the deacidification of single documents in cases where aqueous solutions can not be used, e.g., for water-labile inks and vellum" [74, pp. 8–9].

With this background, we can define two requirements for an ideal nonaqueous deacidification treatment: (1) The deacidification and alkaline buffering agent deposited in the treated papers should be a benign inorganic chemical, demonstrably compatible with paper and books over long periods of time. (2) The solvent for and the carrier of the deacidification agent should be benign to operators and to books under the conditions of treatment and easy to dry from the wetted books.

4.41 *Theory of method.*—The deacidification agent and the solvents used in the Chicago Process of deacidification meet these two ideal requirements. This point will be expanded by first considering the deacidification agent and then discussing the solvent system.

Many organic and inorganic chemicals are effective deacidification agents, but both kinds of chemicals have limitations that work against their wide application. The advantages of organic and inorganic chemicals are combined in certain metal organic compounds. These compounds are partially organic and partially inorganic. One kind of metal organic compounds is called alkoxides. Alkoxides are formed by the reaction of alcohols with many metals [75, 76]. Alcohols react with metals and form their own families of alkoxides just as water forms hydroxides. Many alkoxides are soluble to some degree in their parent alcohol and other organic solvents. One characteristic property of alkoxides is their inclination to react with water and form a hydroxide and the parent alcohol.

Magnesium methoxide is an alkoxide which readily reacts with water. It is commercially available[3] and can be produced in the laboratory [77–82]. Solutions of magnesium methoxide in methanol are stable up to concentrations of 8 percent by weight and metastable from 8 to 11 percent.

Nonaqueous deacidification treatments using magnesium methoxide introduce the same chemicals into paper as are found in stable papers produced in the seventeenth and eighteenth centuries. Magnesium methoxide reacts immediately with moisture to form magnesium hydroxide. Magnesium hydroxide, more familiarly called milk of magnesia, has been known to improve the stability of acidic paper since 1935 [83, p. 437]. Practically speaking, there is no difference between the chemicals produced in paper by the Gear [68] or the Barrow Laboratory [69] aqueous magnesium bicarbonate treatments and my nonaqueous magnesium methoxide deacidification treatment. Magnesium bicarbonate, carbonate, and hydroxide are not stable in paper. The equilibrium compound is a complex mixture of these chemicals and water. Magnesium sulfate, better known as Epsom salts, is a major reaction product on the neutralization of paper, and its effects are not dangerous. It may be concluded, therefore, that the equilibrium deacidification products that result from the introduction of magnesium methoxide meet or exceed the specified ideals. There are other alkoxides that could be used for deacidification work, but they will not be considered at this time. The selection of a nonaqueous solvent system will be discussed next.

Methanol has advantages as an alcohol because it is the smallest and most volatile of all alcohols. Unfortunately, methanol has many of the undesirable properties of water. In addition, it is flammable and toxic and dissolves ink, paper dyestuffs, and pyroxylin. On the other hand, magnesium methoxide is soluble in methanol, and the hazards of flammability, toxicity, and solubility can be circumvented.

The chlorofluorohydrocarbons are nontoxic and about as nonreactive as an organic material can be. As liquefied gases, they are used as foodstuff propellants and in refrigeration. The bigger chemical relatives of these gases are liquids that retain these benign properties and are widely used for dry cleaning greasy dirt from delicate fabrics. Chlorofluorohydrocarbon solvents and methanol are completely soluble in one another, and the hazards of methanol fall off as the proportion of methanol in the mixed solvent is reduced. For example, a solution containing seventy-five parts of a chlorofluorohydrocarbon solvent and twenty-five parts of meth-

[3] From Callery Chemical Co., Callery, Pennsylvania 16024; Morton Chemical Co., 110 North Wacker Drive, Chicago, Illinois 60606; and Stauffer Chemical Co. 380 Madison Avenue, New York, New York 10017.

anol will not support combustion. The vapor from the solution in an open container can be ignited under appropriate conditions, but it is nonexplosive and self-extinguishing.

The Chicago Process is aimed at the deacidification of whole books. The requirements for this are more complicated than for single sheets of paper, and the use of pressure vessels is essential for efficient treatment. Chlorofluorohydrocarbon solvents containing a small quantity of methanol do not affect most book components like paper and boards; cotton thread, tape, and cloth; hide glues; or inks composed of linseed or tung oil and carbon black. Difficulties with soluble book components are evaded through the use of liquefied gases as the major component of the organic solvent. Leather bindings fall into a special category. Either they are worthless and can be discarded, or the book's binding is valuable and special handling to maintain the integrity of such books is essential.

The time of immersion and the point of solvent evaporation are essential considerations when deacidifying whole books. Minimizing the time of immersion protects soluble plastics, such as the cellulose nitrate in pyroxylin-coated book cloths, because they must soften and swell before going into solution. Many soluble resins in binding-cloth coatings are also protected from solvent attack during impregnation of the treatment solution by a tight layer of grime. After impregnation, staining is minimized because the liquefied gases evaporate rapidly throughout the book. The liquefied gas solvent, including the methanol, evaporates from in and on the fibers and other components of the leaves and binding. The soluble dyestuffs in some printing inks and paper as well as the colorants in some binding adhesives are evenly redeposited throughout the book or practically on the same spot where they were dissolved. Little, if any, staining is apparent. Insofar as I know, the problems which organic solvents can cause are readily observable, and conservators are familiar with them from their use of dry cleaning solvents.

The selection of an organic solvent system is dependent upon the kind of material to be deacidified. The treatment of single sheets can be accomplished by immersion, spraying, coating, brushing, sponging, etc., by diluting the methanol solution with methylene chloride or, more preferably, with trichlorotrifluoroethane. The deacidification of whole books is done partly under pressure. Special equipment is required to accomplish the wetting and drying operations. Liquefied refrigerant gases, like chlorodifluoromethane or dichlorodifluoromethane, form the cosolvents, and the procedure can be arranged so the wet book actually dries itself. The mechanical operations required for all of these treatment modes will be apparent from the following discussion of experimental results.

4.42 *Developing the method*—My first steps toward a nonaqueous deacidification process were designed to validate an approach. They have been reported previously [34] and justified my first patent application. Magnesium methoxide was recognized as a better deacidification agent than moderately alkaline salts of weak, volatile organic acids, like magnesium acetate. Nevertheless, a solution of magnesium methoxide in methanol has limitations. The instantaneous reaction of magnesium methoxide with the adsorbed moisture in the paper produced a thick magnesium gel. This gel obstructed impregnation of books by the deacidification solution and hindered the deposition of milk of magnesia throughout the treated books. The books soaked in methanol solutions swelled, and the leaves and bindings occasionally distorted on drying. Inks, dyestuffs, and other colored materials were dissolved, and some bindings and leaves were stained because the methanol transported the colorants to the location where it evaporated. Some of the cellulose nitrate in pyroxylin-coated book cloths dissolved, and the bindings of these books were unattractive after drying. These problems and others were resolved through selection of the solvents and by control of the time and condition of treatment.

I made three major accelerated aging studies evaluating the Chicago Process of nonaqueous deacidification on single sheets of paper according to TAPPI Standard Tests. The six commercial book papers used to evaluate the deacidification treatments are described in table 1. These book papers were manufactured by reputable papermakers and represent well-regarded, commercial book papers. Book papers *A, B,* and *C* were used in the first study, *A* and *C* in the second study, and *A*, *C*, *D*, *E*, and *F* in the third study.

The test samples for the first or sixty-day accelerated aging study were conditioned as recommended by TAPPI [84] and then exposed to the control and deacidification treatments listed in table 2. Afterward, the wetted samples were air-dried, resting freely on a net of mosquito netting, and conditioned [84] before the M.I.T. folding endurance test specimens were cut [85]. The papers treated with aqueous solutions cockled badly. These samples were clamped between sheets of millboard when the fold test specimens were cut in the machine and cross-machine directions. The fold test specimens were used in a sixty-day accelerated aging test at 105° C (221° F) [86]. Table 3 gives the TAPPI cold

TABLE 1

DESCRIPTION OF BOOK PAPERS *A, B, C, D, E,* AND *F*

Code	Type of Paper	Fiber	pH Cold Extract	pH Hot Extract	Comments
A......	Letterpress	Bleached softwood kraft, 34%; bleached hardwood kraft, 66%	6.60	4.60	Filler—25% clay; English finish
B......	Offset	Bleached softwood sulfite, 60%; bleached softwood kraft, 10%; bleached hardwood kraft, 30%	6.90	5.65	Ash, 10%; contains substantial portion deinked fiber
C......	Offset	Bleached softwood sulfite, 60%; bleached softwood kraft, 10%; bleached hardwood kraft, 30%	5.90	4.40	Ash, 10%; contains substantial portion deinked fiber
D......	Offset	Softwood bleached kraft, 20%; hardwood bleached kraft, 10%; groundwood, 70%	6.00	4.98	....
E......	Offset	Softwood bleached kraft, 25%; hardwood bleached kraft, 75%	5.95	5.85	....
F......	Offset	Softwood bleached sulfite, 5%; softwood bleached kraft, 20%; hardwood bleached kraft, 75%	5.85	4.80	....

extraction pH values [87] for certain test specimens at the beginning and at the end of the test.

Two hypotheses were verified by this sixty-day study: (1) Nonaqueous deacidification treatments can improve the permanence of acidic paper just as efficiently as present-day aqueous deacidification treatments. (2) Magnesium methoxide and its reaction products are not detrimental to paper permanence.

The loss of folding endurance [85] with aging for book paper *C* is summarized in figure 3 as an example of the data from this sixty-day test. The regression lines of folding endurance on time were computed according to Brownlee [88, pp. 338–42] from the averages of the logarithms of the folding endurance data and time of aging. The heavy solid lines represent nonaqueous deacidification treatments, and the heavy broken lines represent aqueous deacidification treatments. The light lines represent the untreated standard or controls. The M.I.T. folding endurance data were obtained for each of the times noted on the base line of figure 3. The data for each time represent a minimum of ten measurements in the machine direction of the paper.

Treatment 8 used a 7 percent solution of magnesium methoxide in methanol to fill and encrust book paper *C* with magnesium compounds. The high retention of folding endurance follow-

TABLE 2

FIRST AGING STUDY—THE DEACIDIFICATION TREATMENTS

Treatment	Treatment Solution	Immersion Time (Minutes)
1........	Standard—no treatment	0
2........	Standard—no treatment	0
3........	Control—deionized water, air dried	40
4........	Control—methanol, air dried	20
5........	Control—methanol-trichlorofluoromethane (1:15 parts), air dried	20
6........	Barrow's calcium hydroxide and calcium bicarbonate treatments using deionized water, air dried	40
7........	Gear's magnesium bicarbonate treatment using deionized water, air dried	20
8........	7% magnesium methoxide in methanol, air dried	12
9........	7% magnesium methoxide in methanol, wringer and air dried	12
10........	7% magnesium methoxide in methanol—trichlorofluoromethane (1:3 parts), air dried	12
11........	7% magnesium methoxide in methanol—trichlorofluoromethane (1:15 parts), air dried	12

TABLE 3

TAPPI COLD EXTRACTION pH VALUES FOR THE FOLDING ENDURANCE SPECIMENS OF FIGURE 3 BEFORE AND AFTER SIXTY DAYS OF AGING

TREATMENT	pH VALUE	
	Before Aging	After Aging
1 and 2 (joint sample)..	5.30*	4.80
6....................	7.85	8.10
7....................	8.00	7.60
8....................	10.00	10.00
9....................	10.00	10.00
11....................	8.30	8.00

* The fact that this pH value is 0.6 pH units below the pH value of 5.90 given in table 2 may be due to experimental error or to acidic degradation products. A period of twenty-one months divides the two pH measurements.

ing Treatment 8 indicates that an excessive amount of magnesium methoxide is not deleterious to paper permanence. Treatment 9 was the same as 8 except that the wet paper was placed between two sheets of millboard on removal from the treatment solution. This sandwich was immediately passed through an electric washing machine wringer to squeeze out the excess liquid. Treatments 6 and 7, the Barrow two-stage and the Gear aqueous-immersion processes, improved stability somewhat less than Treatments 8, 9, and 10. Treatment 10 consisted of diluting one part of the magnesium methoxide solution with three parts of trichlorofluoromethane. This 1:3 parts solution was selected because, when ignited in an open pan, it is self-extinguishing. Treatment 11 consisted of diluting one part of the magnesium methoxide solution with fifteen parts of trichlorofluoromethane. This 1:15 dilution was selected to deposit between two and three times the maximum quantity of deacidification agent theoretically required.

The findings of this sixty-day aging study are impressive because the results with book papers *A* and *B* support the findings given in figure 3 for book paper *C*. However, Treatments 9 and 11 did not improve the stability of book paper *A* as much as Treatment 8 did. I believe this anomaly with Treatments 9 and 11 originated in the experimental procedure, which followed established practices oriented toward aqueous rather than nonaqueous procedures. The choice of an immersion time of twelve minutes was arbitrary, and it was necessary to obtain data on the effect of immersion time. These problems were investigated in a subsequent nine-day accelerated aging study.

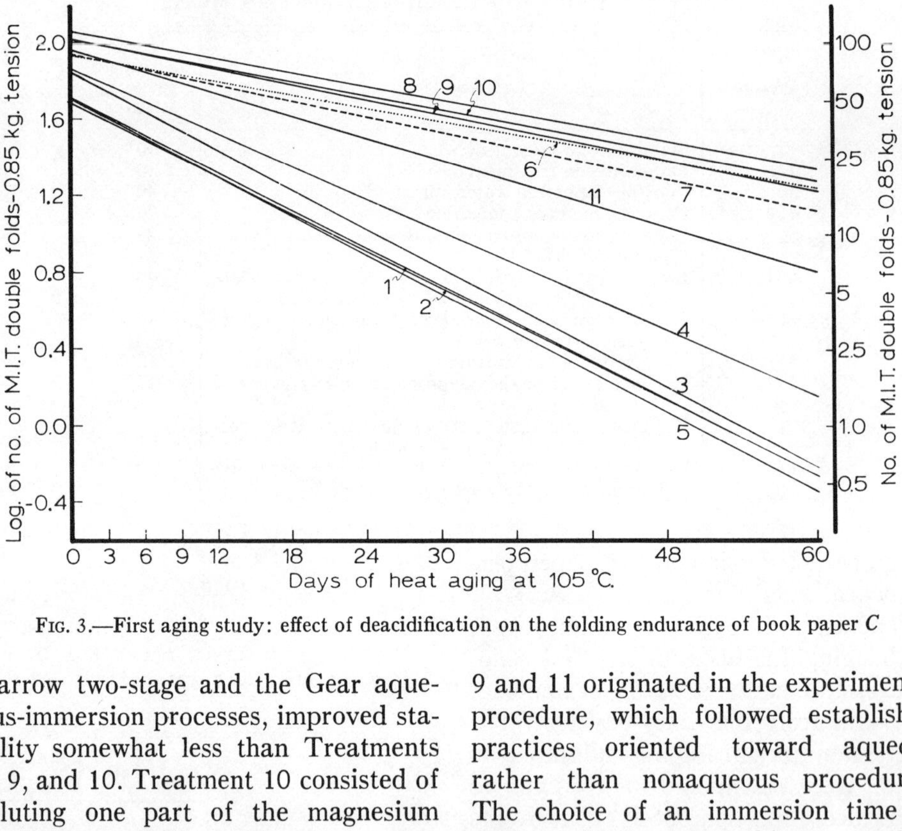

FIG. 3.—First aging study: effect of deacidification on the folding endurance of book paper *C*

In this second study, the effect of soaking time was investigated by immersing book papers *A* and *C* in a solution composed of seventy-five parts of methylene chloride and twenty-five parts of 7 percent magnesium methoxide in methanol. The test papers were immersed in the solution for periods varying from a few seconds up to thirty-two minutes.

The laboratory procedures followed in this nine-day study were more rigorous than the procedures used in the sixty-day study. The test papers and specimens were randomly selected. Treatments 2–11 were dried at 73° F (20° C) in 11 percent relative humidity for twenty-four hours before treatment. The possibility of a weakening effect from condensation of atmospheric moisture was minimized by maintaining a nitrogen-rich atmosphere over the treatment solution and by quickly drying the treated sheets of paper between a number of infrared lamps.

After drying, the test papers were conditioned [84] before the M.I.T. folding endurance test specimens [85] were cut. Next, the test specimens from Treatments 2–10 were exposed to 95 percent relative humidity at 73° F (20° C) for twenty-four hours and then dried prior to dry-heat aging at 100° C (212° F). After heat aging, all samples, with the exception of Treatment 1*a*, were conditioned at 73° F for twenty-four hours in relative humidities of 95 percent, 11 percent, and 50 percent, respectively, to relax dried-in strains before the folding endurance test was made. In general, the test was conducted according to the TAPPI Standard [85], but the M.I.T. fold tester was run through 2,000 or more cycles to provide more constant conditions at the test site.

The findings of this nine-day accelerated aging study indicate: (1) Nonaqueous deacidification solutions are not deleterious to paper when nominal precautions are taken to control moisture effects. (2) The time required for a nonaqueous deacidification treatment is determined by constraints of the equipment and the process rather than by the soaking time.

Figure 4 summarizes the data from book paper *C* with regression lines of folding endurance versus time. The lower group of lines are the control standards. The 1*a*, 1*b*, and 1*c* lines represent untreated controls. The apparent increase in the folding endurance strength of 1*b* and 1*c* compared with 1*a* is a natural consequence of humidity cycling. The fluctuation in the adsorbed moisture relaxes dried-in or other residual strains, and the paper appears to be stronger. (Similar effects occur from aqueous spray and immersion treatments.) Treatment 2 consisted of soaking the samples for thirty-two minutes in the organic solvent and indicates the solvent is not detrimental to paper permanence. Treatment 3 consisted of dipping the samples into the deacidification solution and withdrawing them as rapidly as possible. In Treatment 4, the samples were soaked for thirty seconds, in Treatment 5 for one minute, in Treatment 6 for two minutes, and so on up to thirty-two minutes in Treatment 10. There is no apparent explanation for the gain in strength in Treatment 3 (wetted only) or the more rapid loss of strength in Treatment 4 (immersed for thirty seconds). I believe these lines are extreme examples of the types of folding endurance loss that occur during short-term test periods. If the test had been continued, the rate of decay for Treatment 3 would have temporarily increased and the rate of decay for Treatment 4 would have temporarily decreased. The findings with book paper *A* were similar to those for book paper *C*, and this study clearly indicates that the time of immersion has little effect on the quality of stabilization.

The conclusions regarding requirements for nonaqueous deacidification systems using magnesium methoxide from this nine-day accelerated aging study are: (1) The amount of moisture adsorbed in paper and the ambient atmosphere must be minimized and rigorously controlled. (2) The paper undergoing deacidification must be thoroughly wetted with the treatment solution. (3) The migration of the deacidification agent must be minimized through rapid and controlled drying.

In the third or fifteen-day accelerated aging study, an immersion period of five minutes was selected because this length of time was required for a drying cycle. Three additional book papers *D*, *E*, and *F* (see table 1) as well as *A* and *C* were used in this dry-heat aging study to evaluate refinements in both the aqueous and nonaqueous treatment procedures. The treatments for these book papers are given in table 4.

The saturated aqueous solutions of calcium and magnesium bicarbonate solutions were prepared using cold carbonated water (soda water) as a modification of Schierholtz's suggestion to use carbon dioxide under pressure when concentrated bicarbonate deacidification solutions were desired [54]. These solutions were prepared by discarding a small quantity of carbonated water from bottles of Canada Dry soda water and then adding calcium or magnesium carbonate in excess. The bottles were then sealed, shaken gently, and replaced in a refrigerator. The refrigerator was opened and these carbonated water suspensions agitated from time to time during the next hour. Then the bottles were removed, and the clear, saturated aqueous solutions of the alkaline earth bicarbonates decanted into the treatment pans. During the

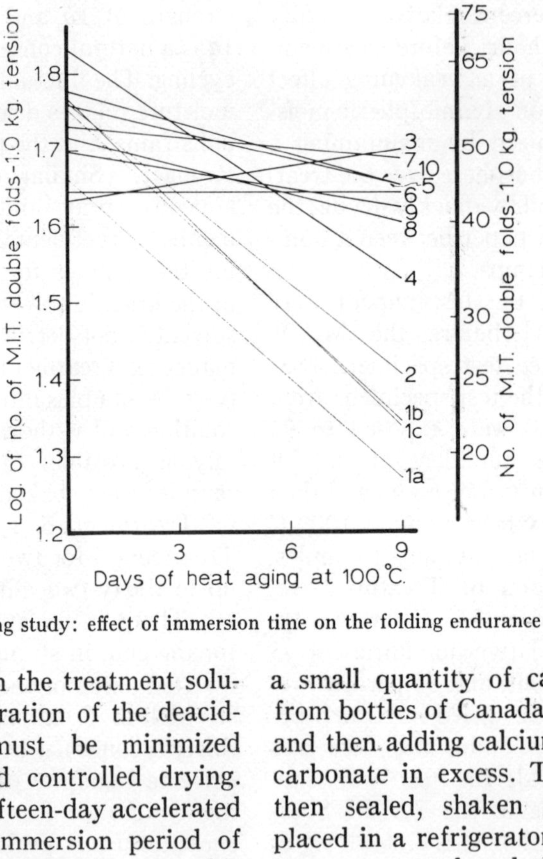

FIG. 4.—Second aging study: effect of immersion time on the folding endurance of book paper *C*

twenty-minute immersion periods, these aqueous deacidification solutions were covered with plastic sheets to maintain a high carbon dioxide atmosphere above the solutions. The high concentration of carbon dioxide in the solution was also maintained by placing the pans containing the treatment solution in an ice bath. The data do not indicate whether calcium or magnesium bicarbonate produces a better stabilization. The magnesium bicarbonate ice bath contained salt and was cold enough to freeze ice in and on the papers undergoing treatment. This ice may have affected the folding endurance of the frozen papers.

In general, this fifteen-day accelerated aging study followed the experimental and analytical procedures outlined above for the nine-day study. The findings confirm the results obtained in the earlier nonaqueous deacidification studies and indicate that water carbonated under pressure is both a convenient and an outstandingly efficient solvent for calcium and magnesium bicarbonates. The data for book paper *C* are summarized in figure 5 as the regression lines of folding endurance on time of aging. The heavy broken lines represent the Canada Dry soda water treatments, and the heavy solid lines represent nonaqueous treatments. The light regression line represents the untreated standard. Treatment 6, a saturated solution of calcium bicarbonate, produced the greatest improvement in folding endurance strength, but its rate of deterioration is the most rapid of the deacidification treatments. The magnesium methoxide Treatments 9 and 10 appear superior to the magnesium bicarbonate Treatment 7. Treatment 9 appears to produce the best results because it has the lowest rate of deterioration. The results with book papers *A*, *E*, and *F* follow the same general pattern as book paper *C* and therefore will not be reported at this time.

The results with book paper *D*, given in figure 6, are worthy of note because 70 percent of the fiber furnish in book paper *D* is groundwood. The permanence of book paper *D*, as measured

TABLE 4

THIRD AGING STUDY—THE DEACIDIFICATION TREATMENTS

Treatment	Treatment Solution	Immersion Time (Minutes)
1........	Standard—no treatment	0
3........	Control—Canada Dry soda water, air dried	20
4........	Control—methanol, wringer-infrared dried	5
5........	Control—methanol–methylene chloride (1:3 parts), infrared dried	5
6........	Saturated solution of calcium bicarbonate in cold Canada Dry soda water, air dried	20
7........	Saturated solution of magnesium bicarbonate in cold Canada Dry soda water, air dried	20
8........	7% magnesium methoxide in methanol, wringer-infrared dried	5
9........	7% magnesium methoxide in methanol—methylene chloride (1:3 parts), infrared dried	5
10........	7% magnesium methoxide in methanol–methylene chloride (1:15 parts), infrared dried	5

by folding endurance retention, compares favorably with that of book paper *C*, as well as many other 100 percent chemical wood pulp papers, both before and after deacidification. The results with Treatment 3 indicate that Canada Dry soda water is naturally an aqueous deacidification solution because it contains a significant quantity of moderately alkaline salts. The results from the other treatments are similar to those with book paper *C* and will not be discussed at this time.

The book papers in this fifteen-day

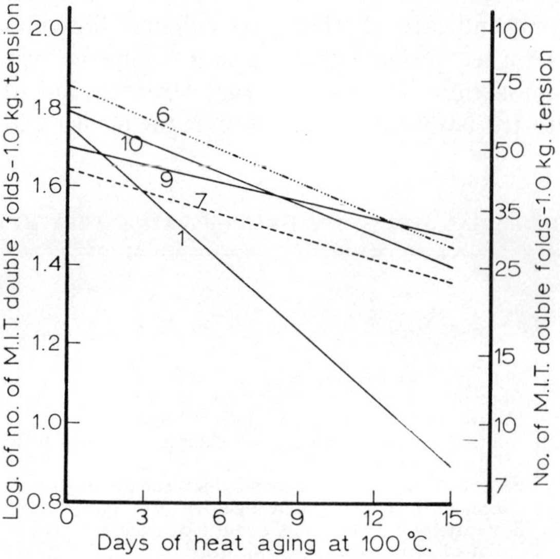

FIG. 5.—Third aging study: effect of deacidification on the folding endurance of book paper *C*

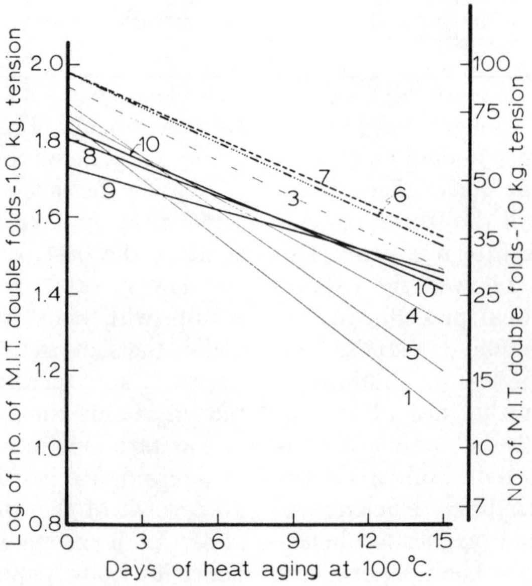

FIG. 6.—Third aging study: effect of deacidification on the folding endurance of book paper *D*

accelerated aging study were tested for resistance to photochemical attack by exposure to a carbon-arc light (Fade-ometer). The deacidification treatments either improved the stability of the papers or had no detrimental effect on them.

There were three major conclusions from the accelerated aging studies on single sheets:

1. Nonaqueous deacidification treatments can improve the stability of acidic paper just as efficiently as, if not more efficiently than, present-day aqueous deacidification processes. Magnesium methoxide and its reaction products are not detrimental to paper permanence as determined by accelerated heat and light aging.

2. The time required for a deacidification cycle is determined by process and equipment constraints rather than by immersion time.

3. The requirements for successful nonaqueous deacidification treatments include (*a*) control of the amount of water capable of reacting with the magnesium methoxide, (*b*) thoroughly wetting the paper with the deacidification solution, and (*c*) drying to deposit the deacidification agent throughout the treated paper.

Conservators presumably will come to use this deacidification process in a manner rather similar to those described in the above tests. Libraries, archives, and other depositories of single-sheet documents could mechanize the process to reduce costs. Presumably, sheets can be laid upon an endless moving belt and dried, deacidified, and dried again as they pass through a tunnel chamber. The deacidification solution could be applied by means of rollers, spray guns, or immersion tanks in a mechanized operation for single sheets.

4.43 *Deacidifying whole books.*—The problems of wetting and drying make the deacidification of whole books more complicated than that of single sheets. The use of pressure vessels (autoclaves) is essential. Figure 7 lists the major

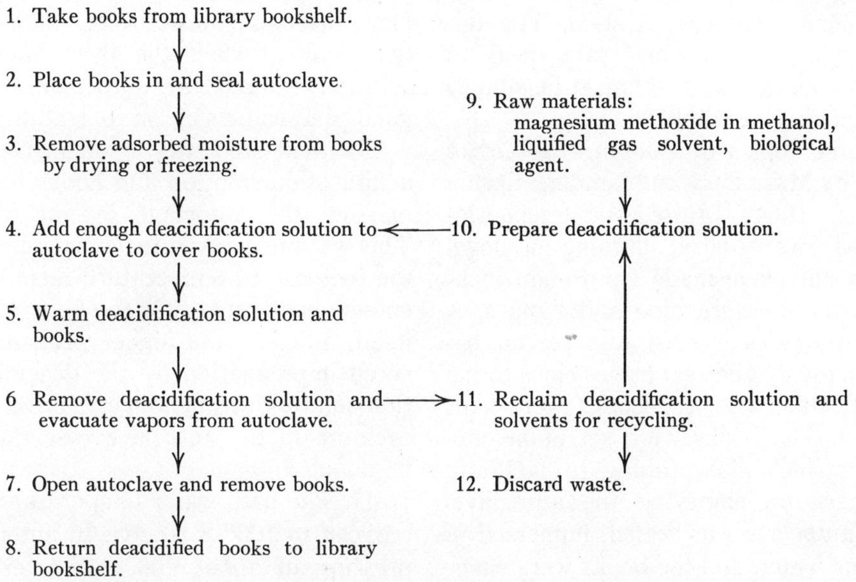
1. Take books from library bookshelf.
2. Place books in and seal autoclave.
3. Remove adsorbed moisture from books by drying or freezing.
4. Add enough deacidification solution to autoclave to cover books.
5. Warm deacidification solution and books.
6 Remove deacidification solution and evacuate vapors from autoclave.
7. Open autoclave and remove books.
8. Return deacidified books to library bookshelf.
9. Raw materials: magnesium methoxide in methanol, liquified gas solvent, biological agent.
10. Prepare deacidification solution.
11. Reclaim deacidification solution and solvents for recycling.
12. Discard waste.

FIG. 7.—Flow chart conception of whole-book deacidification

steps in the Chicago Process of deacidification for whole books. The essential steps of the deacidification treatment proper are noted, as well as the stages required to prepare, reclaim, make up, and recycle the deacidification solution. There has been no experimental work on reclaiming the solution, but there are no foreseeable difficulties in cleaning and recycling it. The importance of recycling the solution cannot be underestimated because the low-cost-per-unit concept of the Chicago Process requires an efficient recovery system. The following experiments and data speak to the commercial and technical feasibility of deacidifying whole books.

Three copies of *Cooking the Greek Way* by Maro Duncan (London: Spring Books, 1964 [printed in Czechoslovakia]), were placed standing top down in an autoclave made from eight-inch-diameter pressure pipe and flanges. A cotton wrapping cord was placed between the fly and text leaves close to the spine. Otherwise, the books were kept closed. The books were set upon one-quarter-inch glass tubing to facilitate drainage on emptying the autoclave. The autoclave was sealed, immersed in boiling water, and the books were vacuum dried for four hours at about five millimeters of mercury. Then, the autoclave was removed from the boiling water and allowed to cool overnight.

The next day the deacidification solution was prepared in a ten-pound propane bottle. First, 500 cubic centimeters of a 7 percent solution of magnesium methoxide in methanol were syphoned into the bottle. Then, the solution was diluted with ten pounds of chlorodifluoromethane (Freon 22, a liquefied refrigeration gas). The liquefied gas flows into the propane bottle more rapidly when the pressure in the propane bottle is substantially lower than the pressure in the refrigeration gas bottle. There was no suitable pump available, so the pressure differential was obtained through cooling the propane bottle by placing dry ice around it. A similar situation existed between the propane bottle and the autoclave. Consequently, the autoclave was cooled by packing it in dry ice and insulating it with a polyurethane foam pad and cotton toweling. The cooling caused a substantial pressure differential, and the deacidification solution flowed rapidly into the autoclave through its lower inlet. (This sudden cooling when the deacidification solution entered the autoclave was a good practical check on its stability.)

The next step was to warm the deacidification solution and books by immersing the autoclave in hot water. This warming served two purposes: (1) the increase in temperature introduced enough heat energy for the book to dry itself, and (2) the higher pressure insured impregnation by the deacidification solution throughout the book. The pressure in the autoclave rose rapidly to about 300 pounds per square inch (psi). The bath water temperature was reduced to 100° F to give an autoclave pressure of about 200 psi. After one hour of immersion, the autoclave was removed from the water bath. The deacidification solution was blown out of the autoclave through the lower outlet on the vessel and discarded. The top outlet was opened when only gas was exhausting from the lower outlet. About ten to fifteen minutes after opening the first valve, the autoclave lid was removed and the books were found to be substantially dry.

In a second test, three copies of *Cooking the Greek Way* were placed in the autoclave as above. This time, however, the adsorbed water was not removed from the books by drying. In this second test, the autoclave was packed in dry ice and the adsorbed water was frozen. The preparation and charging of the deacidification solution was accomplished as in the above test except that twelve pounds of dichlorodifluoromethane (Freon 12) was substituted for the chlorodifluoromethane. The deacidification solution and the books were warmed by squirting the autoclave first with cold and then with hot water. The pressure was about 150 psi and the temperature was about 100° F one hour after charging the deacidification solution. The autoclave was emptied and opened as before, and the books again were found to be substantially dry.

Before discussing the results, it is appropriate to consider why *Cooking the Greek Way* was selected for experimentation. The book was the right size for the autoclave, available in quantity, and inexpensive as a remnant, and it contained colored materials that were soluble in the solvents I wanted to use. These colored materials included blue dyestuffs in the paper, in the stain on the head margin, and in the printing ink, as well as a yellow-brown material in the binding, presumably the softener in the binding adhesive. Moreover, the paper was uncoated and had a fiber content of about 50 percent groundwood and 50 percent softwood sulfite.

The quantity of deacidification solution charged into the autoclave was controlled to fill the autoclave about half the height of the books undergoing treatment. Wetting the books halfway up is more informative than complete immersion. First, the liquid-gas interface is the point where the solvent is most likely to attack the book; and second, I wanted to know the degree to which the solution would wick up the leaves.

The drying under high vacuum caused some of the boards to warp, but the freezing appeared to have no effect. The drying action did not appear to embrittle the paper or otherwise work against its usability. The bowed boards straightened within a few days as they regained moisture from the air. The milk of magnesia powder was more tightly bound in the dried copy than in the frozen copy. The dried book had only a small quantity of powder deposited on its binding. Considerably more was deposited on the binding of the frozen copy. A cloud of powder came from the frozen books if they were opened and smartly clapped shut. No powder came from the dried book under similar conditions. There was little, if any, noticeable difference between the immersed and unimmersed portions of the leaves, and no trace of the liquid-gas interface line. The spines were straight, and the apparent loss of title legibility could easily be fixed with a thin coating of lacquer or varnish. (I believe that the bibliographic data on library books would be more legible and more durable after experiencing the Chicago Process than before.)

The books were standing in the autoclave top edge down in the deacidification solution. Some of the stain on the top edge was dissolved. There appeared to be no damage at the spine and no sign of any dissolved adhesives, etc. The back cover of the dried books did exhibit several faint yellowish marks, and one book had a light bluish streak on the endpaper. The books were a little bulkier after treatment than before, but this effect disappeared a day or so after the books were placed back on the shelves. The dyestuffs in the ink exhibited themselves as strike-through. In other words, the impression to the reader would be that the paper had less ability to hide the type face images on the verso of the pages. (Many ordinary books exhibit a greater degree of strike-through than I produced in *Cooking the Greek Way.*) There was some staining on a few leaves of the books, but it did not appear to be of a serious nature. My belief is that practically all library books could be deacidified in a pressure system and that the ordinary reader or librarian would be unable to tell they had been treated. In the other instances, I do not believe the usefulness of the book as an information source would be impaired. It is remarkable that a book composed of materials like those in *Cooking the Greek Way* was treated as has been described and that, for practical library purposes, no damage occurred.

The contact pH values at various positions on page 128 of an untreated copy of *Cooking the Greek Way* are compared in table 5 with pH values for identical positions in randomly selected copies of a dried and a frozen book from the preceding tests. The contact method of measuring pH is reviewed elsewhere [10;89, pp. 158–59] and has been found to give pH values comparable [12] with those obtained by the TAPPI cold extraction test [87]. The locations where measurements were made are described in table 5. The pH values for the paper in the untreated copy were 4.3 or 4.4 and indicate the paper would be impermanent. The top halves of the other two books were immersed during the treatments. The pH values for the immersed portion of the dried copy were 9.15, 9.8, and 9.05; at the margin of the nonimmersed end values were 7.8 and 7.2. The contact pH values for the frozen copy were 10.4, 10.5, and 10.3 in the immersed portion, and 7.55 and 5.59 at the margins of the nonimmersed end. The fact that some of the deacidification solution traveled vertically up the leaves by capillary action is important. This travel or wicking action verifies the stability and workability of the solution and, together with the pressures of impregnation, guarantees that the treatment solution reached the innermost parts of the book.

TABLE 5

CONTACT pH VALUES FOR PAGE 128 FROM TREATED AND UNTREATED COPIES OF *Cooking the Greek Way*

Contact pH Value at Position:	Untreated Copy	Dried and Deacidified Copy	Frozen and Deacidified Copy
In top margin at center of page	4.4	9.15	10.40
Near fore-edge margin, halfway down page	4.3	9.80	10.50
Near spine, halfway down page	4.3	9.05	10.30
Near fore-edge margin, at tail of page	4.3	7.80	7.55
Near spine, at tail of page	4.3	7.20	7.95

Figure 8 presents the results of an accelerated aging study on the stabilizing effect of these deacidification treatments. The same leaves from all three books were aged according to the TAPPI Standard Test [86], and the change in M.I.T. folding endurance value [87] was observed for the immersed portions of these leaves. Both deacidification treatments were effective in promoting the permanence of the treated books. However, the data are insufficient to decide whether the drying or the freezing method of removing moisture is preferable. I believe the more economic of the two methods should be selected but do not have sufficient data on which to make a decision at this time.

Deacidification is the basic tool of preservation work, but a deacidification treatment is no panacea. A more complete preservation program can justifiably be considered once deacidification is accomplished. In addition to nonaqueous deacidification, the Chicago Process will consider protection against living organisms, paper strengthening, and prolonged storage.

5. PROTECTION FROM LIVING ORGANISMS

The possibility of paper being attacked by living organisms increases as an acidic paper becomes moderately alkaline. A majority of fungi, insects, and rodents prefer to eat neutral or moderately alkaline paper. One consequence of book deacidification, if poor storage conditions exist, is the increased probability of attack by living organisms.

Protection against such attacks can be obtained simply and at practically no expense. A biostat or biocide can be deposited during the deacidification treatment. Commercially available mercuric and tin antibiological agents are soluble in organic solvents, compatible with alkoxides, benign at the required levels of dosage, and presumably effective for many years. The costs would be limited to the chemical itself and to the expense of maintaining the proper dosage level in the deacidification solution.

Two sets of books were prepared for exposure. One set used fifteen copies of the book entitled *The Italian Girl,* and the other used thirteen copies of *The*

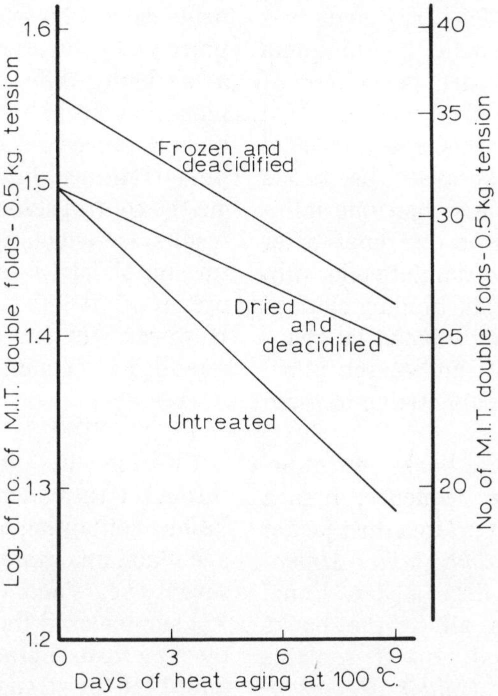

FIG. 8.—Effect of deacidification on the folding endurance of leaves from *Cooking the Greek Way*

Quiller Memorandum. Bis (tri-n-butyltin) oxide[4] was used as the biostat [90–98] in five of the copies from each set. The other copies acted as untreated controls or were treated with solvents or deacidified for purposes of evaluating interactions. The books were exposed to insect and fungus attack in Singapore for five months.[5] After their return, they were examined for insect attack at the Field Museum of Natural History, Chicago, Illinois.[6] The treatment was designed to impregnate the minimum usual dosage of 100 parts per million of bis (tri-n-butyltin) oxide. The actual dosage was below this recommended minimum dosage because the books were evacuated at less than one millimeter of mercury for one hour after drying in an effort to simulate poor production conditions. The binding cloth of these books contained substantial quantities of protein [99] and starch [100] and presumably was appetizing to fungi and insects.[7]

In Singapore, the books were arranged in alternate sequence, first a copy of *The Italian Girl* in a dust jacket and then a copy of *The Quiller Memorandum* without a dust jacket. Fungi attack occurred on all of the books which were exposed. Insect remains were found on *The Quiller Memorandum* copies, but there were no signs of insect attack. The remains of only one insect was found from all the copies of *The Italian Girl*. Again, there was no evidence of insect attack. This lack of insect attack is strange because fungi and insect attack normally occur together. The greatest fungi attack occurred on the deacidified copies without protection. The degree of attack was substantially less on the deacidified copies protected with bis (tri-n-butyltin) oxide.

The degree to which these results were a result of bis (tri-n-butyltin) oxide cannot be established because the untreated controls were not attacked in a markedly different pattern. The explanation probably is that the experimental procedure did not prevent the bis (tri-n-butyltin) oxide from protecting the control standards. I believe these results are encouraging, and the literature on bis (tri-n-butyltin) oxide is impressive [90–98; see also n. 4 above]. However, further study is necessary to establish a recommended procedure.

6. PAPER STRENGTHENING

Interest in strengthening paper through treatment with nonaqueous solutions containing a resin strengthening agent and an organic solvent began over seventy years ago. Grove [101, pp. 369–72] summarized the initial efforts made by American librarians between 1900 and 1918 to strengthen paper by dipping, spraying, or painting the paper with cellulose nitrate lacquers (Cellit or Zampone). Cellulose nitrate lacquers had poor qualities of permanence during the early twentieth century. The breakthrough in producing our *relatively* stable pyroxylin lacquers did not occur until 1927 [102, p. 214].

Gear [68, p. 293] relates that the Library of Congress and the National Bureau of Standards rejected immersion and spray treatment with cellulose acetate and nitrate resins in the early 1930s. They found that these cellulose

[4] M & T Chemicals, Inc., Rahway, N.J., publishes informative literature on "bioM&T TBTO," their bis (tri-n-butyltin) oxide.

[5] D. Koh, higher library officer of the National Library of Singapore, was responsible for testing in Singapore.

[6] R. L. Wenzel, curator of insects at the Field Museum of Natural History, Chicago, Ill., examined the books.

[7] W. A. Wozniak, chief chemist of the Chicago Paper Testing Laboratory, Chicago, Ill., tested the binding cloths for protein and starch.

ester resin coatings did not produce the degree of strengthening which they desired. Experimentation continued, but on lamination with cellulose acetate films. Recommendations were made in 1934, and in 1936 the National Archives established the first laminating operation. A mass production hydraulic press with a heated die was installed and remains in operation today. Barrow [103] was granted a patent for his contributions to lamination technology in 1942. Kathpalia [104] and Langwell [105–107] have proposed cold laminating processes. All of these laminating processes are efficient in strengthening single sheets, but they are not applicable to treating aggregates of single sheets like books.

L. Skřivánek, head of the Conservation and Restoration Department of the State Library of the Czechoslovak Socialist Republic in Prague, recently wrote to me giving a general description of a nonaqueous combination deacidifying, biocidal, and strengthening treatment. Complete details were not available because patent applications are pending on this process for treating whole books. One combination of ingredients for books published before 1900 consisted of magnesium acetate as the deacidification agent, a polyvinyl acetate copolymer as the resin strengthening agent, parachlormetacresole as the biocidal agent, and a lower aliphatic alcohol and butylaldehyde as the solvent components. The immersion procedure appeared straightforward, but the drying operations suggest that individual attention might be required for many books. This would work against mechanization of the process. The testing data and methodology were not provided, and I believe more information is essential before the process can be recommended.

The leaves of books can be strengthened using the same equipment and in much the same way as deacidification takes place in the Chicago Process. Acrylic resins are considered stable resin strengthening agents and are soluble in many organic solvents. I made a number of experiments with different resins dissolved in liquified gas solvents. These strengthening solutions were compounded to deposit 3–5 percent of the resin by weight throughout the treated book. In one experiment, I treated copies of *Cooking the Greek Way* with a 75:25 ratio of low-molecular-weight acrylic resin and ethyl hydroxyethyl cellulose. The M.I.T. folding endurance strength (one kilogram tension) [85] increased from 7.9 folds to 32.3 folds in the machine direction and from 2.8 to 9.1 in the cross direction after deacidification and strengthening. After heat aging under dry ventilated conditions at 105° C for five days [86], the untreated leaves had a folding endurance of 5.6 while the treated leaves had a value of 7.6 in the machine direction. The cross-machine values were 2.2 and 5.0, respectively. The rather sharp decrease in folding endurance retention on aging could be explained by (1) the poor heat stability of the plasticizer, ethyl hydroxyethyl cellulose, or by (2) the 50 percent groundwood content in the paper's furnish.

The leaves in the strengthened books were not bonded together because the escaping gases kept them apart as the book dried and the resin was deposited. After treatment, the paper had a character somewhat similar to that of a sheet heavily sized with gelatin.

This strengthening process is presently envisioned as applicable to books whose paper is not embrittled. Papers which snap or break when they are bent or creased require more support, such as that provided by tissue reinforcement in lamination [103]. The sizing action of resin strengthening agents and a presumable drop in the rate of acidic gas pickup are useful fringe benefits of this strengthening treatment.

7. PROLONGED STORAGE

The final stage of the Chicago Process is conceived as an inexpensive means of providing superior storage conditions over prolonged periods of time. The idea is to store infrequently used books as individual units in cheap, transparent, and disposable containers. The book itself will provide the structure of the unit. The container will consist simply of a clear plastic film wrapped around the book and heat sealed. Cellulose acetate laminating film, polyethylene film, and polyester-polyethelene laminates have properties worthy of consideration.

The interested reader can identify the book number and/or title through the transparent film before breaking the seal, and a new wrapper can easily be applied after the book is used. The plastic film will protect the book from atmospheric pollution, dust and dirt, accidental water damage, and the mechanical wear and tear caused by fluctuations in relative humidity. Chemicals could be incorporated into the plastic film during its manufacture to provide protection against biological and photochemical attack.

8. SUMMARY

In this presentation, I have attempted to outline the problems involved in preserving library materials, to describe an ideal preservation program, to review the several kinds of deacidification treatments which have been developed, and to describe in more detail the nonaqueous deacidification treatment that I have developed in Chicago. In addition, I have tried to describe briefly my ideas about protecting books from fungi, insects, and rodents; about strengthening books; and about storing little-used books in research libraries.

REFERENCES

1. Cerny, J. *Late Rameoside Letters.* Biblioteca Aegyptica, vol. 9. Brussels: Fondation égyptologique Reine Elizabeth, 1939. (Unpublished translation by K. Baer, Oriental Institute, University of Chicago.)
2. Wente, E. F., trans. *Late Rameoside Letters.* Oriental Institute Studies in Ancient Oriental Civilization. Chicago: University of Chicago Press, 1967.
3. Tsien, T. H. *Written on Bamboo and Silk: The Beginnings of Chinese Books and Inscriptions.* University of Chicago Studies in Library Science. Chicago: University of Chicago Press, 1962.
4. Shakespeare, William. *The Works of Shakespeare,* edited by W. A. Wright. 2d ed. vol. 9. London: MacMillan & Co., 1893.
5. Voorn, H. "In Search of New Raw Materials." *Paper Maker* (U.S.) 21 (September 1952):1–14.
6. Chapman, J. A. "An Enquiry into the Causes of the Perishing of Paper." *Calcutta Review,* n.s. (July 1919), pp. 301–7.
7. Chapman, J. A. "The Perishing of Paper, II." *Calcutta Review,* n.s. (July 1920), pp. 233–46.
8. Chapman, J. A. "The Imperial Library, Past and Future." *Calcutta Review,* 3d ser. 2 (March 1922):447–57.
9. American Pulp and Paper Association. *The Dictionary of Paper including Pulp, Paperboard, Paper Properties, and Related Papermaking Terms.* 3d ed. New York: American Pulp & Paper Association, 1965.
10. Browning, B. L. "The Nature of Paper." *Library Quarterly* 40 (January 1970): 18–38.

11. Wessel, C. J. "Environmental Factors Affecting the Permanence of Library Materials." *Library Quarterly* 40 (January 1970):39–84.
12. Smith, R. D. "A Comparison of Paper in Identical Copies of Books from the Lawrence University, the Newberry, and the New York Public Libraries." Manuscript. June 24, 1969. Available from author.
13. Kathpalia, Y. P. "Deterioration and Conservation of Paper. IV. Neutralization." *Indian Pulp and Paper* 17 (October 1962):245–51.
14. Wilson, W. K. "Discussion of New Approaches to Preservation." *Library Quarterly* 40 (January 1970):171–75.
15. Wilson, W. K., and Hebert, R. L. "Evaluation of the Stability of Record Papers." *TAPPI* 52 (August 1969):1523–29.
16. Barry, V. C., and Mitchell, P. W. D. "Properties of Periodate-oxidized Polysaccharides. I. The Preparation of Polymeric Substances Containing Nitrogen from Oxidized Starches." *Journal of the Chemical Society*, pt. 4 (1953), pp. 3610–12.
17. Barry, V. C., and Mitchell, P. W. D. "Properties of Periodate-oxidized Polysaccharides. II. The Structure of Some Nitrogen-containing Polymers." *Journal of the Chemical Society*, pt. 4 (1953), pp. 3631–35.
18. Benn, M. H., and Jones, A. S. "Reaction of Aldoses with Urea." *Chemistry and Industry*, August 1, 1959, pp. 997–98.
19. Burton, H. S.; McWeeny, D. J.; and Biltcliffe, D. O. "Sulfur Dioxide and Ketose-Amino Reactions." *Chemistry and Industry*, April 27, 1963, pp. 693-95.
20. Corbi, J. C. "Oxidation of Cellulose and Color Reversion." Ph.D. diss., University of Toronto, 1963. For abstract, see *Dissertation Abstracts* 3 (September 1964): 1561.
21. Corbi, J. C., and Rapson, W. H. "Color Reversion of Nitrogen Dioxide-oxidized Cellulose." *Pulp and Paper Magazine of Canada* 65 (November 1964):T467–72.
22. Danehy, J. P., and Pigman, W. W. "Reactions between Sugars and Nitrogenous Compounds and Their Relationship to Certain Food Problems." *Advances in Food Research* 3 (1951):241–90.
23. Fletcher, A. P.; Marks, G. S.; Marshall, R. D.; and Neuberger, A. "Carbohydrates in Protein. V. Procedures for the Isolation of Glycopeptides from Hen's Egg Albumin and Their Oxidation by Periodate." *Biochemical Journal* 87 (May 1963):265–73.
24. Lewis, V. M.; Esselen, W. B., Jr.; and Fellers, C. R. "Nonenzymatic Browning of Foodstuffs: Production of Carbon Dioxide." *Industrial and Engineering Chemistry* 41 (November 1949):2587–91.
25. Lewis, V. M.; Esselen, W. G., Jr.; and Fellers, C. R. "Nonenzymatic Browning of Foodstuffs: Nitrogen-free Carboxylic Acids in the Browning Reaction." *Industrial and Engineering Chemistry* 41 (November 1949):2591–94.
26. Lewis, V. M., and Lea, C. H. "A Note on the Relative Rates of Reaction of Several Reducing Sugars and Sugar Derivatives with Casein." *Biochimica et Biophysica Acta* 4 (February 1950): 532–34.
27. Luner, P. "Paper Permanence." *TAPPI* 52 (May 1969):796–805.
28. Ogate, Y.; Kawasaka, A.; and Okumura, N. "Kinetics of the Condensation of Urea with Acetaldehyde." *Journal of Organic Chemistry* 30 (May 1965): 1636–39.
29. Rapson, W. H., and Hakim, K. A. "Carbonyl Groups in Cellulose and Colour Reversion." *Pulp and Paper Magazine of Canada* 58 (July 1957):151–57.
30. Rapson, W. H.; Anderson, C. B.; and King, G. F. "Carbonyl Groups in Cellulose and Color Reversion. 2. Hypochlorite Bleaching and Color Reversion." *TAPPI* 41 (August 1958):442–47.
31. Rapson, W. H., and Corbi, J. C. "Colour Reversion Caused by Degradation Products of Oxidized Cellulose." *Proceedings of the Canadian Wood Chemistry Symposium* 1 (September 1963):27–40.
32. Rapson, W. H., and Corbi, J. C. "Colour Reversion Caused by Degradation Products of Oxidized Cellulose." *Pulp and Paper Magazine of Canada* 65 (November 1964):T459–66.
33. Spinner, I. H. "Brightness Reversion: A Critical Review with Suggestions for Further Research." *TAPPI* 65 (June 1962):495–514.
34. Smith, R. D. "Paper Deacidification: A Preliminary Report." *Library Quarterly* 36 (October 1966): 273–92.

35. Wachter, A., and Skei, T. *Vapor-Phase Corrosion Inhibition with a Mixture of Inhibitors.* U. S. Patent no. 2,711,360. Washington, D.C.: Patent Office, June 21, 1955.

36. Hill, R. O., Jr. "Cellulose Esters, Organic." *Encyclopedia of Polymer Science and Technology: Plastics, Resins, Rubbers, and Fibers.* Vol. 3. New York: Interscience Publishers, 1965.

37. Sadler, F. S. *Thermally Stabilized Cellulose Materials for Electrical Insulation.* U.S. Patent no. 3,135,627. Washington D.C.: Patent Office, June 2, 1964.

38. Millington, J. E. *Thermostable Dielectric Material.* U.S. Patent no. 3,316,178. Washington D.C.: Patent Office, April 25, 1967.

39. Gaines, R. C. "An Investigation into the Ability of Morpholine to Stabilize Cellulose against Heat." Manuscript. March 14, 1966. Available at the Institute of Paper Chemistry, Appleton, Wis.

40. Volgenau, L. "The Effect of Amines on the Thermal Stability of Cellulose." Manuscript. March 12, 1965. Available at the Institute of Paper Chemistry, Appleton, Wis.

41. Langwell, W. H. "The Permanence of Papers." *British Paper and Board Makers' Association, Technical Section: Proceedings* 29 (February 1952): 21–82.

42. Langwell, W. H. "The Vapour Phase Deacidification of Books and Documents." *Journal of the Society of Archivists* 3 (April 1966):137–38.

43. Ede, J. R., and Langwell, W. H. "Sulphur Dioxide and Vapour Phase Deacidification." In *1967 London Conference on Museum Climatology,* edited by G. Thomson. London: International Institute for Conservation of Historic and Artistic Works, 1968.

44. Process Materials Corporation. *Vapor Phase Deacidification of Books and Documents (Langwell Method).* Carlstadt, N.J.: Process Materials Corp., 1968.

45. DuBois, K. P. "Cyclohexylamine." In *Nonnutritive Sweeteners: An Interim Report to the U.S. Food and Drug Administration, Department of Health, Education, and Welfare.* Washington, D.C.: Ad hoc Committee on Nonnutritive Sweeteners, National Academy of Sciences—National Research Council, 1968.

46. Stecher, P. G. *The Merck Index of Chemicals and Drugs.* 8th ed. Rahway, N.J.: Merck & Co., 1968.

47. Sax. N. I. *Dangerous Properties of Industrial Materials.* 3d ed. New York: Reinhold Book Co., 1968.

48. "Toxicology. HEW Bans the Cyclamates." *Time,* October 24, 1969, pp. 84–85.

49. Callaway, S., and Crichton, D. *Toxic Effects of Cyclohexylamine Carbonate* (Ptn/CQ.1101/476/56). Porton: Royal Air Force, 1956.

50. Lemonova, G. V. "Toxicity of Cyclohexylamine and Dicyclohexylamine." *Gigiena Truda i Professional'nye Zabolevaniya* 7 (1961):5156. English translation available in *Federation Proceedings: Translation Supplement* 24 (January-February 1965): T96–98.

51. Lucas, A. *Ancient Egyptian Materials and Industries.* 3d ed., rev. London: Edward Arnold & Co., 1948.

52. Plenderleith, H. J. *The Conservation of Antiquities and Works of Art: Treatment, Repair, and Restoration.* London: Oxford University Press, 1966.

53. Barrow, W. J. *Manuscripts and Documents: Their Deterioration and Restoration.* Charlottesville: University of Virginia Press, 1955.

54. Thomas, J. J. "Alkaline Printing Papers: Promise and Performance." *Library Quarterly* 40 (January 1970):99–107.

55. Byrne, J., and Weiner, J. *Permanence.* Institute of Paper Chemistry Bibliographic Series no. 213. Appleton, Wis.: Institute of Paper Chemistry, 1964.

56. Kantrowitz, M. S.; Spencer, E. W.; and Simmons, R. H. *Permanence and Durability of Paper: An Annotated Bibliography of the Technical Literature from 1885 A.D. to 1939 A.D.* U.S. Government Printing Office Technical Bulletin no. 22. Washington, D.C.: Government Printing Office, 1940.

57. Rafton, H. R. *Paper Manufacture.* U.S. Patent no. 2,115,747. Washington, D.C.: Patent Office, May 3, 1938. Rafsky, H. R. (former name of H. R. Rafton). *White Pigment,* description of early alkaline-filled paper. U.S. Patent no. 1,415,391. Washington, D.C.: Patent Office, May 9, 1922. Rafsky, H. R. *Paper,*

description of early alkaline-filled paper. U.S. Patent no. 1,595,416. Washington, D.C.: Patent Office, August 10, 1926.
58. Rawling, F. G. *Method of Producing Sized Papers*. U.S. Patent no. 2,114,809. Washington, D.C.: Patent Office, April 19, 1938.
59. Reichardt, G. "The Durability of Paper." *Library Quarterly* 8 (October 1938): 510–20.
60. Kimberly, A. E., and Scribner, B. W. *Summary Report of National Bureau of Standards Research on Preservation of Records*. U.S. National Bureau of Standards Miscellaneous Publication M154. Washington. D.C.: Government Printing Office, 1937.
61. Wilkie, J. B. "Laundry 'Winter Damage.'" *U.S. Bureau Of Standards Journal of Research* 6 (April 1931):593–602.
62. Smith, R. D. "Paper Permanence as a Consequence of pH and Storage Conditions." *Library Quarterly* 39 (April 1969):153–95.
63. Schierholtz, O. J. *Process for the Chemical Stabilization of Paper and Product*. U.S. Patent no. 2,033,452. Washington, D.C.: Patent Office, March 10, 1936. The British Patent was issued to the Ontario Research Foundation. *Improvements in Processes for the Chemical Stabilization of Paper and Product*. Patent no. 443,534. London: His Majesty's Stationery Office, March 2, 1936.
64. Barrow, W. J. "Deacidification and Lamination of Deteriorated Documents, 1938–63." *American Archivist* 28 (April 1965):285–90.
65. Church, R. W., ed. *Deterioration of Book Stock: Causes and Remedies, Two Studies on the Permanence of Book Paper Conducted by W. J. Barrow*. Virginia State Library Publication no. 10. Richmond: Virginia State Library, 1959.
66. Barrow, W. J. *The Barrow Method of Restoring Deteriorated Documents*. Richmond, Va.: W. J. Barrow, 1965.
67. Barrow, W. J. *Procedures and Equipment Used in the Barrow Method of Restoring Manuscripts and Documents*. Richmond, Va.: W. J. Barrow, 1965.
68. Gear, J. L. "Lamination after 30 Years: Record and Prospect." *American Archivist* 28 (April 1965):293–97.
69. W. J. Barrow Research Laboratory. *Permanence/Durability of the Book*. Vol. 3. *Spray Deacidification*. Richmond, Va.: W. J. Barrow Research Laboratory, 1964.
70. W. J. Barrow Research Laboratory. *Permanence/Durability of the Book*. Vol. 5. *Strength and Other Characteristics of Book Papers 1800–1899*. Richmond, Va.: W. J. Barrow Research Laboratory, 1967.
71. Pravilova, T. A., and Istrubsina, T. V. "Preservation of Paper Documents by the Buffering Method." In *Preservation of Documents and Papers*, edited by D. M. Flyate and translated by J. Schmorack. Jerusalem: Israel Program for Scientific Translations, 1968. Available from U.S. Department of Commerce, Clearinghouse for Federal Scientific and Technical Information, Springfield, Va., as TT 67-51400, and in *Chemical Abstracts* 62 (1965):2911.
72. "Report of the Committee for Paper Problems." *Bulletin of the American Group—The International Institute for Conservation of Historic and Artistic Works* 9 (October 1968):29–30.
73. Langwell, W. H. "Methods of Deacidifying Paper." *Journal of the Society of Archivists* 3 (April 1969):491–94.
74. Baynes-Cope, A. D. "The Nonaqueous Deacidification of Documents." *Restaurator* 1 (1969):2–9.
75. Anderson, A. R., and Thomas, I. M. "Alkoxides, Metal." In *Encyclopedia of Chemical Technology,* edited by R. E. Kirk and D. E. Othmer. Vol. 1. 2d ed. New York: John Wiley & Sons, 1963.
76. Bradley, D. C. "Metal Alkoxides." In *Metal-organic Compounds*. American Chemical Society Advances in Chemistry Series no. 23. Washington, D.C.: American Chemical Society, 1959.
77. Browning, B. L. *Methods of Wood Chemistry* Vol. 1. New York: Interscience Publishers, 1967.
78. Cohen, C. A. *Process for Producing Magnesium Alcoholates*. U.S. Patent no. 2,287,088. Washington, D.C.: Patent Office, June 23, 1942.
79. Hunter, E. A. *Preparation of Magnesia*. U.S. Patent no. 2,570,058. Washington, D.C.: Patent Office, October 2, 1951.
80. Kimberlin, C. N. *Process for Producing Magnesia*. U.S. Patent no. 2,593,314.

Washington, D.C.: Patent Office, April 15, 1952.

81. Lund, H., and Bjerrum, J. "Eine einfache Methode zur Darstellung wasser-freier Allkohole." *Berichte der Deutchen Chemischen Gesellschaft* 1, pt. B (1931): 210–13.

82. Suchoff, L. A. *Method of Forming an Adherent Film of Magnesium Oxide.* U.S. Patent no. 2,796,364. Washington, D.C.: Patent Office, June 18, 1957.

83. Richter, G. A. "Relative Permanence of Papers Exposed to Sunlight. II." *Industrial and Engineering Chemistry* 27 (April 1935):432–39.

84. Technical Association of the Pulp and Paper Industry. *TAPPI Standard Test T 402 m-49: Conditioning Paper and Paperboard for Testing.* New York: Technical Association of the Pulp & Paper Industry, 1949.

85. Technical Association of the Pulp and Paper Industry. *TAPPI Standard Test T 423 m-50: Folding Endurance of Paper.* New York: Technical Association of the Pulp & Paper Industry, 1950.

86. Technical Association of the Pulp and Paper Industry. *TAPPI Standard Test T 453 ts-63: Relative Stability of Paper (by Effect of Heat on Folding Endurance).* New York: Technical Association of the Pulp & Paper Industry, 1963.

87. Technical Association of the Pulp and Paper Industry. *TAPPI Standard Test T 509 su-68: Hydrogen Ion Concentration (pH) of Paper Extracts—Cold Extraction.* New York: Technical Association of the Pulp & Paper Industry, 1968.

88. Brownlee, K. A. *Statistical Theory and Methodology in Science and Engineering.* 2d ed. New York: John Wiley & Sons, 1965.

89. Browning, B. L. *Analysis of Paper.* New York: Marcel Dekker, Inc., 1969.

90. "A Review of Organotin Compounds in the Control of Pests." *Tin and Its Uses: Quarterly Journal of the Tin Research Institute* 66 (1965):1–5.

91. Arnold, M. H. M., and Clarke, H. J. "The Evaluation of Some Fungistats for Paint." *Journal of Oil and Colour Chemists' Association* 39 (December 1956):900–908.

92. Blum, M. S., and Bower, F. A. "The Evaluation of Triethyl Tin Hydroxide and Its Esters as Insecticides." *Journal of Economic Entomology* 50 (February 1957):84–86.

93. Negherbon, W. O. "Triethyl Tin Hydroxide and Its Esters; Insecticidal Activity." In *Handbook of Toxicology.* Vol. 3. *Insecticides.* Philadelphia: W. B. Saunders Co., 1959.

94. Fahlstrom, G. B. "Organo-Tin Compounds: Evaluation of Preservative Properties by Soil-Block Techniques." *Journal of American Wood-Preservers' Association* 54 (1958):178–84.

95. Hartmann, E.; Hardtmann, M.; and Kümmel, P. *Process for Protecting Wool, Fur, Rugs, and the Like against the Attack of Moths and Products Thereof.* U.S. Patent no. 1,744,633. Washington, D.C.: Patent Office, January 21, 1930.

96. Hirshland, H. E., and Banks, C. K. "Organotin Compounds." In *Metal-Organic Compounds.* American Chemical Society Advances in Chemistry Series no. 23. Washington, D.C.: American Chemical Society, 1959.

97. Ingham, R. K.; Rosenberg, S. D.; and Gilman, H. "Organotin Compounds." *Chemical Reviews* 60 (October 1960): 459–539.

98. Lewis, W. R., and Hedges, E. S. "Applications of Organotin Compounds." In *Metal-organic Compounds.* American Chemical Society Advances in Chemistry Series no. 23. Washington, D.C.: American Chemical Society, 1959.

99. Technical Association of the Pulp and Paper Industry. *TAPPI Standard Test T 417 os-68: Proteinaceous Nitrogenous Materials in Paper (Qualitative).* New York: Technical Association of the Pulp & Paper Industry, 1968.

100. Technical Association of the Pulp and Paper Industry. *TAPPI Standard Test T 419 su-68: Starch in Paper.* New York: Technical Association of the Pulp & Paper Industry, 1968.

101. Grove, L. E. "Paper Deterioration—an Old Story." *College and Research Libraries* 25 (September 1964):365–74.

102. Haynes, W. *Cellulose: The Chemical That Grows.* New York: Doubleday & Co., 1953.

103. Barrow, W. J. *Method for Preserving Documents and the Like.* U.S. Patent no. 2,301,966. Washington, D.C.: Patent Office, November 17, 1942.

104. Kathpalia, Y. "Hand Lamination with Cellulose Acetate." *American Archivist* 21 (July 1958):271–74.
105. Langwell, W. H. "The Postlip Duplex Lamination Processes." *Journal of the Society of Archivists* 2 (October 1964): 471–76.
106. Langwell, W. H. *Improvements in or Relating to the Preservation of Documents in Storage.* Great Britain Patent no. 1,000,981. London: Her Majesty's Stationery Office, October 22, 1965.
107. Langwell, W. H. "Recent Developments in Postlip Lamination Processes." *Journal of the Society of Archivists* 3 (April 1966):360–61.

DISCUSSION

WILLIAM K. WILSON

Records research in the last few years has been on the upswing and is being conducted in many laboratories over the world. I am aware of work in progress at the following institutions: (1) Graduate Library School, the University of Chicago; (2) the Institute of Paper Chemistry, Appleton, Wisconsin; (3) W. J. Barrow Research Laboratory, Richmond, Virginia; (4) British Museum Research Laboratory, London; (5) Biblioteca Nazionale Centrale, Florence; (6) Empire State Paper Research Institute, Syracuse; (7) institutions in Poland, Rumania, and Russia; (8) Imperial College, London; (9) Timber Research Unit, Council for Scientific and Industrial Research, Pretoria, South Africa; and (10) U.S. National Bureau of Standards, Washington, D.C.

Two journals devoted to records preservation are (1) *Restaurator,* edited by Poul Christiansen, University Library, Copenhagen, Denmark, and (2) *Mitteilungen der Internationalen Arbeitsgemeinschaft der Archiv-, Bibliotheks-, und Graphik-Restauratoren,* Freiburg im Breslau, West Germany.

During a recent discussion of research on the stability of paper and the preservation of records, it was pointed out that the records of the future are not likely to be made on paper. This certainly is partly true, as many record materials other than paper are in use today. The production of printing and writing papers has increased steadily, and its growth rate has not seemed to reflect the impact of these newer materials. The annual need for about 15 million tons of printing and writing paper is not likely to disappear overnight.

Now I should like to make some remarks concerning the data Smith presented in his paper and to discuss some implications of the data, and where he might go from here.

Smith has presented data showing that nonaqueous deacidification is effective on single sheets of unprinted book paper. These data are convincing.

He has shown that books can be deacidified by a nonaqueous procedure in a pressure system. The data from these tests, while indicating that the procedure was effective, are limited, as he restricted his work to one title that did not degrade as rapidly as expected. Further work with a more acidic book, including a comparison with an aqueous deacidification procedure, might be desirable.

Assuming that this qualification is met or that one accepts his work on single sheets as meeting the need for comparison, the next step would be to design a pilot apparatus, similar to that which might be used in a library, in order to develop information on: (1) effectiveness of various solvent systems, (2) optimum time of treatment, (3) cost per unit of deacidified material, (4) effect of solvents on various materials used in books, and (5) methods for recovering and recycling solvents.

The design, construction, and testing of a pilot apparatus is not a small task. It is difficult to set precise time limits on this kind of investigation because all of the problems cannot be anticipated, and Smith will probably want to evaluate a variety of treatment procedures. A nonaqueous pressure system should be useful for the mass-production deacidification of archival and library materials.

I should like to offer the following as *opinions:*

1. Any problems that might occur should develop from the solvent and not from the magnesium methoxide. The latter would end up as magnesium carbonate in the paper. Some of the same types of solvents that Smith used are recommended for cleaning of documents.

2. Any difficulties would be likely to occur immediately and not a year or more later.

3. Many sizing materials would be soluble.

4. A water deacidification method might be preferable in those cases where the paper must be wet anyway for cleaning, bleaching, or repair.

5. Although I feel that moisture should play a greater part in a laboratory aging method for paper, it is very unlikely that the use of a method involving moisture would have resulted in different conclusions. Smith used a standard method, and indeed he would be open to criticism if he had not.

6. Humidity cycling (95 percent, 11 percent and then 50 percent relative humidity) is a preferred procedure prior to physical testing. Smith has utilized this technique in his more rigorous work.

Smith's study of aqueous deacidification methods is timely, and I hope this work will be pursued. Most procedures, I believe, consume entirely too much time. Some data obtained about two years ago indicate that a major part of the pick-up of magnesium bicarbonate occurs in the first five minutes. If this is true for most papers, soaking time could be drastically reduced. This may be academic, as the time of soaking may not be the rate-determining step in the procedure. As part of the overall study, boundary conditions and preferred procedures should be worked out for all methods of deacidification. Much of this information is available and waiting to be assembled.

Smith has found differences in performance of several of the deacidified papers with time of aging. Although these differences are real, I doubt if they are significant. I should prefer to lump the deacidified papers together and conclude that, in the absence of an exhaustive study of deacidification methods, all of them appear to serve the purpose. The variables are endless, and we do not have all of the information.

Smith would have a more dramatic story to tell if he had used papers that were more acidic. He proved his point but made his task a little more difficult.

Presumably it will be desirable to dry paper to a low moisture content prior to *nonaqueous* deacidification. Paper is more susceptible to damage from handling at low moisture contents because it is less flexible. This is a matter of degree rather than kind, but paper that already is weak must be handled very carefully. During *aqueous* deacidification the wetted paper retains only a small fraction of its dry strength and is even more susceptible to damage from handling.

The heats of vaporization of the chlorofluorohydrocarbon solvents are low enough that their removal from paper should be easy and economical. The heat of vaporization of water is almost 600 calories per gram (2.5 megajoules per kilogram), methyl alcohol requires 263 calories per gram (1.10 megajoules per kilogram), and the chlorofluorohydrocarbon solvents range from thirty-five to fifty-six calories per gram (0.15–0.23 megajoules).

Now I should like to leave Smith's paper and make a few remarks concerning research on preservation of records in general.

The first point I wish to emphasize is that we really do not understand everything that happens when a sheet of paper deteriorates. Some of the possibilities have been discussed by Luner [1].

The second point is that the evaluation of materials and processes should be done on a continuing basis. New materials and new processes are constantly appearing on the market. A prime example is the revolution that has occurred in the past twenty years, or even in the past ten years, in office copying machines.

The third point is that cooperation is needed among manufacturers, research laboratories, libraries, printers, and publishers. An excellent example of informal cooperation is Smith's work. The University of Chicago, the Institute of Paper Chemistry, the Council on Library Resources, Inc., and the Chicago Testing Laboratory, as well as industry and overseas institutions, have contributed to his research.

The fourth point is that specifications for stable papers are needed. Manufacturers and consumers, with specifications, can communicate in quantitative language.

Now I should like to make a few comments concerning accelerated or laboratory aging. Laboratory aging represents a compromise, and we should never expect the full story from any accelerated aging procedure. However, this is the only practical approach to evaluating the relative stability of various materials.

How does one select samples of paper for aging studies? It one writes down all of the variables, a program of such magnitude emerges that it would require a staff of ten people working for the next ten years. In the meantime, newer materials would be on the market, and modifications in the manufacture of the papers being studied might have occurred.

Smith mentioned that laboratory aging had indicated that sodium bicarbonate was not a good material for deacidification. He also pointed out that sodium bicarbonate apparently had come into contact with cloth in which some mummies were wrapped, and after several thousand years this cloth was still in excellent condition. This is an example of a material that performed well in normal aging but not in accelerated aging. Situations like this call for the utmost in knowledge and judgement in order to avoid errors.

Laboratory aging methods must be developed to suit the material. Several years ago one of my colleagues and I developed the information necessary to write specifications for a stable laminating film formulated from cellulose acetate [2]. We concentrated on oxidative degradation, as cellulose acetate is degraded principally by an oxidation process. At the end of an induction period during which little measurable degradation occurs, the degradation

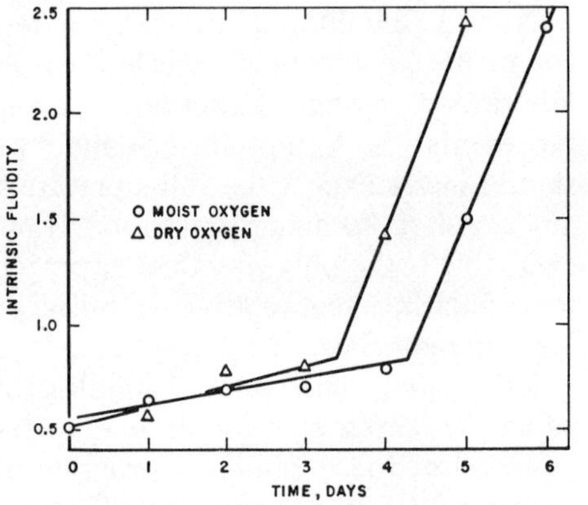

FIG. 1.—Degradation of a plasticized cellulose acetate film (one mil) in moist and dry oxygen at 110° C.

rate greately increases. Data on the degradation of film aged in moist oxygen and in dry oxygen at 124° C are plotted in figure 1 [2]. This plot shows why one should not rely on a one-time one-temperature aging method. A three-day test would show little difference between the two aging conditions, but a four-day test would indicate that dry oxygen caused much more degradation than moist oxygen.

Different papers may react differently with respect to additives that contribute to the bonding of the fibers. One additive might be susceptible to oxidative degradation but not to hydrolytic degradation. Another additive might be susceptible to hydrolytic degradation but not to oxidative degradation.

One of the best ways to obtain information on stability is to examine the characteristics of an artifact that has survived for a long time. Hanson's work at the Institute of Paper Chemistry in the late thirties was a very significant contribution in this area [3].

Numerous studies have shown that there is a correlation between pH and stability, but some examples have been selected to show that there are exceptions to this relationship. The pH of these examples was measured according to the TAPPI cold extraction procedure [4]. Data on the decrease in folding endurance of four papers during aging at 90° C and 50 percent relative humidity and plotted in figure 2.

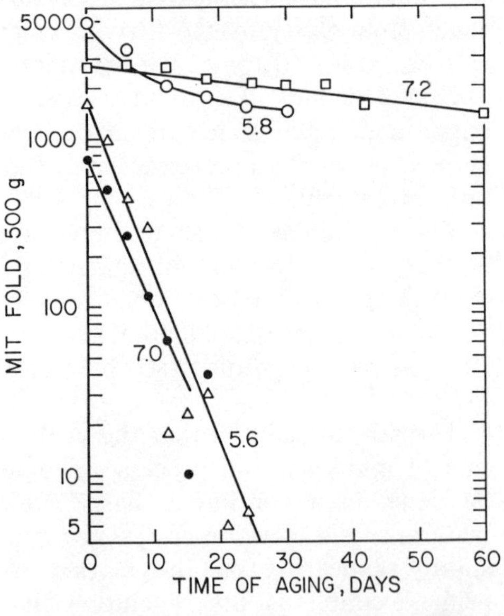

FIG. 2.—Change in machine-direction folding endurance (M.I.T., 500 grams tension) with time of aging at 90° C and 50 percent relative humidity; pH values, TAPPI Standard T 509, are indicated on plots.

The papers with pH values of 5.6 and 5.8, respectively, have the same fiber furnish but degrade at greatly different rates. These two papers were sized differently, and the sizing materials apparently affected the rates of degradation differently. This difference in rate of deterioration or the stability of the paper with a pH of 5.8 would not be anticipated on the basis of a knowledge of pH alone. The paper with a pH of 7.2 contains an alkaline filler, and the paper with a pH of 7.0 is an acid paper with an alkaline coating. Therefore, although there is a correlation between pH and stability, these data show that pH alone is not the final answer.

Data on the change in folding endurance with time of aging at 90° C and 50 percent relative humidity of a group of manifold papers are plotted in figure 3. Number 104 is an alkaline paper, number 107 is a neutral paper, and the others are acid papers. As expected, the rate of degradation of number 104 is very low. The rate of degradation of number 107 is about what one would expect in relation to the alkaline paper and the acid papers. There is some indication that the rate of degradation of number 107 increases with time, but it is possible that this increase would not occur during normal aging. This may be similar to the situation mentioned earlier where sodium bicarbonate appeared to contribute to stability during normal aging but did not perform well during laboratory aging. These examples show that laboratory aging data must be interpreted carefully.

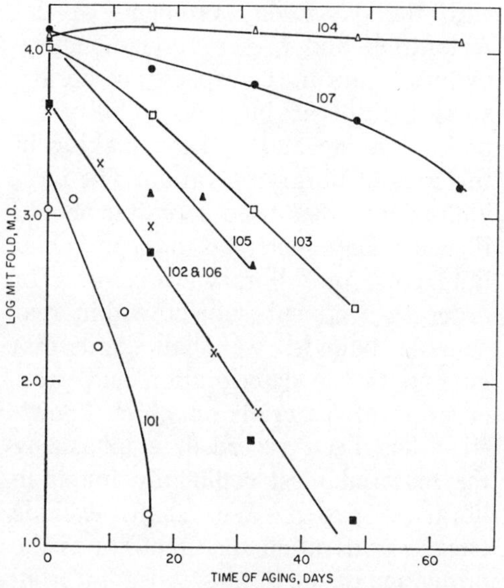

FIG. 3.—Changes in machine-direction folding endurance (M.I.T., 500 grams tension) with time of aging at 90° C and 50 percent relative humidity of a group of manifold papers.

REFERENCES

1. Luner, Philip. "Paper Permanence." *TAPPI* 52 (February 1969):796–803.
2. Wilson, W. K., and Forshee, B. W. *Preservation of Documents by Lamination.* U.S. National Bureau of Standards Monograph no. 5. Washington, D.C.: Government Printing Office, 1959.
3. Hansen, Fred S. "Resistance of Paper to Natural Aging." *Paper Industry and Paper World* 20 (February 1939):1157–63.
4. Technical Association of the Pulp and Paper Industry. *TAPPI Standard Test T509 su-68: Hydrogen Ion Concentration (pH) of Paper Extracts—Cold Extraction* New York: Technical Association of the Pulp Industry, 1968.

THE LIBRARIAN AS CONSERVATOR

JAMES W. HENDERSON AND ROBERT G. KRUPP

We have been asked to consider the librarian as conservator, not in the role of specialist or technician dealing with the day-to-day problems of deterioration and preservation of libary materials, but in the capacity of library administrator having responsibility for policy making and decision making in this area of library operation. The term "librarian" when used hereafter should therefore be understood to mean "chief librarian" or "library director." In order to keep our subject within reasonable bounds, we shall limit discussion to the deterioration and preservation of materials on which knowledge has been recorded, emphasizing the material most commonly found in libraries—paper. We shall exclude from consideration such matters as the protection of the library collection from theft, mutilation, fire, and acts of God, since those aspects of preservation require their own sets of administrative policies.

The librarian faced with the problem of deterioration and perservation of materials needs to know, above all, what to do. He will be able to act with greater efficacy, however, if he has some understanding of the historial context in which he will be working. For this reason we shall take time to review the effort librarians and others closely associated with them have made, individually and collectively, in dealing with this problem.[1] We shall then attempt to indicate the extent to which librarians need to familiarize themselves with technological aspects of the subject. Finally, we shall turn our attention to the business of administering a conservation program, an area somewhat less well charted than others in the field of library science.

I. HISTORICAL AND TECHNICAL BACKGROUND

In 1876, John William Wallace, then president of the Historical Society of Pennsylvania, addressed the Conference of Librarians which assembled in Philadelphia and which gave birth to the American Library Association. It was the nation's centennial year, and it was only natural for Wallace to try to look ahead to see what the next hundred years held in store for libraries and the library profession. At the conclusion of his address, he said: "I see before me in the future many questions in regard to the subjects upon which I have spoken; and yet upon another subject which I have not touched, the conduct of and management of these vast libraries themselves when everything else has been adjusted. You . . . I doubt not must have seen and now behold a hundred more. Before another century rolls by they will be practical questions" [4, pp. 9–10]. In another part of this same speech, Wallace had referred to some recent advances in the papermaking industry: "The increase of books . . . is to be attributed in some part . . . to the

[1] A partial review of historical developments relating to book deterioration and preservation appears in [1]. Walton [2] offers an extraordinarily useful bibliography covering the period to 1929. See [3] for a bibliography of the period from 1921 to the present.

facility with which of late times, in consequence of the application of chemical agencies instead as formerly of mechanical ones alone, to the paper-makers' art, paper itself is made" [4, p. 3].

At least one of those in Wallace's audience concerned with the "conduct . . . and management" of libraries knew that the paper being made by these new processes constituted one of the "hundred more" practical questions that would have to be dealt with before another century had passed. He was Justin Winsor, librarian of the Boston Public Library, who was elected president of the conference immediately following Wallace's opening remarks. Winsor had tried, unsuccessfully, to induce the editors of the leading Boston newspapers to publish a few copies of each issue on good paper.[2] This was perhaps the first attempt by a library administrator to solve a preservation problem still manageable at the time but later astronomical in scale. On the other side of the water, J. Y. W. MacAlister, librarian of the Leeds Library, had approached some of the leading British publishers on the question of the durability of modern book papers but "with no useful result" [6]. Neither of these attempts came to the attention of the library world, however, until a good many years after they had been made. Winsor's effort seems first to have become known through an editor's note to an article by Rossiter Johnson in the August 1891 issue of the *Library Journal* (reprinted from the *New York World*) in which Johnson sounded the alarm that inferior paper was a menance to the permanency of literature [5]. MacAlister did not make a public report of his concern until 1897 in an address to the Library Association [6].

Although we are not concerned here primarily with technological questions, it would be misleading to go further without alluding to the fact that there were a number of investigations of paper deterioration during the nineteenth century, especially in Great Britain and Germany. One of these studies deserves to be mentioned because of the involvement of a librarian, Richard Garnett, keeper of printed books at the British Museum. Garnett was a member of the Committee on Paper Deterioration formed by the Royal Society of Arts to ascertain whether the fibrous raw materials introduced into paper manufacture were inferior to the older celluloses with respect to relative permanence of the paper made from them. The committee found that disintegration occurs in all grades of paper as the result of chemical change of the fibers themselves and in some cases because of pollution of the atmosphere. The disintegration of rag paper seemed to be due to acid bodies either present in the original paper as made or resulting from atmospheric pollution. Disintegration of paper made from mechanical wood pulp, the committee reported, was due to oxidation [7].

For a good many years, discussion among librarians centered on two aspects of preservation: the idea of special library editions of publications printed on high-quality paper, and problems connected with one form of paper in particular—newsprint.

In 1898 the Conference of Italian Librarians resolved to ask the government to control the standard of paper for government publications and for a given number of books, periodicals, and

[2] See note signed "Eds. L. J." at the end of [5].

newspapers for government libraries [8]. In the same year John Russell Young, then librarian of Congress, proposed an amendment to the copyright law requiring the printing of copies on paper of a fixed grade for important libraries [9, pp. 45–6]. The International Congress of Librarians meeting in Paris in 1900 heard the suggestion that governments and libraries refuse to purchase works other than those printed on paper conforming to official specifications, an idea that MacAlister also had advanced [10]. A 1909 report of the U.S. Department of Agriculture argued for printing a small edition of each publication on high-grade paper for distribution to public and institution libraries [11, p. 11].

The problem of paper deterioration seems to have been brought to the attention of the American Library Association for the first time in 1909 by Cedric Chivers [12], a bookbinder from Brooklyn, and again in 1910 by Frank P. Hill [13] of the Brooklyn Public Library. Hill was particularly concerned with newsprint and suggested the formation of an ALA committee to confer with newspaper publishers on the problem. The committee, consisting originally of Hill, Chivers, and H. G. Wadlin of the Boston Public Library, reported in 1912 [14] and again in 1913 [15]. These reports dealt primarily with the possibility of treating newspapers with a preservative, and with the attitudes of both publishers and librarians toward special library editions of newspapers printed on good paper.

Leadership during the period from 1915 through 1925 came in the person of Harry Miller Lydenberg, then chief reference librarian, and later director, of the New York Public Library. In 1915 Lydenberg described a method of treating paper developed at the New York Public Library using Japanese tissue paper applied with rice paste [16]. Although this was the cheapest and most practical method that had been devised up to that time, it was a manual procedure and still too expensive (at thirty-five dollars a volume) for general use. By 1918 Lydenberg was able to announce a mechanical method utilizing a pasting machine adapted for the purpose and reducing the cost by ten dollars per volume [17]. A sample of this technique can be found in Robert E. Binkley's *Manual on Methods of Reproducing Research Materials,* published in 1936. The piece of newsprint in the copy of this book we examined was still intact, but the entire leaf—Japanese tissue and all—was very brittle, especially the discolored outer margin areas [18]. In 1918, also, Lydenberg published a bibliography on paper deterioration [19], and experimentation under his direction at the New York Public Library continued and was widely publicized [20, 21, 22, 23]. In 1925 Lydenberg called for a permanent paper for printing trade statistics, legal records, and public documents [24, 25].

By 1927 the work of these men had begun to bear fruit. In January of that year the *New York Times* started publishing a rag paper edition for archival purposes [26]. The rag paper edition was continued, incidentally, through June 30, 1953, when it was abandoned because of high production costs—and therefore a high subscription price—and because of the preference of many subscribers for the microfilm edition [1, p. 372]. The *Detroit News* also published a rag paper edition during roughly this same period. (In April 1969, the *New York Times* informed a number of library administrators that it was considering the possibility of publishing a "compact" edition, reduced in size, with advertising excised, and printed on "acid free, long life" paper.)[3]

By 1928, the problem of preserving manuscripts and printed books had become a matter of official international concern. Early that year, a committee of experts—both technical and bibliothecal—met and adopted resolutions to be presented to the Section on Preservation of Manuscripts and Printed Books of the International Institute of Intellectual Cooperation (the predecessor of UNESCO). Archivists and librarians on the committee included the director of the National Archives of the Netherlands, the general administrator of the Bibliothèque Nationale, and the officer in charge of repairs of the Public Record Office, London. After exhorting governments to recognize their responsibilities with respect to the preservation of knowledge, the committee called for a new process of paper manufacture to assure unquestioned length of life, the establishment of standards and watermarking, the encouragement of research toward the development of harmless inks and other writing materials, and precautions against improper storage conditions, binding, and handling [27].

The U.S. government was not slow to respond. At the joint request of the American Library Association and the American Association of Book Publishers, the National Bureau of Standards undertook a study of book papers. Through the efforts of Lydenberg and other librarians, funds were made available by the Carnegie Corporation for an extension of the research to include library storage conditions. The results of these studies were made known in a series of reports issued by the bureau in the early thirties and summarized in its Miscellaneous Publication no. 144 [28]. This report, dated 1934, was brought to the attention of librarians that same year by B. W. Scribner of the bureau staff in an article in the *Library Quarterly* [29]. The main causes of deterioration, according to this report, were light, adverse temperature and humidity, acidic pollution of the air, and low-grade paper.

In spite of a period of adverse economic conditions, efforts toward progress in conservation technology continued. The Division of Repair and Preservation was created in 1936 in the newly established National Archives under the direction of A. E. Kimberly [30]. The professional literature reported with frequency on the work of the Istituto di Patologia del Libro, founded in Rome in 1938 (e.g. [31]).

We must not leave the thirties without mentioning a development of great significance—the application of microphotography to the techniques of preserving and disseminating library materials. Although not inexpensive, and not suitable for the preservation of all types of publications, microfilming appeared to be a solution to the newspaper problem, at least, and the new process made it possible for libraries to share their resources in a new way. By 1932 a number of libraries had installed microfilming equipment [32], and two research libraries—the Library of Congress and the New York Public Library—ultimately became major microfilm publishers [33]. The publication of large bodies of material in microfilm by libraries and commercial publishers over the years has permitted libraries to acquire new materials and to replace old sets and files.

Another important development af-

[3] Letters from Robert S. November, director, Library Services and Information Division, *New York Times,* and Arnold Zohn, Arno Press; dated, respectively, May 12, 1969 and June 10, 1969.

fecting the preservation of library resources is the mushrooming reprint publishing industry which, taking advantage of new technology developed in the late fifties, has brought back into print thousands of volumes of serial sets and scholarly editions.

In the case of both microtext and reprint publishing, research library resources have been tapped for the original documents which had to be copied, and librarians have cooperated with publishers in making these resources available.

As we look at book conservation today, we see everywhere the long shadow of the late William J. Barrow. Barrow's research is known to most of us and need not be gone into here except to call attention to its wide range—lamination, deacidification, storage conditions, adhesives, and the development of permanent/durable paper—and to note its importance in pointing the way to new solutions.[4] Under the sponsorship of the Council on Library Resources, Barrow worked closely with librarians, and his research led to the Association of Research Libraries' recommendations for a national preservation program, described in a report by Gordon Williams released in 1964 [35] and dealt with in some detail at this conference by Edwin Williams. The work of the William J. Barrow Laboratory continues, as does that of the Institute of Paper Chemistry, the Istituto di Patologia del Libro, and other centers for book conservation research in England, France, the USSR, and other European countries. The research of Richard D. Smith [36, 37] of the Graduate Library School, University of Chicago, and that to be undertaken by the Imperial College, London [38, pp. 14–15], promise further insights into the nature of the problem as well as effective and economical methods for deacidifying books en masse. The Library Technology Program of the American Library Association has issued a number of useful publications on conservation in the larger sense of the term and has announced plans for other publications in the field. A major step forward was taken in 1967 when the Library of Congress recognized its growing responsibility for the development of a national program and reorganized its preservation activities in order to take leadership in the field [39, p. 60]. Finally, two currently proposed studies, if carried out, will advance our knowledge and move us closer to a national program. One of these, proposed by the Association of Research Libraries' preservation committee, will outline a detailed plan for the administrative, operational, and bibliographical organization of a national preservation program [40]. The other is a proposal by the National Archives and the National Bureau of Standards for empirical and basic research to develop information on the chemical stability of archival paper and related materials, to develop specifications for such materials, and to determine proper environmental conditions for archival paper [41].

So far we have avoided more than bare mention of technological developments in the field of conservation of library materials. Our reasons for this are several. First, the subject is enormously broad, covering as it does such varied types of material as paper, leather, cloth, adhesives, animal skin, clay, acetate, shellac, vinyl, laminating tissues and film, mending tape, ink, etc., each with its own technology. Second,

[4] For a brief description of Barrow and his research as well as a partial bibliography of his work, see [34, pp. 45–49].

real understanding of this aspect of the subject requires scientific knowledge of such phenomena as the thermodynamics of the cellulose molecule, which apparently is not understood thoroughly even by scientists, let alone by librarians. The National Archives–National Bureau of Standards study just referred to indicates the need for substantial research in such incompletely investigated areas as degradation rates at various temperatures, the effect of moisture on aging, and the role of bleaching agents, alum, and aluminum chloride in papermaking.

There is a question, then, as to how far into the subject the librarian can and should go. Much will depend on his own scientific background and understanding, but a perusal of the current literature on the preservation of these materials will help eradicate misconceptions—it is remarkable how many incorrect statements have been made, often by librarians, as Gospel truth—and point to areas of general agreement. It is agreed, for example, that the most significant cause of paper impermanence is acidity resulting from the manufacturing process and also from polluted atmosphere. We know, too, that the conditions under which books are stored (temperature and probably also relative humidity) have a significant effect on their life-span, but we have not yet determined what storage conditions are optimal. We know that *all materials* are affected by the manufacturing process and storage conditions to a greater or lesser degree, and that nothing is immune to deterioration. As for paper, it would seem that deacidification, strengthening, and air-conditioning are indicated for the preservation of materials still intact and that a combination of publication on paper with permanent qualities, deacidification, and air-conditioning will be necessary for the preservation of those publications of the future that are to be retained in library collections in book form.

II. ADMINISTERING THE CONSERVATION PROGRAM

A. ORGANIZATION

In the history of the conservation of library materials, ours is not the first voice to speak of the need for an overall conservation program within the library or the first to argue that conservation be given its proper place in the library's scheme of organization. Nevertheless, the number of times this concept has been promulgated is few. In 1946, Pelham Barr, then executive director of the Library Binding Institute, spoke of the need "for reorienting administrative thought on the whole subject of book conservation and binding" [42, p. 218]. Pointing out that binding is only one part of conservation, he said:

> Some strange phenomena in the evolution of library administration have resulted from this neglect of conservation. It became harder and harder to develop a program and procedures for book conservation, and therefore, it was more and more neglected. As it withered away, it left binding supervision without any fundamental place in some library organizations. . . . Some administrators have tried to dispose of the annoying department by attaching it to all kinds of other functions, which are frequently not closely related. But few have realized that it could "logically" be attached to so many other library functions for the very reason that it is essentially a conservation function and therefore fundamental in all library administration. [42, p. 219]

Barr called for recognition of an "overall program of book conservation" [42, p. 215] and the need to "plan and provide for a truly broad program" [42, p. 219]. "Where are the administrators" he asked, "who can become library custodians in the true and effective sense of the title, when the function has for so many years atrophied?" [42, p. 219]. In this same article Barr outlined the scope of a conservation program as follows:

> (1) selecting material before purchase with respect to usability and useful life; (2) examining condition and probable future condition of all material received . . . and prescribing conservation treatment, if necessary, before use; (3) providing proper housing of all material, in accordance with its conservation needs as well as its accessibility; (4) assuming responsibility for its condition at all times; (5) assuring its proper handling by staff and patrons; (6) organizing systematic inspection so that need for conservation attention is promptly recognized; (7) deciding on the proper treatment of all material needing attention; (8) supervising the treatment; and (9) deciding on storing or discarding. [42, p. 215]

One could not draw up a better outline of conservation procedures today.

Maurice F. Tauber and his associates devoted three chapters of *Technical Services in Libraries,* first published in 1954, to various aspects of conservation and mentioned the necessity "to emphasize the essentials of an over-all program" [43, p. 313].

Library Trends chose "Conservation of Library Materials" as the subject of its January 1956 issue, and the introductory article, written by Tauber, was entitled "Conservation Comes of Age." Here Tauber pointed to the "many areas . . . still in need of basic investigation" and said that librarians were "compelled to pay heed to the future disposition of their collections" [44, p. 221]. In this same issue of *Library Trends,* Edward Connery Lathem, dealing with the subject of binding and conservation personnel, wrote: "It is not enough that everyone should constantly and vigilantly direct attention to the condition and care of all library materials; there must be, as well, someone specifically responsible for the binding and conservation program as a whole. And this responsibility, moreover, must be backed by a degree of authority adequate to assure the program's proper functioning and success" [45, p. 321]. Although the articles in this conservation issue of *Library Trends* were concerned largely with binding, most of the ingredients of a total conservation program were, in fact, discussed. In addition to binding, the contributors wrote about the applications and potential uses of microreproductions and other photographic media, restorative practices, the treatment of special and nonbook materials, discarding, storage conditions and practices, personnel, and the possibility of cooperative projects.

In spite of almost a quarter-century in which the need for administrative attention to conservation has been recognized, few libraries in the nation today have anything resembling a total conservation program or a conservation unit of significance. What emerges clearly is the need for librarians to recognize now that conservation is as important to preparation for service as acquisition and cataloging and that the conservation unit should take its place as one of the library's principal technical services. We believe that it is within this part of the library's structure that conservation will have its best chance to become a matter of continuing professional attention and concern. Librarians who do not see the urgency of facing up to such an organizational requirement at this time will be well advised to begin to lay the groundwork for a conservation program. Those who are about to consider establishing a conservation unit may wish to use the Preservation Office of the Library of Congress as a model. There the conservation function has been placed in the Administrative Department, with the principal preservation officer an assistant director of that department. The office has responsibility for five activities, each of which is represented by a subunit: binding, restoration, preservation microfilming, collections maintenance (by which is meant physical care, including cleaning of books and stacks, monitoring environmental conditions in stack areas, and the like), and preservation research [46]. All but the last of these are appropriate activities for the conservation unit of any research library. (Because of its cost and also because of the shortage of research personnel in the field, book conservation research should probably be concentrated in only a relatively few centers.) The conservation unit will almost certainly become responsible also for other activities such as lending to reprint and microform publishers, since their publications may result in the replacement of deteriorating materials in the library's collections.

B. MANAGEMENT

Selection; acquisition.—The conservation program begins with the selection for acquisition, whenever possible, of materials printed on permanent/durable paper. The librarian will need to understand the meaning of this term. According to the Committee on Permanence and Durability of Paper of the Technical Association of the Pulp and Paper Industry, "*permanence* is the degree to which paper resists chemical action which may result from impurities in the paper itself or agents from the surrounding air; *durability* is the degree to which a paper retains its original qualities under continual usage" [47, p. 33]. Tentative specifications for sixty-pound, uncoated permanent/durable paper were developed by Barrow [48, p. 31; 49, p. 851]. These specifications have been referred to the Joint Committee on a Permanent/Durable Paper established in November 1961 by the American Library Association with representation from the publishing, printing, and papermaking industries as well as from the library and scholarly world. Unhappily this committee has not been able to report on recommended specifications. Until it does, librarians will have to check the specifications of the various papers that are purportedly permanent/durable with Barrow's tentative specifications referred to above. Since paper manufacturers find watermarking economically prohibitive, checking specifications will not be accomplished easily unless publishers can be persuaded to make reference to the paper manufacturers and the manufacturing specifications in the colophons of the books they publish. Ultimately, it is hoped, publishers will need to refer only to an ALA or United States of America Standards Institute (USASI) standard. Meanwhile, the Association of Research Libraries has urged publishers to use permanent/durable paper for works of more than ephemeral interest and has asked the U.S. Government Printing Office to publish a selected list of most important government publications on permanent/durable paper [50, p. 3]. The joint committee already referred to has reported that "a number of book publishers are using permanent/durable paper for more titles than was earlier recognized" [38, p. 20].

Screening.—It is unlikely that permanent/durable paper will ever be used universally. Examination and testing of books, therefore, will need to become a routine part of the library's processes. Paul N. Banks has suggested that the traditional dichotomy of books as rare or ordinary be given up and that a category designated as books of permanent research value be recognized [51]. This may be possible in some libraries, but in most archival collections there is little that is not regarded as having permanent value. Even libraries of record discard some materials that are superseded in one way or another, however, and the fact that an item is to be discarded eventually is sometimes known at the time of initial processing. The examination process might result in a division of materials into three categories: (1) those known to have been printed on permanent/durable paper and presumably to be retained permanently, (2) those to be retained permanently and printed on paper of unknown quality, and (3) materials to be discarded. Books in the second category will need to be inspected and tested to determine whether they may be sent to the shelf without treatment or whether they must be deacidified or restored. Spot testing for permanence is a first step in the process. According to a report [52] just issued by the Barrow Laboratory, paper should be tested for groundwood, acidity, alum, and rosin. The tests can be applied quickly without sophisticated equipment and by persons with no special training so long as due caution is taken in handling chemicals and interpreting results. Samples of the paper to be tested must be removed from the book, but only four square inches of paper from an area at least one-eighth inch inside the margin is needed. As a result of these tests, paper may be rejected as unstable; or it may be accepted; or, in some cases, it may be found to require further laboratory testing.

Treatment.—Until such time as effective and economical techniques for the mass treatment of materials become available, librarians will need to be highly selective in the materials they preserve and will have to make decisions with respect to the best and most appropriate means of preserving them. Priority should be given to materials that are unique or believed to be not commonly held and to materials of local significance. Rare materials in need of preservation probably ought to be restored and possibly also deacidified and laminated. If these processes cannot be afforded, however, such materials should be microcopied, with a master negative retained for archival purposes and a positive microcopy made for general use so as to protect the originals from excessive handling. This procedure is advisable even when the originals have been preserved. Few libraries in the United States have made use of restoration, deacidification, and lamination techniques in preserving materials. Of some sixty-two libraries answering a questionnaire on this point, eleven reported that they had had paper restored; two reported owning deacidification equipment, and four had sent materials to a deacidification shop; ten owned laminating equipment, and twelve had sent materials to an outside shop for lamination. Most of the libraries answering the questionnaire, on the other hand, own microfilming equipment or have sent materials to an outside photographic laboratory.

When mechanized deacidification of books becomes feasible, the conservation unit will have the task of working through the collection in some systematic way for the purpose of identifying those materials which cannot be saved by such a process; then a choice will have to be made between replacement, restoration, microrecording, and discarding.

If restoration is decided upon, it is essential that the reconditioning of bindings and paper be carried out under the supervision of an expert because a number of specialized techniques are involved: rebinding, repair, cleaning, washing, bleaching, resizing, fumigating, and the use of preservatives. A choice must be made of the method of deacidification to be employed. Care should be taken that materials are not laminated without deacidification and that laminating tissues and plastics are of the proper pH value. The number of expert restorers is few, and since formal professional training in this field is not given in the United States, individual libraries having conservators on their staffs can count themselves fortunate. George Cunha [53, p. 165] has suggested, for this reason, that cooperative regional library conservation associations be formed to carry out restoration work and to train conservators.

If microrecording is chosen as a method of preservation, the *National Register of Microform Masters* should be consulted to make certain that a microform of the material does not already exist. The type of microform to be utilized—roll or fiche—will also have to be decided. Preparation of material for filming and the photoghaphic work itself should be done in accordance with accepted bibliographic and technical standards [54, 55], and a master microform should be created to be used only for the purpose of generating additional service copies. In like manner, a library receiving an order for a microform should make a master negative for its own purposes and supply the individual or institution placing the order with a positive copy. Although optimal storage conditions for microforms have not yet been determined, guidelines for the storage of microforms exist and should be followed in the absence of more authoritive information [56, 57]. There is no convincing objective evidence that protective coating of microfilm is effective or that so-called rejuvenation of microfilm is possible [58]. Master microforms should be reported to the *National Register of Microform Masters* so that their existence may become known and so that they may play their part in the national preservation program [59].

The bibliography of binding conservation is as extensive as the bibliography of the conservation of paper, and if binding seems to have been neglected in this discussion, it is because the conservation of the material on which knowledge has been recorded has to be regarded as primary. Binding is one of several means toward that end. Bindings deteriorate too, but they are, or ought to be, more easily replaceable than the printed page. Problems arise when paper is too poor to bind or when the binding method originally employed has been so destructive as to make rebinding impossible. Matt Roberts [60] and Paul Banks [61] have warned librarians about the evils of the destructive oversewing process which, alarmingly, is the only method in use in commercial library binderies in the United States today. Roberts's essay on oversewing and its alternatives, "perfect" binding and flexible sewing, ought to be required reading for all librarians. Roberts describes the shortcomings of oversewing as follows: (1) an oversewn book does not open easily and will not lie flat;

(2) oversewing presumes the destruction of the original sections, thus making further rebinding all but impossible; (3) the oversewn book has a greatly diminished inner margin; (4) a book that is tightly sewn and has little inner margin is difficult to photocopy and is frequently damaged in the attempt; (5) paper that is even a little brittle will break due to the unyielding grip of oversewing. So-called perfect binding has some of the same disadvantages as oversewing and would not seem to be well suited to volumes to be retained permanently. Flexible binding, on the other hand, has only a single disadvantage—cost [60, p. 18]. Banks points out that even the standards for library binding developed by the Library Technology Program [61] do not insure nondestructive binding, since they do not preclude oversewing. "There is only one way," he says, "in which non-destructive binding . . . will become more easily and cheaply available, and that is for librarians to assume the responsibility for learning more about the technical aspects of the care of books in their charge, and to put pressure—the pressure of buying power—onto the library binding industry" [61, p. 334]. Clearly a "conservation standard" is needed for binding materials of permanent value. Librarians will have to insist that this standard be met, when appropriate, and will have to be able and willing to pay for it.

Other binding practices and methods of protecting materials physically will need to be reexamined to guard against acid migration from paper of poorer quality to higher-quality paper. End papers should be made of permanent/durable paper, and folders, envelopes, and other containers in which library materials are kept should be made of materials meeting archival specifications. The practice of binding together pamphlets printed on paper of varying quality should be discontinued.

Collections maintenance.—Library materials should be stored under conditions where they will be protected from particulate matter and pollutants in the atmosphere and from variations of temperature and humidity. Here librarians have made considerable progress. Thirty-four of the sixty-two libraries replying to a questionnaire reported from 75 percent to 100 percent of their space as being air-conditioned. Nevertheless, three of the major research collections in the country—those of Harvard, Yale, and the New York Public Library—are, in the main, without such protection, and the collections of the Library of Congress have been air-conditioned for only two or three years. Very little of the space that is air-conditioned, however, is under humidity control, and not all installations include adequate filtering systems. Librarians are of the opinion that a temperature of about 70° Fahrenheit and a relative humidity of 50 percent are optimal for book storage, but these are questions in need of further investigation. Barrow's studies indicate that cooler temperatures are desirable [62], and research on optimal temperature and relative humidity is still being carried on by the Barrow Laboratory. It is probable, too, that optimal storage conditions will vary for different kinds of papers, and almost certainly different types of materials will require different storage conditions. Good collections maintenance calls for monitoring of bookstacks for temperature and humidity control on a twenty-four-hour basis. Although a good deal has been said about the damaging effects of ultraviolet rays on paper, further research is needed also on optimal lighting conditions for book storage.

Books are rarely handled properly in libraries. The conservator should prepare instructions as to how books should be vacuumed and dusted and how they should be removed from shelves [63, pp. 5–8]. Stack personnel and copying machine operators should receive instructions on the handling and care of books. Special care must be exercised during the copying process. As John Alden has said, "in his anxiety to please, whatever the cost to his collections, the American librarian has, in permitting and even encouraging reproductions, too often abrogated his responsibility to the future in maintaining the materials in his care" [64, p. 5321]. Copying should not be permitted without professional approval. Face-down copying from bound volumes should be avoided, since it always involves a certain amount of pressure, resulting in injury to the book's spine and hinges or the breakage of brittle leaves. If face-down copying must be used for bound volumes, personnel of the reprographic department should be trained in techniques designed to minimize damage [65, pp. 20–32]. Face-up copying is preferable for all bound volumes and mandatory for rarer items. For rare items, too, master negatives should be retained so as to prevent further exposure of materials to the hazards of reproduction.

Personnel.—A serious problem in administering a conservation program arises because of the dearth of qualified personnel in the field. The conservation unit will have to be directed by a person of unusual qualifications: a background in science and technology is fundamental; specialized formal training and experience in book restoration, binding, and photography is mandatory; and some knowledge and appreciation of libraries and the role of the librarian is desirable. It may not be necessary for the library conservator to be the product of a library school, especially if the conservation program is under the general direction of the head of the technical services department. It should be possible to train restoration, binding, and photographic technicians through a combination of formal instruction and on-the-job experience. If qualified personnel are to be produced, however, a share of the cost of training will have be be underwritten. Some forty libraries answering a questionnaire on this point expressed a willingness to help finance such training. The Council on Library Resources has almost single-handedly supported the work accomplished in the book conservation field over the past decade, thanks in large measure to the interest and concern of its first president, Verner Clapp. Perhaps the time has come for the establishment of a library conservation foundation to sponsor book conservation research and to offer scholarships and fellowships in the field. It is incredible that there is, in the United States, no academic center for library conservation; nor, for that matter, are there many courses relevant to conservation in current library school curricula [66, p. 612]. A first step for such a foundation might be to establish a library conservation school. Whether such training should be part of the library school curriculum may be left open for now, but such a school should certainly be operated in conjunction with a strong center for education in librarianship.

Costs; budgeting.—Conservation is expensive. The installation and operation of air-conditioning, with humidity control, on a twenty-four-hour cycle, the maintenance of an adequate cleaning schedule, the utilization of proper binding, book restoration, and microrecording techniques, and the administration of the conservation program may have to compete with other, seemingly more pressing, items in the library budget. Frazer Poole [67, pp. 617–18] has given us some recent indicative costs. Deacidification and lamination will cost about $1.25 for an average sheet of 8½ × 11 inches; microforming costs about $12.00 a volume for both negative and positive copies. Robert E. Kingery [68 p. 40] identified certain costs that may not be immediately apparent and that have to be taken into consideration, especially when microrecording is selected as the means of preservation. These are the costs of recataloging, shelf preparation, and binding (if electrostatic reproductions are made). Kingery showed that electrostatic reproduction is the costliest of conservation measures, with short-run reprinting, deacidification/lamination, and microrecording following in that order. He showed also that immediate conservation is less costly than delayed conservation, since recataloging and rebinding costs do not occur when immediate conservation steps are taken.

It is impossible to say how much is spent on library conservation in the United States today. The costs of air-conditioning, cleaning, binding, and microrecording run into many millions, no doubt. There are, however, only about ten libraries that have budgetary allocations for preservation, and these funds are used mostly for the purchase of replacement copies, reprints, and microforms and for the microrecording of material. In most cases conservation funds are included entirely in other budgetary allocations. Conservation budgeting is not likely to become standard until the conservation program is firmly established in the organizational structure.

External involvement.—The librarian and the conservator will need to keep abreast of developments in the conservation field and should participate in common conservation endeavors. It may be important, for example, for the librarian to become active in such organizations as the Air Pollution Control Association and to make certain that local and state public officials are aware of the effects of air pollution on library materials. To be effective, too, librarians concerned about conservation will need to be better organized than they are at present. The Association of Research Libraries Committee on the Preservation of Library Materials has been the only professional group in the library field seriously interested in this problem.[5] At a time when restructuring is the order of the day, it may not be inappropriate to suggest that the American Library Association and other library associations take official cognizance of conservation. It is true that ALA has a bookbinding committee and a committee on permanent/durable paper, and much of the Library Technology Program's laudable work has been in the conservation area. But should there not be a conservation section within the ALA Resources and Technical Services Division? Or possibly the scope of the Reproduction of Library Materials Section should be enlarged and the

[5] An ad hoc committee on preservation, of the Resources and Technical Services Section, New York Library Association, was established May 5, 1969. This committee has been actively surveying preservation programs and needs in New York State and is planning cooperative workshops and conferences. The Resources and Technical Services Section of NYLA sponsored a symposium on preservation in 1967.

section renamed the Conservation and Reproduction of Library Materials Section.

Although conservation of library materials seems to be a somewhat neglected area, there are about twenty agencies in the United States and Canada and about twice as many foreign and international agencies having some interest in the field [53, pp. 190–97]. The librarian and the conservator will need to be acquainted with these agencies and their work. The newly established international journal, *Restaurator* [69], should play an important role in bringing together reports of current developments in conservation research and practice.

The librarian will want to cooperate, wherever possible with other libraries engaged in microrecording projects, and he should encourage and support regional and national conservation programs, especially in the areas of research and development, training, and the coordination of programs for the reproduction of library materials. He will want to work with commerical microform and reprint publishers in putting private capital behind the creation of materials needed by libraries in general, making certain that his library receives a master microform or reprint of materials used.

Policies and procedures.—The foregoing discussion of the management of a conservation program may be useful to the librarian in constructing a set of policies and procedures to govern his institution's conservation program. Only a very few libraries have developed written statements of any kind in this area of library operation.

We have tried to provide some guideposts for the librarian who seeks his way in establishing a total program of conservation but have left a good many bypaths unexplored. Only indirectly have we referred to the peril we face—the loss of recorded knowledge which, together with man's art and artifacts, provides the only link between the generations. If we may end on a hortatory note, we urge librarians to recognize the importance of conservation within their own institutions and, because it is an area which cries out for cooperative solutions, we ask librarians to begin to work actively in helping establish library conservation as one of the high priorities of the national obligation.

REFERENCES

1. Grove, Lee E. "Paper Deterioration—an Old Story." *College and Research Libraries* 25 (September 1964):365–74.
2. Walton, Robert P. "Causes and Prevention of Deterioration in Book Materials." *Bulletin of the New York Public Library* 33 (April 1929):235–66.
3. *Library Literature* (1921–), s.v. "Books—Conservation and Restoration" (a bibliography).
4. Wallace, John William. *An Address of Welcome from the Librarians of Philadelphia to the Congress of Librarians of the United States, Assembled October 4, 1876, in the Hall of the Historical Society of Pennsylvania.* Philadelphia: Sherman & Co., 1876. Reprint Boston: G. K. Hall & Co., 1965. Also found in *Library Journal* 1 (November 30, 1876):92–95.
5. Johnson, Rossiter. "Inferior Paper, a Menace to the Permanency of Literature." *Library Journal* 16 (August 1891):241–42. Reprinted from the *New York World.*
6. MacAlister, J. Y. W. "The Durability of Modern Book Papers." *Library* 10 (October 1898):295–304.
7. "Report of the Committee on the Deterioration of Paper." *Society of Arts Journal* 46 (May 20, 1898):597–601.
8. "Conference of Italian Librarians." *Library Journal* 23 (December 1898):667.
9. U.S. Library of Congress. *Report of the*

Librarian of Congress for the Fiscal Year Ended June 30, 1898. Washington, D.C.: Government Printing Office, 1898.

10. Dauze, Pierre. "La question de la conservation du papier dans les bibliothèques publiques et privées et un moyen de la résoudre." *Procès-verbaux et mémoires*. Congrès international des bibliothécaires tenu à Paris du 20 au 23 août 1900. Paris: Welter, 1901, pp. 227–31.
11. Wiley, Harvey Washington, and Merriam, C. Hart. *Durability and Economy in Papers for Permanent Records*. U.S. Department of Agriculture, Report no. 89. Washington, D.C.: Government Printing Office, 1909.
12. Chivers, Cedric. "The Paper and Binding of Lending Library Books." *ALA Bulletin* 3 (September 1909):231–59.
13. Hill, Frank Pierce. "The Deterioration of Newspaper Paper." *ALA Bulletin* 4 (September 1910):675–78.
14. "Preservation of Newspapers." *ALA Bulletin* 6 (July 1912):116–18.
15. "Preservation of Newspapers." *ALA Bulletin* 7 (January 1913):22–26.
16. Lydenberg, Harry Miller. "Preservation of Modern Newspaper Files." *Library Journal* 40 (April 1915):240–42.
17. Lydenberg, Harry Miller. "Present Discontents with Newspaper Stock." *ALA Bulletin* 12 (September 1918):211–16.
18. Binkley, Robert C., et al. *Manual on Methods of Reproducing Research Materials*. A survey made for the Joint Committee on Materials for Research of the Social Science Research Council and the American Council of Learned Societies. Ann Arbor, Mich.: Edwards Brothers, Inc., 1936.
19. Lydenberg, Harry Miller. "Bibliography of Paper Deterioration." *Paper* (July 17, 1918):12–13.
20. "Newspaper Files Disintegrate Soon." *New York Times*, September 3, 1917.
21. Lydenberg, Harry Miller. "Saving the Newspaper Files for Posterity." *New York Evening Post*, April 2, 1921, p. 11.
22. "Times Files Saved by New Method." *New York Times*, August 12, 1921, p. 12.
23. "Some Experiments toward the Preservation of Paper Made by the New York Public Library." Printed at the New York Public Library for distribution at the Paper Industries Exhibition, Grand Central Palace, New York City, April 9–14, 1923.
24. Lydenberg, Harry Miller. "Inferior Paper Endangering the Permanence of the Printed Page." *Pulp and Paper Magazine of Canada*, August 27, 1925, p. 985.
25. Lydenberg, Harry Miller. "Inferior Paper Endangering the Permanence of the Printed Page." *New York Times Book Review*, August 2, 1925, p. 2.
26. "Times to Print Copies on Durable Rag Paper." *New York Times*, December 5, 1926.
27. "On the Preservation of Manuscripts and Printed Books." *Library Journal* 53 (1928):712–15, 710 [sic].
28. Kimberley, A. E., and Scribner, B. W. *Summary Report of Bureau of Standards Research on Preservation of Records*. U.S. Bureau of Standards, Miscellaneous Publication no. 144. Washington, D.C.: Government Printing Office, 1934.
29. Scribner, B. W. "Preservation of Records in Libraries." *Library Quarterly* 4 (July 1934):371–83.
30. U.S. National Archives. *Annual Report of the Archivist of the United States for the Fiscal Year Ended June 30, 1936*. Washington, D.C.: Government Printing Office, 1936.
31. Gallo, A. "L'Istituto di Patologia del Libro." *Accademie e Biblioteche d'Italia* 13 (April 1939):318–35.
32. Henry, Edward A. "Books on Film: Their Use and Care." *Library Journal* 57 (1932):215–17.
33. Diaz, Albert. "Microreproduction Information Sources." *Library Resources and Technical Services* 11 (Spring 1967): 211–14.
34. Council on Library Resources, Inc. *Annual Report for the Year Ended June 30, 1967*. Washington, D.C.: Council on Library Resources, 1968.
35. Williams, Gordon. *The Preservation of Deteriorating Books: An Examination of the Problem with Recommendations for a Solution*. Report of the Association of Research Libraries Committee on the Preservation of Research Library Materials. September 1964. This study also appears, in two parts, as "The Preservation of Deteriorating Books." *Library Journal* 91 (1966):51–56, 189–94.
36. Smith, Richard Daniel. "Paper Deacid-

ification: A Preliminary Report." *Library Quarterly* 36 (October 1966):273–92.
37. Smith, Richard Daniel. "Paper Impermanence as a Consequence of pH and Storage Conditions." *Library Quarterly* 39 (April 1969):153–95.
38. American Library Association, Library Technology Program. *Ninth Annual Report,* 1967–68. Chicago: ALA Library Technology Program, n.d.
39 U.S. Library of Congress. *Annual Report of the Librarian of Congress for the Fiscal Year Ended June 30, 1968.* Washington, D.C.: Government Printing Office, 1969.
40. Association of Research Libraries, Committee on Preservation of Deteriorating Library Materials. "Preparation of Detailed Specifications for a National System for the Preservation of Library Materials." Draft, April 4, 1969. Available from Association of Research Libraries, 1527 New Hampshire Avenue, N.W., Washington, D.C. 20036.
41. "The Permanence of Paper—Archives and Related Materials: A Research Proposal." Based on a proposal requested and received by the National Archives and Records Service from the National Bureau of Standards. Revised March 1969.
42. Barr, Pelham. "Book Conservation and University Library Administration." *College and Research Libraries* 7 (July 1946):214–19.
43. Tauber, Maurice F., et al. *Technical Services in Libraries: Acquisitions, Cataloging, Classification, Binding, Photographic Reproduction, and Circulation Operations.* New York: Columbia University Press, 1954.
44 Tauber, Maurice F. "Conservation Comes of Age." *Library Trends* 4 (January 1956):215–21.
45. Lathem, Edward Connery. "Some Personnel Considerations for Binding and Conservation Services." *Library Trends* 4 (January 1956):321–34.
46. U.S., Library of Congress. *Library of Congress Regulations,* nos. 212–14. October 23, 1967.
47. "Report of the [Technical Association of the Pulp and Paper Industry] Committee on Permanence and Durability of Paper." *Paper Trade Journal,* July 27, 1933, pp. 33–36.
48. Church, Randolph W., ed. *The Manufacture and Testing of Durable Book Papers.* Virginia State Library Publications, no. 13. Richmond: Virginia State Library, 1960.
49. Clapp, Verner W. "'Permanent/Durable' Book Papers." *ALA Bulletin* 57 (October 1963):847–52.
50. Association of Research Libraries. *Minutes of the Seventy-first Meeting, Held January 7, 1968.*
51. Banks, Paul N. "Some Problems on Book Conservation." *Library Resources and Technical Services* 12 (Summer 1968): 330–38.
52. W. J. Barrow Research Laboratory, Inc. *Permanence/Durability of the Book.* Vol. 6. *Spot Testing for Unstable Modern Book and Record Papers.* Richmond: Virginia State Library, 1969.
53. Cunha, George Daniel Martin. *Conservation of Library Materials: A Manual and Bibliography on the Care, Repair and Restoration of Library Materials.* Metuchen, N.J.: Scarecrow Press, 1967.
54. Salmon, Stephen R. *Specifications for Library of Congress Microfilming.* Washington, D.C.: Library of Congress, 1964.
55. Library Standards for Microfilm Committee of the Copying Methods Section, Resources and Technical Services Division, American Library Association. *Microfilm Norms.* Chicago: ALA Resources and Technical Services Division, 1966.
56. *U.S.A. Standard Practice for Storage of Microfilm,* USAS no. PH5.4. Approved July 2, 1957. New York: American Standards Association, 1957.
57. McCamy, Calvin S. *Summary of Current Research on Archival Microfilm.* National Bureau of Standards Technical Note 261. Washington, D.C., 1965.
58. Peiz, Gladys T. "Film Coatings—Do They Really Protect Microfilm?" *National Micro-News* 67 (December 1963): 125–39.
59. Applebaum, Edmond L. "Implications of the National Register of Microform Masters as Part of a National Preservation Program." *Library Resources and Technical Services* 9 (Fall 1965):489–94.
60. Roberts, Matt. "Oversewing and the Problem of Book Preservation in the Research Library." *College and Research Libraries* 28 (January 1967):17–24.

61. American Library Association, Library Technology Project. *Development of Performance Standards for Binding Used in Libraries, Phase II.* LTP Publications, no. 10. Chicago: American Library Association, 1966.

62. Grove, Lee E. "What Good Is Greenland? New Thinking on Book Preservation and Temperature." *Wilson Library Bulletin* 36 (May 1962):749, 757.

63. Horton, Carolyn. *Cleaning and Preserving Bindings and Related Materials.* Chicago: American Library Association, Library Technology Program, 1967.

64. Alden, John. "Reproduction vs. Preservation." *Library Journal* 91 (1966): 5319–22.

65. Hawken, William R. *Photocopying from Bound Volumes: A Study of Machines, Methods, and Materials.* LTP Publications, no. 4. Chicago: American Library Association, Library Technology Project, 1962.

66. Friedman, Hannah B. "Preservation of Library Materials: The State of the Art." *Special Libraries* 59 (October 1968): 608–13.

67. Poole, Frazer G. "Preservation Costs and Standards." *Special Libraries* 59 (October 1968):614–19.

68. Kingery, Robert E. "The Extent of the Paper Problem in Larger Research Collections and the Comparative Costs of Available Solutions." In *Permanent/Durable Book Paper, Summary of a Conference Held in Washington, D.C., September 16, 1960.* Virginia State Library Publications, no. 16. Richmond: Virginia State Library, 1960.

69. *Restaurator: International Journal for the Preservation of Library and Archival Material.* Published by Restaurator Press, Copenhagen.

DISCUSSION

PAUL N. BANKS

So thoroughly did Henderson and Krupp do their homework and so clearly did they present the position of the librarian as conservator that it has taken hard thought on my part to compose additional relevant comment. Instead of reiterating their well-made points, I should like to talk about one aspect of book conservation to which they have alluded but which they have not discussed. That is book conservation as a professional discipline. Before expanding on this, however, I should like to make two points that are basic to my further discussion.

First, I believe that it needs to be emphasized that the frame of reference of the authors' paper and of my remarks (as indeed of this conference as a whole) is the research library, where it is desired to keep indefinitely at least broad classes of material. I make this point because I believe that one of the problems in developing programs and standards for the care of books has been the "lowest common denominator" principle, that is, the lack of objective thinking about the aims of the library in question in determining the approach to the care of its collections. Some of the ideas which the authors have presented or I will propose would certainly not be defensible in the case of a junior college library, for example. I have commented more fully on this idea in the article cited by the authors [1].

The second point concerns the book as an artifact. While *the* big problem in research libraries is the preservation of the intellectual content of the books, by preserving the original paper and print or by some form of copying or replacement, nevertheless there are many books which have value as artifacts—records of their own history and of the history of technology, aesthetic or bibliographical values—and should be conserved accordingly. Most, if not all, research libraries have rare book rooms, and I believe that it is safe to say that in deciding on treatment for most rare books, their value as artifacts should be taken into account. There is, of course, gradual attrition of the copies of any given edition of any book in its original condition, and unless artifactual value is kept in mind as decisions are being made about the care of the books, Victorian publishers' bindings, for example, may become very rare indeed.

ATTEMPTING A DEFINITION OF BOOK CONSERVATION

Henderson and Krupp have referred to book conservators, have mentioned some aspects of the conservator's function, and have decried the lack of training facilities for book conservators. In my opinion, we have a more basic problem than simply lack of training facilities: to my knowledge, book conservation has nowhere been described or defined as a discipline or profession.

In an attempt to establish the scope of book conservation, we might examine what Sheldon Keck said to an international conservation meeting in Rome in 1961. Keck, whose credentials as an art conservator and educator of art conservators place him in the top rank of that profession, said: "Conservation may be . . . described as a concept including (a) 'preservation'—namely, action taken to prevent, stop or retard deterioration—and (b) 'restoration'—action taken to correct deterioration and alteration" [2, p. 199].

To divide book conservation in another, although similar, way, we might say that it consists of, on the one hand, control of the environment in which books live—that is, "climatology," as museum people call it—and handling and use. The other half, in this breakdown, would be the actual treatment of books: preventive treatment (such as deacidification, stabilization of leather, and binding journals, for example) and curative treatment (lamination, rebinding, restoration, and the like). In both cases, an understanding of the nature of the materials used in the production and the treatment of books is essential.

In order to help keep our thinking as clear as possible, I would like to exclude replacement with microforms, reprints, etc., from my definition of conservation or preservation. Although they are clearly, for the time being at least, necessary to the retention of our body of knowledge, it does not seem to me that replacing a book is preserving it. In addition, Gordon Williams has pointed out a number of reasons why replacement is not totally without hazards in attempting to retain just the intellectual content of books [3].

THE QUALIFICATIONS OF THE BOOK CONSERVATOR

Henderson and Krupp state that the head of the conservation unit of a library should be a person of unusual qualifications. I can only say, "Hear, hear!" To further try to define book conservation, I would like to present my thoughts, in somewhat idealistic terms, about what sort of a person the book conservator should be.

This person should have some knowledge of science, as the authors point out, although I doubt that he would have time to be a scientist as such. He must, however, be able to communicate with the scientist; that is, he must be able to put questions to the scientist in such a way that the scientist can provide useful answers from research, and he must be able to translate the scientist's findings into guidelines for practical action. (By the same token, we certainly need also more scientists who specialize in various aspects of conservation).

The book conservator must have a strong background in the history and aesthetics of the book—something akin to the "connoisseurship" which art conservators study. He must have (as the authors point out) an understanding of the function and purpose of the library he is dealing with, though he does not necessarily have to be a librarian. This should certainly include, in most research libraries, some knowledge of the aims and methods of analytical bibliography, if the values of books which bibliographers study are not to be unnecessarily destroyed.

This ideal man whom we are discussing should have a bent for engineering, because he is dealing with, after all, physical—one might say mechanical—structures, and he will probably have to be concerned with small mass-production procedures and equipment. He has to have a modicum of administrative ability, as he will undoubtedly be directing the work of others and be involved in paperwork and other administrative procedures. And he must be a craftsman.

I would like to expand upon—and emphasize—this last point for a moment, because I believe that it has been seriously neglected. Our body of verbal and intellectual knowledge of bookbinding, and especially of book and paper restoration, is thus far extremely limited. As the authors have pointed out, the literature on these subjects is inadequate. I shall have more to say on that point in a moment. In addition, we do not have handbooks of strain factors of book materials, or formulas—much less computer programs—for the stresses on various components of a book in use. In other words, there is not an engineering of book structures as there is of buildings or automobiles. Since we cannot as yet base the mending of a leaf or the design of a library binding on precise formulas, the treatment of books and manuscripts—both as mass and as individual problems—must be guided or executed by a person who has an intimate tactile, manual knowledge of books and papers, as well as a strong intellectual background in the subject. Like the surgeon, he must have highly developed hands as well as mind. While it seems almost inevitable that the qualified book conservator will become principally an administrator, Peter Waters has stated: "The conservator should have a workshop of his own, as his ideas grow out of practical experimentation."[1] I do not know that this point has been made formally before, although it is taken or granted—to the point of hardly needing mention—in the field of art conservation.

In addition, the supply of properly trained and flexible craftsmen, particularly in restoration, is practically nonexistent. As I have discussed elsewhere [4], the role of the artisan is an anomalous one in our society, and the traditionally trained artisan, even where he exists, may be too inflexible to serve the modern conception of book conservation as well as he might. In many fields, he is being replaced by skilled technicians, but this has not really begun to happen in book conservation, except in Florence. This, combined with the fact that in America there are

[1] Peter Waters, private communication. Address: The Slade, Foxfield, Petersfield, Hampshire, England.

no programs for training artisans of any caliber, means that at this moment in history the conservator must train his own craftsmen-technicians. This he obviously can do only if he himself has a good grounding in technique.

I believe, then, that we can say that the ideal book conservator is a specialist who has considerable depth in the area of actual treatment of books, and considerable breadth in a variety of fields which bear on the care of books. He should have well-developed synthesizing powers: the ability to integrate bits of knowledge from disparate disciplines—historical, aesthetic, scientific, technological, philosophical—into effective courses of action for the care of research library collections.

COMPARISON OF BOOK CONSERVATION WITH ART CONSERVATION

Another way to attempt to define, or to assess, a profession is to compare it with professions with which it has features in common. The field to which book conservation is (or perhaps it would be more realistic to say "should be") most similar is the conservation of art and ethnographic objects.

The authors state that the literature of book conservation is full of pitfalls. This is an understatement: a recent article warns us to protect books from damage by moonlight. Despite the expressed interest in the moon, such pronouncements hardly place us in the sophisticated age of the moon walk. By contrast, the field of art conservation has had an international professional journal for twenty-seven years, and published abstracts of relevant literature covering a thirty-seven year period [5–7]. The monographic literature, while burdened with junk, is balanced with a substantial body of significant material. For example, a 500-page monograph has just appeared, under international auspices, on the design and equipment of the museum laboratory.

A profession can be to some extent measured by its training programs; its schools have a strong bearing, both direct and indirect, on establishing and maintaining recognizable standards. In addition to training, they often perform such important secondary functions as conducting research, acting as clearing houses for information, providing faculty and clerical time for writing, editing journals, operating professional societies, and so forth. There has been a graduate-level training school for art conservators for ten years, and another is opening next year.[2] There are other programs of various types and calibers for training art conservators. There is no program whatsoever in America for professional training of bookbinders or book restorers, much less book conservators.

An important American museum would no longer conceive of sending its paintings to the local picture framer who cleans and restores paintings as a sideline; yet the majority of important American libraries entrust their rare books to people with exactly analogous qualifications. A museum of any size has a highly sophisticated conservation laboratory, and at least four have research laboratories as well. Libraries do not yet have comparable facilities, although there is reason to hope that the Library of Congress may soon have them, as the authors point out. Although we still have a very long

[2] The Conservation Center of the Institute of Fine Arts, New York University, awards graduate degrees and was opened in 1959–60. A graduate program in art conservation cosponsored by the New York State Historical Association and the State University of New York is opening in 1970 in Cooperstown, New York.

way to go, I believe that we have at the Newberry Library the beginning of a well-balanced program in relation to our size.

Art conservation has had an influential international professional society for nearly twenty years, which has an extremely active American group.[3] The latter has promulgated suggested standards of professional ethics and is gradually working up to the point when it may be able to propose accreditation. There is no form of standard for treatment of library materials or for those who treat them; there is not even a generally accepted if unwritten consensus.

It is true that the art conservator tends to deal with individual objects of great value, and that he is concerned with aesthetic values. These two facts, needless to say, are not true of the vast majority of research library books; yet, as I have pointed out, virtually every research library has some books—perhaps even large numbers—which have high aesthetic or monetary value, or both. It is thus my firm belief that part of the book conservator's responsibility is to bring the same ideals, standards, and level of professional competence to his problems that the museum conservator brings to his. Moreover, I do not see why we should not expect the same level of sophistication in the treatment of those library conservation problems which must be dealt with on a mass basis as is expected to be brought to individual problems in the library or in the museum.

[3] International Institute for Conservation of Historic and Artistic Works (IIC), 176 Old Brompton Road, London S.W. 5, England. The American group (IIC-AG) may be addressed in care of the Conservation Center of the Institute of Fine Arts, New York University, 1 East 78th Street, New York, New York 10021.

THE ROLE OF THE CONSERVATOR IN THE LIBRARY

We might try to further define this ideal book conservator whom we have been talking about by examining what his role in the library should be if he is to have a significant impact on the care of its collections.

As Henderson and Krupp have pointed out, the librarian needs to know what to do, and he cannot rely on the existing literature. What can he rely on? I believe that he must create within his organization the post of conservator, and attempt to fill it with a specialist whose sole responsibility is to study and administer all aspects of a broad conservation program. This, as we have heard from Keck, should include preservation—that is, control and monitoring of the environment—and treatment—binding, lamination, deacidification, restoration. It should include both mass-production binding of nonrare materials, to help insure that this is done nondestructively where possible, and the meticulous fine binding or restoration of rare books. I believe that "preservation" in the form of microfilming and the like is, administratively, primarily a bibliographical problem, and need not be the concern of the conservator except that he should participate in formulating guidelines for what is preserved intact and what is replaced.

Part of the conservator's job, at this moment in history, will have to be traveling, talking, visiting, attending meetings, reading, serving on committees, and engaging in related matters that are not immediately productive. It is the only way that he can learn.

The conservator should also be given enough rank and support within the library to enable him to alter or eliminate existing bad practices and initiate desirable new ones where necessary. Part of the reason for this is that he must interact with many other departments of the library: the engineering department on control of environment, curators on aesthetic and historical questions, technical processes on bibliographical questions, public service on use and handling patterns, and the top-level administration on basic policy matters such as degree of public access. If we could consider the library as a sort of court, with the books being gradually (perhaps very gradually) destroyed by a "prosecution" of perfectly legitimate demands—need for funds, acquisition needs, heavy use by readers, expediency, and so on—balance to the proceedings can probably be brought only by a defending advocate who is charged with such a job.

THE EDUCATION OF CONSERVATORS

I am well aware that the fine-sounding advice which I have just given you is counsel of perfection for the time being. There exists now the barest handful of competent conservators in America, and those who exist are, I believe, committed to their present positions. I firmly believe, however, that each large research library should have the type of specialist I have outlined, as museums now do, if libraries are effectively to approach their conservation problems in all of their complexity.

Richard Buck, director of the Intermuseum Conservation Laboratory at Oberlin, said recently that the IIC-AG committee on the nation's needs in art conservation "has concluded that trained personnel is the basic need on which depends any significant expansion in [restoration] laboratory or analytical-research facilities. Its recommendation is to mobilize the national resources for training [8, p. 5]. I believe that a similar statement should be made about book conservation, except for one glaring fact: we have no national resources for training book conservators. What, then, do we do?

The first order of priority toward beginning to solve our pressing conservation problems is, in my opinion, the establishment of training facilities for conservators. This is not going to be easy because we are trying to start something from nothing. It would be easier, perhaps, if we had some bookbinding schools, or if there were a library school which had taken an active interest in conservation. If the will is developed, however, I am convinced that we can begin to train some conservation specialists by engaging the experience of those few who now exist and by utilizing people in related fields—from paper chemistry to art conservation—to broaden and round out the training program.

CONCLUSION

In conclusion, then, I have to say that I believe that the head librarian cannot effectively be the conservator of the research library, any more than he himself can effectively be head of technical processes. In both cases, a specialist is needed who can devote his full attention to the subject, and, in both cases, this specialist needs both broad background and intensive technical training.

I have fully persuaded you, I trust, of the type of person who is needed in the research library, and of what his role in the library should be, and we have seen that the supply of such people is, to put it mildly, inadequate. To interpret slightly Henderson and Krupp's sentiments, one of the most pressing concerns of the librarian must be the conservation of his collections if there are to be collections extant for the scholar of the future to consult, and it is incredible that there is, in the United States, no academic center for library conservation.

REFERENCES

1. Banks, Paul N. "Some Problems in Book Conservation." *Library Resources and Technical Services* 12 (Summer 1968): 330–38.
2. Keck, Sheldon. "Training for Engineers in Conservation." In *Recent Advances in Conservation,* edited by G. Thomson. London: Butterworths, 1963.
3. Williams, Gordon. "The Preservation of Deteriorating Books: An Examination of the Problem and Recommendations for a Solution." *Library Journal* 91 (1966):51–56, 189–94.
4. Banks, Paul N. "The Scientist, the Scholar and the Book Conservator: Some Thoughts on Book Conservation as a Profession." In *Atti della XLIX Riunione della Società Italiana per il Progresso delle Scienze.* Rome: SIPS, 1968.
5. *Technical Studies in the Field of Fine Arts.* Published for the Fogg Art Museum, Harvard University, Cambridge, Mass., 1932–42.
6. *Studies in Conservation.* Published by the International Institute for Conservation of Historic and Artistic Works, 1952–.
7. (*a*) Abstracts for 1932–42. In *Technical Studies in the Field of Fine Arts.* (*b*) Abstracts for 1943–52. In *Abstracts of Technical Studies in Art and Archaeology* ("Freer Abstracts"), by Rutherford J. Gettens and Bertha M. Usilton. Washington, D.C.: Freer Gallery of Art, Smithsonian Institution, 1955. (*c*) Abstracts for 1953–. In *IIC Abstracts* (became *Art and Archaeology Technical Abstracts* in 1966), published by the International Institute for Conservation of Artistic and Historic Works, 1955–.
8. Anonymous news note. *ICA Newsletter* 7 (June 1969):5. Published by the Intermuseum Conservation Association, Oberlin, Ohio.

THE CONTRIBUTORS

GREER ALLEN: manager, University of Chicago Printing Department, Chicago, Illinois. Born New York City, 1924. B.A., Yale, 1947. Member, Johnson Society of Midwest Region. Editor, *Manuscripts,* quarterly publication of the Manuscript Society, 1960–68.

PAUL N. BANKS: conservator, Newberry Library, Chicago, Illinois. Born Montebello, California, 1934. Carnegie Institute of Technology, 1953–56. Member, Guild of Book Workers, American Institute of Graphic Arts, American Library Association. Fellow, International Institute for Conservation of Historic and Artistic Works. Publications include various articles in scholarly periodicals.

BERTIE L. BROWNING: senior research associate, Institute of Paper Chemistry, Appleton, Wisconsin, 1933–68. Born Appleton City, Missouri, 1902. B.S., 1925; M.S., 1926; Ch.E., 1931, University of Missouri; Ph.D., University of Wisconsin, 1928. Member, American Chemical Society, American Association for the Advancement of Science, Technical Association of the Pulp and Paper Industry. Publications include *The Chemistry of Wood* (New York: Wiley, 1963), *Methods of Wood Chemistry* (New York: Wiley Interscience, 1967), *Analysis of Paper* (New York: Marcel Dekker, 1969).

FORREST F. CARHART, JR.: director, Office for Research and Development; and director, Library Technology Project, American Library Association, Chicago, Illinois. Born Sheffield, Iowa, 1917. A.B., Drake University, 1939; A.B.L.S., 1941; A.M.L.S., 1943, University of Michigan. Member, American Library Association, Special Libraries Association, Illinois Library Association, Illinois Chapter of Special Libraries Association. Publications include various contributions to encyclopedias.

GEORGE T. EATON: assistant division head, Applied Photography Division, Research Laboratories, Eastman Kodak Company, Rochester, New York. Born Edmonton, Canada. B.A., Brandon College, Brandon, Manitoba, Canada, 1932; M.A., McMaster University, 1933; B.S., Acadia University, 1933; graduate work, University of Toronto, 1934–37. Member, Society of Photographic Scientists and Engineers, Society of Motion Picture and Television Engineers, Photographic Society of America. Publications include scientific papers on various aspects of photographic chemistry and a series of articles on photography and photographic processes for encyclopedias.

JAMES WOOD HENDERSON: chief, Research Libraries, New York Public Library, New York City. Born 1917. B.A., 1939; M.A., 1941, University of Oklahoma; B.S., Columbia University, 1948; M.P.A., New York University, 1958. Member, American Library Association, Bibliographical Society of America, American Association of Museums, Manuscript Society, Phi Beta Kappa. Publications include coediting *Library Catalogs; Their Preservation and Maintenance by Automated and Photographic Techniques* (Cambridge, Mass.: M.I.T. Press, 1968).

ROBERT G. KRUPP: chief, Science and Technology Division, Research Libraries, New York Public Library, New York City. Born Buffalo, New York, 1920. B.S., University of Buffalo, 1942; M.L.S., Columbia University, 1955. Member, American Chemical Society, Special Libraries Association, American Library Association, American Society for Information Scientists. Publications include miscellaneous papers on chemistry and chemical nomenclature and contributions to *Special Libraries.*

LEONARD SHATZKIN: vice-president for manufacturing, research, and development, McGraw-Hill Book Company (noted for experimentation with publishing on permanent paper), New York City. Born Warsaw, Poland, 1919. B.S., Carnegie Institute of Technology, 1941. Member, Institute of Management Sciences, American Institute of Graphic Arts, Technical Association of the Pulp and Paper Industry.

RICHARD DANIEL SMITH: co-director of the Conference. Fellow, University of Chicago, Graduate Library School. Born South Bethlehem, Pennsylvania, 1927. B.S., Pennsylvania State University, 1952; M.A., University of Denver, 1964. Publications include "Paper Impermanence as a Consequence of pH and Storage Conditions," *Library Quarterly* 39 (April 1969):153–95. For further biographic information, see the *Library Quarterly* 39 (April 1969):197.

KENNETH W. SODERLAND: associate director for preparations, University of Chicago Library, Chicago, Illinois. Born Snohomish, Washington, 1923. B.A., 1948; M.A., 1951; M.A.L.S., 1952, University of Washington; Certificate, University of Stockholm, 1949. Member, American Library Association.

JOSEPH J. THOMAS: vice-president and research director, S. D. Warren Co. (a division of Scott Paper Co.), Westbrook, Maine. Born Columbia, Pennsylvania, 1909. B.S., 1930; M.S., 1932; Ph.D., 1935, Pennsylvania State University. Member, American Chemical Society, Technical Association of the Pulp and Paper Industry, Sigma Xi. Publications include articles in trade journals.

HAROLD W. TRIBOLET: manager, Department of Extra Binding, and hand binder/conservator, R. R. Donnelley & Sons, Co., Chicago, Illinois. Born Chicago, Illinois, 1911. Member, International Institute for Conservation of Historic and Artistic Works. Publications include "Trends in Preservation," *Library Trends* 13 (October 1964); *All the King's Horses* (Chicago: R. R. Donnelley & Sons, 1954); and *Florence Rises from the Flood* (Chicago, R. R. Donnelley & Sons, 1967).

CARL J. WESSEL: chief scientist, John I. Thompson & Co. (a subsidiary of TRACOR, Inc.), Washington, D.C. Born Pittsburgh, Pennsylvania, 1911. B.S., Canisius College, Buffalo, New York, 1934; M. S., University of Detroit, 1938; Ph.D., Catholic University of America, 1941. Member, American Chemical Society, American Association for the Advancement of Science, American Institute of Chemists, American Society for Information Sciences, Institute of Environmental Sciences, Society for Industrial Microbiology, Air Pollution Control Association, American Institute of Biological Sciences. Publications include contributions to various books, technical publications, scholarly journals, and encyclopedias. In addition, he coauthored, with G. A. Greathouse, *Deterioration of Materials: Causes and Preventive Techniques* and has presented papers at numerous conferences.

EDWIN EVERITT WILLIAMS: associate university librarian and member of the Faculty of Arts and Sciences, Harvard University, Cambridge, Massachusetts. Born Los Angeles, California, 1913. A.B., Stanford University, 1932; A.M., University of California at Berkeley, 1936. He has written *Racine depuis 1885: bibliographie . . .* (Johns Hopkins University Press, 1940), *Farmington Plan Handbook* (Association of Research Libraries, 1953; revised, 1961), *A Serviceable Reservoir* (United States Book Exchange, 1959), and *Resources of Canadian University Libraries for Research in the Humanities and Social Sciences* (National Council of Canadian Universities & Colleges, 1962). In addition, he has edited *Conference on International Cultural, Educational and Scientific Exchanges* (Chicago: American Library Association, 1947), *Problems and Prospects of the Research Library* (Association of Research Libraries, 1955), *Libraries and Universities,* by Paul Buck (Harvard University Press, 1964), and *Harvard Library Bulletin*, 1968–present.

WILLIAM K. WILSON: chief, paper evaluation section, National Bureau of Standards, U.S. Department of Commerce, Washington, D.C. Born Harrisville, West Virginia, 1913. A.B., Salem College, Salem, West Virginia, 1934; M.S., West Virginia University, 1938. Member, American Chemical Society, Technical Association of the Pulp and Paper Industry, American Society for Testing and Materials. Fellow, Washington Academy of Sciences. Publications include various articles in the *Journal of the National Bureau of Standards, TAPPI,* and other chemical periodicals.

HOWARD W. WINGER: co-director of the Conference. Managing editor of the *Library Quarterly* and professor in the Graduate Library School, University of Chicago.